IN THE NEW WORLD

Lawrence Wright

IN THE NEW WORLD

Growing Up with America
1960-1984

Alfred A. Knopf   New York   1988

Portions of this book were originally published in slightly different form as "Why Do They Hate Us So Much" in the *Texas Monthly.*

"The Nixon Age" was originally published in slightly different form as "Why We Liked Dick" in *The Washington Monthly.*

Grateful acknowledgment is made to the following for permission to reprint previously published material:

CHAPPELL & CO., INC.: Excerpt from the song lyrics "Camelot" by Alan Jay Lerner and Frederick Loewe. Copyright © 1960 by Alan Jay Lerner and Frederick Loewe. All rights administered by Chappell & Co., Inc. International copyright secured. All rights reserved. Used by permission.

DECAY MUSIC: Excerpt from the song lyrics "Riot" by the Dead Kennedys. Copyright © 1982 by Decay Music.

TREE INTERNATIONAL: Excerpt from the song lyrics "Okie From Muskogee" by Merle Haggard and Roy Edward Burris. Copyright © 1969 by Tree Publishing Co., Inc. Used by permission of the publisher. International copyright secured. All rights reserved.

Library of Congress Cataloging-in-Publication Data
Wright, Lawrence [date]
In the new world.
Bibliography: p.
1. United States—Civilization—1945–
2. United States—Social conditions—1960–1980.
3. United States—Social conditions—1980–
4. Wright, Lawrence [date]. I. Title.
E169.12.W75   1987   973.92   87-45234
ISBN 0-394-54282-7

To my father and mother,
Don and Dorothy Wright

For there is a new world to be won—a world of peace and good will, a world of hope and abundance; and I want America to lead the way to that new world.

JOHN F. KENNEDY
(*July 4, 1960*)

My friends, it is because we are on the side of right: it is because we are on God's side: that America will meet this challenge and that we will build a better America at home and that that better America will lead the forces of freedom in building a new world.

RICHARD NIXON
(*Last speech of the 1960 campaign*)

CONTENTS

IN THE NEW WORLD

1 / A NEW AMERICA

My first sighting of the new world came from the back of the family station wagon, in the late afternoon as the slanting sun behind us lit up the city skyline with fierce and brilliant color. Now, of course, the vista of skyscrapers that awed me as a child is buried in the shadows of modern Dallas; the buildings that seemed so monumental then against the flat horizon were the pale blue Southland Center, the Mobil Building with the neon winged horse atop, the Republic Bank, largest bank in the Southwest. When I come upon these structures today they seem petite and almost historical. Foremost, as we approached the city, was an unpretentious cubical edifice with a large billboard on the roof advertising Hertz rental cars and blinking the time and the temperature. The building itself was anonymous, and afterward, when the world knew it as the Texas School Book Depository, people in Dallas identified it by the Hertz sign and said, "Oh, *that* one."

We were moving from Abilene, Texas, where my father was vice president of the largest bank in town. My sisters and I had been in mourning for weeks, since Daddy returned from his mysterious trip to announce that he had gotten a new job—at last he would be president of his own bank. It was small, he warned us, but it was in Dallas, and Dallas was growing, and as the city grew so would his bank. Dallas was a place where dreamers like my father would be given a chance.

As in all boomtowns, tension in Dallas was high. Some people were zooming through society like race cars, giving the world an impression of Dallas as a city of affluent hicks—you could see them flaunting their greenbacks at the gaming tables from Las Vegas to Monte Carlo, or talking too loudly in restaurants that were really too good for them. They were moneyed, naive, too eager, democratic, yes, but socially pretentious. For an astounding number of people Dallas was just such a jackpot. They formed a rough society of nouveaux millionaires; they built gorgeous Gatsby-like mansions on the north side, enrolled their children in Hockaday or St. Mark's, bought their minks and their Cadillacs, and joined the Republican party. The winners were easy to spot.

The losers made their own headlines. Dallas was the murder capital of Texas, and Texas itself led the United States in homicides. We were reminded that Dallas killed more people in a year than all of England—a statistic with little effect, for wasn't England a sound-asleep society, and weren't we exploding with new force, making millions by the minute, and did you expect a new world to be born without death and broken hearts?

It was not just Dallas, of course. New cities were forming, cities without traditions, with only the blind instinct to grow, to add wealth. Already in the fifties the urban centers of the Northeast had begun their long decline. A great migration was taking place, out of Boston, for instance, which lost 13 percent of its population in the fifties; and New York, which diminished by one hundred thousand people; and Cleveland and Providence; all of them great industrial centers, union towns, politically liberal. A million immigrants settled in the newly built suburban tracts surrounding Phoenix, San Diego, Albuquerque, Orlando, Los Angeles, Houston. Middling towns such as Tulsa, Amarillo, Mobile, Charlotte, doubled in population; Tucson grew five times its size, Anaheim nearly ten times. And yet this was only a prelude to the sixties, when the new world that was arising in the South and the West erupted like Atlantis, a civilization that seemed to pop up overnight.

What distinguished Dallas from the other cities of the new world (this was the legend we told ourselves) was that there was no reason for its existence. It did not float atop an ocean of oil; there was no seaport, no mighty river; there were no paper mills or stockyards or coal mines; it was essentially a low-water crossing on a muddy creek, no more than that. Dallas had pressed itself into existence through force of will and public relations. During the construction of the Texas & Pacific Railroad the city fathers had tricked the legislature into bending the tracks toward Dallas, and on that fragile concession they made the city the transportation and distribution depot of the Southwest—a city of warehouses and regional offices, and soon of banks and insurance companies, which piped the dollars out of the oil fields and ranchlands; a city then of magnificent stores, which fed the material aspirations of the newly moneyed; a city finally of commerce, information, and trade, self-created like no other city in the world.

And because there was finally no reason for Dallas, there was anxiety among its citizens. It might all disappear tomorrow: the customers would go elsewhere, the companies would relocate, the train wouldn't stop here anymore. Dallas was a fire that might go out at any time. To keep it alive the citizens advertised it far and wide, and even to ourselves; it was "Big D, my oh yes!," the city that works, et cetera. We were blowing on the coals.

My father, John Donald Wright, was typical of the men who made that new world. The youngest of five children, he went to a one-room schoolhouse in central Kansas, and saw his family farm blow away in the same wind that brought the Depression. He was sixteen when he left home, and with no resources other than fear and determination he put himself through Central State Teachers College in Edmond, Oklahoma, then through law school at the University of Oklahoma. When World War II broke out he dutifully joined the infantry. He met my mother, Dorothy Peacock, while he was in Officer Candidate School at Fort Benning, Georgia, and proposed to her after a three-week courtship. She was a hostess at the Officer's Club, and boldly at ease in society—warm, immediate, playful, his opposite in so many critical ways. For most of their first decade of marriage, my father was off fighting in Europe, the

Pacific, and then Korea. He did not think of himself as a brave man or a natural warrior. Twice his hair turned completely white, but returned to its wavy black when he was discharged as a major in 1952 at the age of thirty-six. He was a civilian now with a wife and three children. He had not even begun to make a career. He hit the ground running.

Eight years later he had learned the frustration of small-town banks with sleepy family management, so when he was finally offered the presidency of the Lakewood State Bank in Dallas he accepted at once. In 1960 it was a small and troubled storefront bank on Gaston Avenue, between Doc Harrell's drugstore and Kirk's Beauty Salon. To see it now—three entire city blocks of land, a tower, a parking garage, fountains, expensive art on the walls, and a modern, amalgamated name, Allied Bank of Dallas—is to realize my father's aspirations in their most tangible form. He built this bank, with the help of people like him, people who came out of nowhere with nothing, who came to Dallas because Dallas would give them a chance.

Wasn't this the American dream? And wasn't Dallas a new America for all those frustrated farmboys like Don Wright, who found life too small in their places of origin, and who came to Dallas to grow beyond themselves, to transform themselves—Dallas, a city chrysalis where the poor, backward, and ambitious were transmogrified into the rich, conservative, and satisfied.

By comparison with Abilene, Dallas seemed wide open, but it wasn't, as we soon learned. Politically, it was shut up tight. Hungry newcomers like my father found the leadership of the city distant and mysterious. You had to prove yourself, endure probation. If you did, you'd be noticed; you'd be brought along slowly, like a colt being trained to a bridle. One day someone would approach you. You'd be asked to "do something for Dallas." You'd get an assignment. For my father it was to head up a bond election to air-condition the public schools. People were surprised when the bond passed; the secret circle opened and admitted Don Wright.

The cabal he entered was the Dallas Citizens Council, which

was once defined as "a collection of dollars represented by men." There was not a doctor or a practicing lawyer on the council, and not a single woman. These were the board chairmen, men who could commit money without consulting anyone else, the "yes-or-no men," as Mayor R. L. Thornton, Sr., who founded the council, called them. The men on the council chose the candidates for local office and made decisions for the good of the city, without consulting the voters or the elected representatives. When, for instance, Chance Vought Aircraft was considering relocating in Dallas, the head of the company announced that the runways at Dallas's Love Field were two thousand feet too short for its purposes. Three hours and forty minutes later a council member called him and said that the city had approved an emergency bond and that work would start on the runways Monday morning. That's the way Dallas operated. As a political model the city was ruled from the top down, by corporate junta, but by and large it was well ruled.

It was that same firm rule, however, that caused life in Dallas to go, subtly, quite wrong. If you had come to Dallas in 1960 from any other American town of comparable size, you would have found it much the same as your city. Its people dressed alike, talked alike, and thought alike, as did the preponderance of middle-class citizens everywhere; the country had after all a very homogeneous culture in 1960. What would have struck you, if you were keen enough to observe it, was that similarity had been carried too far in Dallas. America was a conformist society, perhaps, but conformity had been taken to extremes in Dallas. I don't ever remember seeing a bearded man, other than Santa Claus, until Stanley Marcus decided to grow a beard two years after the Kennedy assassination. When the famously bearded Commander Whitehead came to Neiman-Marcus for a British Fortnight celebration, the president of our most famous department store decided to give a party for bearded men only. He found he didn't know any; he wound up serving a roomful of strangers.

Dallas was a city of believers, a city of eight hundred churches, among them the largest Methodist, the largest Baptist, and one of the largest Presbyterian congregations in the world. While everyone was religious, some were superreligious, and they thought of themselves as a spiritual vanguard. They were contemptuous of the rest of us; we might as well have been agents of the devil. In the face of so much belief, honest doubt hid itself; skeptics and heretics were one and the same.

My family was conventionally religious—Methodists—although my father was devout. God had spared his life several times on the battlefield, and he repaid Him by living righteously and teaching Sunday school. But even my father was scared off by the fanaticism of the first church we joined. The preacher was a Holy Roller with a red face and sulfurous eyes, so that when he pounded the Bible and screamed about damnation, he truly had the aspect of a man roasting on the coals of hell. He also had a taste for Savile Row suits and alligator shoes, which was satisfied by the hypnotized widows in the front pews.

We later moved downtown to the First Methodist Church, and when we were brought into the congregation we knelt before the choir as they sang the final verse of "The Battle Hymn of the Republic." They began in a melodic whisper—"In the beauty of the lilies Christ was born across the sea"—but the sound swelled and grew thunderous, and I felt my skin turn to gooseflesh as the refrain "Glory, glory hallelujah!" nearly levitated me above the organ pipes. I asked God to bless me and keep me, and save me from my evil nature.

Dallas was filled with suspicious Protestants. In 1960, when John Kennedy had not yet secured the Democratic presidential nomination, the Reverend W. A. Criswell of the First Baptist Church declared in a sermon that "the election of a Catholic as president would mean the end of religious freedom in America." One of Criswell's 18,500 parishioners was billionaire H. L. Hunt, who took the trouble to have 200,000 copies of Criswell's sermon mailed to Protestant ministers all over the country. We never made the mistake of underestimating the power and influence of the First Baptist Church. In 1964 there was a brief flurry on the part of Hunt to get the Republican presidential nomination for another of Criswell's parishioners, evangelist Billy Graham, and I wonder how far this scheme might have gone if a Texan had not been occupying the White House at the time.

Everybody knew informally that Criswell was growing wealthy off his investments, which were guided by some of the enormously powerful members of his congregation. All of our pastors were well-to-do. The biblical injunction that it is easier for a camel to pass through the eye of a needle than for a rich man to enter the kingdom of God was not the subject of many sermons. In Dallas, success meant money, even in theology, and it would have been simply embarrassing to see a preacher struggle to send his children to private school, or have to drive a secondhand car.

The richest man in the world lived only a few blocks from us, in a reproduction of Mount Vernon on the shore of White Rock Lake. You could see H. L. Hunt in the morning raising the flag in his front yard, or sitting on the porch in the late afternoon, in a white shirt and a clip-on bow tie, playing checkers. It was part of Dallas lore that Hunt's Mount Vernon was twice as large as George Washington's—or even ten times as large (size always being important in Texas, a state with few other admirable physical qualities). Hunt actually went to the trouble to have his mansion measured, and found it merely 2 percent larger than the original.

In his front yard he posted a billboard advertising his superpatriotic radio show called "Life Line." He hired a former FBI agent named Dan Smoot as his commentator, who later founded his own conservative newsletter and opened an account in my father's bank. The Dallas extremist fringe found its voice and radio ambassador to the rest of the nation in Smoot. He talked about the enemies within, and their names were Eleanor Roosevelt, Walter Reuther, Edward R. Murrow, Earl Warren. He opposed mental health programs because they were a Communist form of mind control. He urged the repeal of the income tax, abandonment of disarmament plans and foreign aid, and eventually the election of a Congress that would "bring a bill of impeachment against John F. Kennedy." On the very day of the assassination, "Life Line" editorialized that if Kennedy succeeded in his plan to communize America, we would find ourselves living in a country where "no

firearms are permitted the people, because they would then have
the weapons with which to rise up against their oppressors."

My father used to dream about landing an account from Hunt,
whose wealth was spread all over the globe but not in his neighborhood bank. He was famously tight with his money. He drove to
work every day in an Oldsmobile 88 and carried a sack lunch. One
of the legends I heard about Hunt is that his net worth increased
$11,000 per minute, most of it from his oil wells but also from his
diverse investments in real estate, broadcasting, agriculture, health
food products (under the HLH label), and even a sandwich shop
in downtown Dallas. At that rate, one week's earnings would more
than match the total assets of the Lakewood State Bank. My father
finally cajoled Hunt into taking a tour of the facilities. He appeared
one autumn day, a genial old gent with wispy white hair and
chipmunk cheeks, in the company of several dark-suited young
men. He spent his time flirting with secretaries. One of the girls
was getting married, and her friends were celebrating the occasion
with a coffee cake. "Here, Mr. Hunt, you can have a piece," offered
the bride-to-be. The cake was intercepted by one of the dark suits,
who tasted it and passed it on to Hunt. He pronounced it delicious.
"Now, honey, I've got a little sump'n for yew," he said, and
reached into his pocket. Two pecans.

Hunt never really fit into the city; he loathed charity and all civic
functions—you would never see him at a symphony ball, mingling
with the sophisticates, but you might catch him at the state fair,
personally hawking his HLH Gastro-Majic indigestion pills. Despite his wealth and radically conservative politics, he was essentially bohemian and wildly out of place in a city where pretense
mattered. He was not only a notorious philanderer, he was a biga-
mist with three sizable families. One of his girlfriends was the diva
Lily Pons, who settled briefly in Dallas and tried to reform its
cultural prejudices. Hunt never lost his appetite for women, even
in his eighties when he was boasting of his potency and hoping, by
eating healthy food, to live another eighty years. I can remember
seeing him standing on his head on the television news, with a
nubile instructor grinning beside him, advertising the benefits of

yoga. He also liked to crawl, or creep, as he called it, and he invited the *Dallas Morning News* to photograph him on his hands and knees racing around his living room. "They call me the 'Billionaire Health Crank,' " he joked. He was terribly afraid of death.

It's a measure of how small my world was that I had no experience with any person of another race in Dallas, except for our weekly maid. I was an unconscious racist, a fact I discovered in Dr. Criswell's church. I was invited there on a blind date by friends who introduced me to Linda, and we sat together and listened to Dr. Criswell deliver the evening sermon with his usual nineteenth-century theatrics. He wore a cream-colored suit and swayed in the pulpit, tears in his eyes, praising our material prosperity and condemning godless Communism. With his white hair parted down the middle, he reminded me of Our Gang's Alfalfa grown old. Linda was not black, of course, or she would never have entered the sacred nave; Criswell had once called race mixing "a thing of idiocy and foolishness." Linda's mother was a Filipino, and she had inherited an Asian caste of skin. As I sat next to her, liking her, the racist inside me noticed that she was not entirely white. I never called her; her color frightened me.

We said that Fort Worth was "where the West begins," and we might have said of Dallas that it was where the South ends. The slave culture had run aground in East Texas; past Houston and Dallas blacks were rarely seen. We fought school desegregation with the same cleverness as the rest of the South. In 1954 the Supreme Court had ruled in *Brown* v. *Board of Education of Topeka* that public schools should be desegregated "with all deliberate speed"; eleven years later I graduated from high school without ever having had a black classmate.

In 1965 the Davis Cup came to Dallas, in the form of a challenge round between the United States and Mexico. Tennis was my sport, and my hero then was Arthur Ashe, the NCAA champion from UCLA. He was the first black man in what was still a country-club sport. Ashe had the biggest serve since Pancho Gonzales and a backhand that no one had ever equaled; it was the strongest stroke in the game. But he was not a powerful-looking man. He was

lithe and tall, and he whipped his shots with abandon. This was a
new game to us, power tennis; there was nothing leisurely about
it, nothing cunning. It was a raw and, I suppose, angry game,
played by an intellectual with delicate manners. He was the most
exciting player in the world, but when he made the Davis Cup
team, the Dallas Country Club refused to host the match. Rather
than be disgraced, the city quietly built a splendid municipal court
in Samuell Park, near my neighborhood. The inadvertent effect of
this decision was to democratize the sport in Dallas, and to make
the city one of the great international centers of the game.

Understanding that integration of public facilities was inevitable, the Citizens Council arranged a coup. One day a black couple
was seated for lunch at the Neiman-Marcus Zodiac Room. That
was it—a signal to the entire city that desegregation had arrived.
It was typical of Dallas that social change would be accomplished
in the parlors of power, and not at the lunch counters of Wal-
green's.

The subject of sex was never unbuttoned in my house. My father
was puritanical; he walked out of Dr. Zhivago because it was too
racy, and after that we never took him to movies. Mother, on the
other hand, had a taste for potboilers and French films, but it was
a taste seldom satisfied, for Dallas was as publicly antisex as it was
anti-Communist. In fact there seemed to be a subliminal link
between the two, having to do with -verting, either per- or sub-.
There was a high level of hypocrisy in sexual affairs, which was not
surprising, given the go-go egos of the big winners in this sanctimonious city and the idle and pampered status of its women. The
city fathers, publicly pious, were in private a rough and jaunty
bunch, with thick knuckles and heavy appetites, men who were
used to grabbing what they wanted. There was a tacit understanding, in those tall buildings, that the flesh was weak. Even our
neighborhood pharmacist was known to trade out the cost of a
prescription drug for a few hot moments behind the curtain that
led to his "office"—a lonely daybed. My prudish father forgave this
offense on the grounds that it was done in a charitable spirit (and
because the druggist was on his board of directors).

The city never, in my memory, went to the trouble of formally banning a work of art or literature, as we heard had been done in Boston, although in the fifties the local art museum removed from display some of its collection of "Communist" art, including paintings by Picasso and Rivera. In 1962, after Henry Miller's erotic novel *Tropic of Cancer* was published, the Dallas police swept through the city's bookstores and the book simply disappeared. We were sexually sanitized. I can remember my furtive astonishment when I read James Michener's *Hawaii.* I couldn't believe a book as lusty as that had fallen into the hands of an unguarded teenager. I had sexual luaus in my dreams for weeks. Between readings I hid the book in a cigar box behind an air-conditioning vent, where it no doubt still reposes.

The prevailing ethic in the city was not hard work but high risk. The big money had been made by the wildcatters in the oil fields. All of my life I had heard stories about men who had been through several fortunes; the attitude of these men toward money, and themselves, was highly romantic. They courted great wealth, grasped it briefly, then lost it again, usually through some preposterous investment. Anyone who worked too hard to make money or who seemed to be too cautious in holding on to it was regarded as a drudge or a scrooge. Money was supposed to be inconsequential, and although our millionaires didn't light their cigars with fifty-dollar bills like Daddy Warbucks, they enjoyed wasting money, buying up entire store window displays from Neiman-Marcus, or his-and-her submarines.

Dallas had been a wide-open town, filled with mobsters and prostitutes and numbers runners, until 1948 when Bill Decker became sheriff and turned back the mob. He was our Wyatt Earp, and as grateful as the city was for his service, one had a sympathetic feeling for the citizens of Tombstone once the shopkeepers and churchgoers got control. We had an overdose of righteousness. In Texas, juries set the sentences in criminal trials, and in Dallas they assessed such terrific penalties (especially for property crimes, not so much for murder) that you supposed they must believe in reincarnation. One habitual offender got a thousand years for possessing marijuana. In 1972 the Ransonette brothers, Woodrow and Franklin, kidnapped Amanda Dealey, the daughter-in-law of our newspaper publisher. Since the death penalty was not in effect, the jury sentenced them each to five thousand years.

Dallas was so straitlaced it got a national reputation as a lousy spot for conventions. Outsiders couldn't get over the way pedestrians froze into place in front of a DON'T WALK sign on an empty street. Edna Ferber once went to jail for jaywalking in Dallas, and many people suspect she wrote *Giant* in revenge—a theory I endorse, having received two jaywalking tickets myself during a teenaged crime spree.

Despite its reputation for regimentation and hard justice, Dallas had an underground love of criminality. Belle Starr, the Bandit Queen, settled near Dallas in 1860. Bonnie Parker and Clyde Barrow, the romantic desperadoes of the Depression, were from Dallas, and are buried there—still, no doubt, the most famous dead people in town (Lee Harvey Oswald lies in Fort Worth). The hero of my own youth was the King of Diamonds, a jewel thief who operated in North Dallas for several years. He must have been an avid reader of society columns, because he usually struck when the homeowners were off at a charity ball. Reporters loved him; they even threw their own party in his honor and demanded costume jewelry at the door. During debutante season the cops staked out all of North Dallas, but he always slipped through them, leaving behind his distinctive waffle-soled shoe prints. I remember learning the word "impunity"—that's what the King of Diamonds operated with.

We were orderly, if not always law-abiding, but all the clean living and upstanding behavior bred a secret taste for the low life. This was not simple perversity. I had the feeling, growing up in Dallas, that real life was being hidden from me. There was a curtain drawn over human travail and ugliness, which I longed to fling away. But for a schoolboy in Texas, about the only glimpse behind the curtain came each October during the Texas State Fair (the nation's largest, of course), when the tattooed ladies rolled into town. Each year we were let out of school one day during the fair, a sanctioned excursion into the world of midgets and two-headed calves. For me, the smell of corruption was never the brimstone that the preachers hollered about but the vomity odor of corn dogs that wafted through the midway. I spent most of my summer's allowance throwing softballs at Kewpie dolls, thrilled to know *for certain* that I was actually being cheated.

The political scale in Dallas began with Eisenhower conservatism and ran well past fascism into such utopian notions as H. L. Hunt's belief that the power of a person's vote should depend on the amount of taxes he paid. (He articulated this vision in a novel titled *Alpaca.*) Although Dallas was predominantly Republican, the Democrats were also intensely conservative—the local party leadership hadn't supported the national ticket since 1932. Such were the politics of the new world. The motto of its citizens was "unlimited opportunity," and anything that hindered the advance of the ambitious, the clever, and the talented was seen as an infringement of liberty. The choking liberalism of the East was not appropriate for this frontier society of ours. We had cities to build and roads and schools and businesses that no one had ever imagined. We wanted to be left alone to make our new world. Our enemies were bureaucracy, regulation, legalisms. We felt ourselves to be a colony of an older civilization, and we resented the weight of its laws and strictures.

Dallas never went as far in its antigovernment stance as the voters in Houston, who rejected zoning as a Communist plot. The archconservatives of Dallas were no more rabid than those in Los Angeles or Miami, nor was the political climate of Texas much different from that of Southern California, or Florida, or Arizona. Across the country, but particularly in this new world, there was a certain adolescent bitterness, a suspicious feeling of impending betrayal, a willingness to find conspiracy lurking in every corner. "The mood," as Arthur Schlesinger, Jr., described it, "was one of longing for a dreamworld of no communism, no overseas entanglements, no United Nations, no federal government, no labor unions, no Negroes or foreigners—a world in which Chief Justice Warren would be impeached, Cuba invaded, the graduated income tax repealed, the fluoridation of drinking water stopped and the import of Polish hams forbidden."

No, it was not just Dallas, but my hometown was already gaining the reputation of being the capital of this new world. There was something scary brewing in my city. People were demanding certitudes no sane man could offer. Military solutions—invading Cuba, annihilating Russia—were crisp, definitive responses to problems that seemed too damn much trouble to understand. "Fuzzy" was the word for any response other than a straightforward invasion of a foreign country when American interests (there were always American interests) were threatened. Fuzzy responses were what you came to expect from the bow-tied intellectuals at the State Department. In that atmosphere strident attitudes, even crazy ones, were appealingly clear.

Our politicians were always on the run from the smears of the right. Our mayor, Earle Cabell, who later served in Congress, was a far-right Democrat who was present at the founding of the Dallas chapter of the John Birch Society (he actually did not join), and yet he was routinely described as "the socialist mayor of Dallas." The leader of the American Nazi party, George Lincoln Rockwell, offered that Dallas had "the most patriotic, pro-American people of any city in the country." The compliment may have embarrassed a few, considering its source, but we believed that about ourselves. To the radical conservatives, Dallas had become a kind of shrine, a Camelot of the right.

The superheated political climate in the city brought ordinary life to a rolling boil. It was hysterical, yes, but after a point there seems to be little difference between hysteria and festivity. One sensed the appeal of fanatical movements. They begin like this, in a city where anxiety is high, where the opposition is cowed, where there is only one public voice and it is filled with certainty and hate. The brakes were off in Dallas. We had the giddy feeling that we were careening toward some majestic crack-up, but it was a thrilling ride, and who had the nerve to say slow down?

Once again—it wasn't just Dallas. But we who lived there began to feel that we were in the middle of a political caldera, a grumbling, reawakening fascist urge that was too hot to contain itself. I wonder what might have happened in Dallas if Kennedy hadn't died there.

2 / 1960

Soon after we moved to Dallas my mother set out to become a "Dallas Woman." The phrase carried freight in Texas, where it signified a stylishness and sophistication that were uncommon in the rest of the state. Women advanced themselves in the city through a network of clubs and auxiliaries, such as the Bankers Wives, which Mother joined as a matter of course, and bridge clubs, which were her passion. She loved society and bright talk. She had been a part of the smart set when she was growing up in Atlanta; her scrapbooks are filled with handsome athletes who played forward for Vanderbilt or wide receiver for West Point, and girls who wore slouch hats and smoked cigarettes and drove in open roadsters. At the University of Alabama she wrote a society column and briefly dated Bert Parks, before he became the perennial master of ceremonies of the Miss America Pageant (I'm unendingly grateful she didn't marry him). She read *The New Yorker* and the novels of John Cheever. In her ideal life she would have been sipping Manhattans with Dorothy Parker at the Algonquin.

In Dallas she joined the Jane Douglas chapter of the Daughters of the American Revolution, which was the largest DAR chapter in the country. There she learned about the politics of the Dallas Woman. It was a politics of paranoia. The female patriots of the DAR were obsessed with "Communist plots"—which, decoded, meant fluoridation of the drinking water and desegregation of the public schools. Once a week Mother attended the Public Affairs

Luncheon Club, a women's group sponsored by H. L. Hunt, which concentrated on bringing conservative speakers to town. George Wallace came, and Ronald Reagan, and Dr. Fred Schwarz, the right-wing California educator. Barry Goldwater came so frequently that he got to be known as the "third senator from Texas." But the most popular speaker was the only elected Republican in Texas, Dallas congressman Bruce Alger.

Alger was a Princeton man, a bomber pilot in World War II, and the handsomest man in town. Even in his own party he was ridiculed as a hopeless extremist. In the ten years he represented Dallas in the House of Representatives there was never an important piece of legislation with his name on it. He was the only man in Congress to vote against giving free milk to schoolchildren. Pork barrel projects that might have gone to Dallas went to Fort Worth instead. It was said of Alger that he "couldn't even get a streetcar transfer in Washington"—and that was during a Republican administration. In the last four years of Alger's congressional reign, Dallas lost eight federal agencies. Despite his record, Alger survived political challenges by two of the most popular Democrats in the city, first by District Attorney Henry Wade, and then by Barefoot Sanders, a state legislator who became a federal district judge. In all of his contests Alger was carried along by a formidable cadre of angry right-wing women. His relation to those women was a matter of legend and speculation in the city. Alger was their prince. He was an extraordinary sexual presence, and he found power through the fears and the sublimated desires of the right-wing Dallas Woman.

In that season the entire country was learning about sex and politics through the presidential campaign of John F. Kennedy. We had heard about the Kennedy magic and glamour, but these terms only described his highly polished exterior self; they said nothing about the man inside, who was a mystery to us all. After a generation of old men in the White House, Kennedy suffused the country with the musk of vigorous youth. There was a phenomenon in the 1960 campaign known as "jumpers." Newsmen noticed that as Kennedy traveled around the country, women in crowds would jump to get a look at him; this was mentioned in the newspapers, and soon it became a mass phenomenon, an almost involuntary response on the part of women as the candidate's motorcade passed: jumping, some wildly, some, it seemed, obediently—even nuns would give a little hop. A sexual wave was running through America, and the candidate was Pan, and his music was visible in the oscillation of women's bodies.

It is strange now to remember that there was actually a dispute in 1960 over who was the better looking, Kennedy or his opponent, Richard Nixon, who was greeted on the campaign trail by "Nix-onettes." Magazines spoke of him almost as a matinee idol. He had a beautiful "movie star" smile, and his eyes, which later became so hooded and furtive, seemed then warm, innocent, almost roman-tic. Perhaps he thought of himself that way. He had begun a modest career in community theater before turning to the larger stage of politics. It was in Whittier, California, while playing a small role in *The Dark Tower,* by George S. Kaufman and Alexan-der Woollcott, that Nixon met his future wife, Pat Ryan, a local actress who had occasional bit parts in Hollywood. He told her the first day they met that he would marry her someday.

Both Nixon and Kennedy would come to represent profound trends in American politics that would divide the electorate for decades after the 1960 election, and yet during the campaign itself the great complaint was that there was no difference between them. Soviet chairman Nikita Khrushchev called them "a pair of boots—which is better, the right boot or the left boot?" Kennedy spoke of change, of moving forward, and yet he ran a campaign based on anti-Communism, military buildups, and economic growth—themes remarkably similar to those that Ronald Reagan would campaign for twenty years later. Kennedy spoke louder on the subject of civil rights, but his opponent's record on the matter was as good as his. Nixon found little to attack in the Kennedy platform, so he concentrated his fire on Kennedy's relative inex-perience. The most prominent issue in the televised debates between the candidates was the defense of Quemoy and Matsu, two negligible islands in the Formosa Strait.

Had they exchanged parties we might have understood them better. Both men had joined the parties of their fathers. Joseph Kennedy had grown up in the Democratic ward politics of Boston, and married the mayor's daughter. He was a Democrat in the same way he was a Catholic and an Irishman. It was part of his ethnic identity, almost an accident of birth. Frank Nixon's Republicanism, on the other hand, was a peculiar conversion. At the age of thirteen he possessed a beautiful filly, which was drafted to ride in a parade behind William McKinley, then running for governor of Ohio. At the end of the parade McKinley commented, "I never did see such a fine, pretty horse." Then he asked Frank Nixon to always vote Republican, and Nixon said he always would.

And so the sons took on their fathers' politics, despite circumstances that might otherwise have inclined them in a different direction. John Kennedy was—far more than his father—a product of the liberal, moneyed, prep-school Eastern Establishment. In 1960 the backbone of that Establishment was still largely Republican. Richard Nixon grew up on the opposite side of the continent, the son of a man who, he said, "was a streetcar conductor in Ohio, worked on a wheat ranch in Montana, was an oil-field worker, a carpenter, ran a lemon ranch that failed and lived out his years as a small grocer." All of his life Richard Nixon claimed to speak for the common man, what he called the Forgotten American.

It was characteristic of Nixon that the qualities he shared with Kennedy—his youth, his looks, his Irishness—seemed in him entirely unremarkable, but distinctive in Kennedy. One never heard, for instance, about Nixon's religion, which was Quakerism, a pacifist sect that might have stimulated more controversy than Kennedy's less exotic Catholicism. Like Kennedy, Nixon was Irish on both sides of his family, a fact that was scarcely noticed in the campaign—he seemed to have no ethnic coloration at all. With the Kennedy and Fitzgerald clans, being Irish had been a source of power, a political base in Irish Catholic Boston, but it was also a wellspring of resentments. Rose Kennedy complained that the "nice people of Boston"—that is, the Back Bay, Protestant, Republican Brahmins—had never accepted the Kennedys, despite the family's money and political influence. Of course, to us in the new world, the Kennedys *were* the Eastern Establishment, no matter how much they felt themselves to be frustratingly apart from it. There was still about the Irish the stamp of the immigrant, although again, one never thought of the Nixons that way. California washes away such distinctions, which are nursed in Boston. The Kennedys were upstarts; they threatened the social balance by being too successful. The Nixons, on the other hand, were quiet failures who threatened no one.

This should have been one of the great political contests; we were entering a decade of dramatic change, and yet it was a campaign in which real issues scarcely surfaced at all. "Of the great civil rights battle that was to mark the decade, of the war in Vietnam, of the surge of female consciousness, of the eruption of youth, of the changes in life-styles, of abortion, of drugs, of the vast revolution in the tax system—not a single memorable speech or text comes down to me, either in recollection or in my notes," Theodore White would write in his memoirs. It was not, in any real sense, a political campaign at all. On the surface it was an apparent personality contest, and in that respect Nixon was absurdly overmatched. But under the surface—down, down among the primitive fears and prejudices—there were warning sounds, and they were evoked by Kennedy. These emanations had little to do with his politics. They had to do with his family, his religion, his education, his taste, his looks, his accent, his wife. Kennedy gave off threatening vibrations to millions of Americans, and no one was more finely attuned to that frequency than the right-wing Dallas housewife.

Kennedy's crowd included the Hollywood friends of his brother-in-law Peter Lawford. They were all, as one would say then, very advanced in their attitudes. Of course Nixon had movie stars in his entourage, but one never felt that he was at ease with them. Right after the election, Lawford's close friend Sammy Davis, Jr., married a white woman, the Swedish actress May Britt. "How do you feel,

Chicky Baby?" asked Kennedy's sister, and Sammy Davis said, "Man, I'm electric." We had never heard talk like that. Although Nixon was only four years older than Kennedy, with his boxy suits and homilies he was a thoroughgoing expression of the fifties. Kennedy, on the other hand, was sleek and cool and frighteningly modern. One sensed a chronological border falling between them—the boundaries of two ages, two sensibilities. With Kennedy, the sixties would break loose from the square, central, Nixonian values of the past and become morally unbound, experimental, open to change and sensation—in a word, hip.

In this feverish season John Wayne's epic movie, *The Alamo*, came to the Capri theater in Dallas, after its world premiere in San Antonio. With its budget of $12 million, *The Alamo* was billed as the most expensive movie of all time, a fact that seemed entirely appropriate to Texans, since it celebrated the central event in our history: the deaths of Jim Bowie, Davy Crockett, and 180 some-odd martyrs who died to make Texas a republic. I didn't know anyone who failed to see that movie. *The Alamo* became a talisman of our defiance. If John Wayne died to keep us from becoming Mexicans, who could doubt it was better to be dead than Red?

At the peak of the 1960 campaign, Nikita Khrushchev arrived at the United Nations in New York, loudly demanding the resignation of Secretary General Dag Hammarskjöld, and even pounding on his desk with a shoe—a gesture of such swaggering boorishness that it justified every qualm the Dallas Woman felt about Russia, the United Nations, and American foreign policy. Castro came too. There was an air of mischief about the pair of them invading this sanctuary of high diplomacy. Khrushchev would hold court from the balcony of the Soviet mission, cracking jokes and scaring everybody to death with his casual chatter about nuclear war. Castro checked out of his fancy midtown hotel, claiming he'd been badly treated and overcharged, and moved into the Hotel Theresa in the middle of Harlem. He received guests in his pajamas. I secretly liked Khrushchev and Castro. They reminded me of two of the Three Stooges, Curley and Moe; they were obviously having a great time. After all his attacks on capitalism, Khrushchev left the country with a freighter full of merchandise, including a Cadillac limousine, an Oldsmobile, a Mercury Comet, two television sets, and a pair of washing machines.

Dallas liked Nixon because he stood up to Khrushchev in the kitchen debates. He had brought down Alger Hiss, the exemplar of the Eastern Establishment. Kennedy talked tough—a lot tougher than Nixon—but in Dallas the national Democratic party was thought to be weak on Communism. Former governor Allan Shivers, who had led Democratic defections in the last two presidential elections, claimed that the Democratic platform in 1960 promoted "socialistic measures that socialist Norman Thomas never dreamed of." A group called Texans for Nixon took out an ad in the *Morning News* with a warning from Barry Goldwater about the influence of organized labor in the Democratic party, which he said was "something new, and something dangerous— born of conspiracy and violence, sired by Socialists, and nurtured by the general treasury of the UAW-CIO." The enemy was Walter Reuther, head of the auto workers union, who had spent time in Russia during his youth. "The campaign for President in 1960 is not the usual contest between old-time political parties. It is a life and death struggle between Vice President Richard Nixon on the one hand, upholding American principles, and the candidate of the Walter Reuther party, on the other hand, with what this plainly implies."

The Democratic candidate made an obligatory visit to Dallas, drawing a surprisingly large crowd, estimated at 175,000 people (Nixon, the day before, attracted only 100,000). Kennedy had just come from Houston, where he had spoken to a large group of Protestant ministers about the issue of his Catholicism. There was a widespread fear that Kennedy's election would be tantamount to letting the pope rule America. Since Catholics believe the pope to be infallible (the argument went), Kennedy would have to do whatever he instructed. Dr. Norman Vincent Peale, the apostle of positive thinking, gloomily wondered if American culture could survive a Kennedy presidency. There was some irony in this, since Kennedy was, as his wife privately admitted, an awfully poor Catholic. In Houston Kennedy had given a fine, important speech that seemed to have settled the matter. He won over House Speaker Sam Rayburn, who was escorting the candidate through his native state. However, the Protestants in Dallas weren't so easily persuaded. "The more I listen to him, the more I 'ha-ha,' " said Dr. Criswell.

No Democratic candidate had ever won the White House without carrying Texas; Kennedy knew that—that's why he picked Lyndon Johnson as his running mate, to the outraged dismay of the Eastern press and many of Kennedy's advisers, who regarded Johnson as a hard-shell Southern conservative, a native racist, a drawling, backslapping political whore with no guiding lights other than the oil-depletion allowance. They despised Johnson in the East because he represented the insurgent Southwest. They had no idea how much more we hated Johnson in Dallas. Here he was called a closet socialist, a leftover New Dealer, a bleeding heart in domestic matters and a weak sister when it came to standing up against Communist aggression. Was there ever a man in public life with such a divided image?

Four days before the general election Lyndon Johnson came to town. It was November 4, 1960, Republican Tag Day in Dallas, and the downtown lunch crowd was being canvassed by three hundred women in red, white, and blue. They were Bruce Alger's women. Many of them were in the Junior League, and they looked disarmingly girlish in their patriotic outfits and their red coif hats with ribbons streaming down the back. They were passing out literature for the Nixon-Lodge campaign. It was chilly, and some of them wore their minks.

Johnson had spoken earlier that morning in Arlington, and as he entered Dallas a city policeman pulled over his Lincoln to warn him of a "little disturbance" awaiting him at the Baker Hotel, where the Johnsons traditionally stayed. Commerce Street in front of the hotel was filling up with tag girls, who had now transformed themselves into an eager mob, complete with placards that Alger had stored in the Baker overnight. The cop advised Senator Johnson to use the hotel's Akard Street entrance to avoid the demonstration.

Several women spotted the Johnsons arriving and rushed over to surround their car. As Lady Bird was stepping out, one of the pickets impulsively snatched Mrs. Johnson's gloves from her hands and threw them in the gutter. Lady Bird went white. It was still a time when incivility was rare in politics, when public figures felt safe in crowds. No one, perhaps not even the tag girls themselves, was prepared to understand the ferocity and the anger of these apparently happy and well-cared-for women.

Johnson rushed Lady Bird into the lobby of the Baker, which was packed with jeering tag girls. As he entered the elevator Johnson turned and said, "You ought to be glad you live in a country where you have the legal right to boo and hiss at a man who is running for the vice presidency of the United States." There was an instant of silence, then a voice in the back of the crowd yelled, "Louder and funnier, Lyndon."

Johnson was expected to speak at a luncheon across the street in the Adolphus Hotel. Congressman Jim Wright of Fort Worth accompanied the Johnsons, and he forayed ahead. As he passed through the mink-coated rabble in the street, he encountered his colleague Bruce Alger grinning hugely and holding a sign saying LBJ SOLD OUT TO YANKEE SOCIALISTS. Wright told him that it was inappropriate for a United States congressman to be standing in the middle of a mob, and that no matter what Alger might think of a man's politics, Johnson was the Senate majority leader and was due the respect of his office. "I went to hear your man [Nixon] in my city this morning," Wright said. "I listened with courtesy. I wouldn't do what you're doing even if I felt that way."

"We're gonna show Johnson he's not wanted in Dallas," Alger replied, and the tag girls cheered.

As the Johnsons made their way through the Baker lobby, the crowd closed ranks behind them, becoming bolder. There were more of them waiting in the street, and beyond that, in the lobby of the Adolphus. This was an odd political gauntlet to pass through. It recalled the stoning of Vice President Nixon's motorcade by Communist students in Caracas, Venezuela. But this wasn't South America; this was Lyndon's own state.

The demonstrators in Commerce Street waited with placards and catcalls. Most of them were carrying Nixon-Lodge and TOWER FOR SENATE signs (one of the peculiarities of that election being that Johnson was entered in both races, thanks to a special dispensation from the Texas Legislature). THINK ONCE AND SCRATCH LYNDON TWICE, said one sign. Also: LBJ TRAITOR, JUDAS JOHNSON, and LET'S GROUND LADY BIRD. The Johnsons moved inside a small capsule of personal distance that grew smaller and threatened to collapse entirely under the crush of protesters. In retrospect it was that violation of private space that heralded our new, tragic political era. Years later, as president, Johnson would become accustomed to seeing hateful signs with his name on them; indeed, he would know the fury of the public as few men ever have, but in 1960 it was something new, something unheard of.

What was more surprising was that the sign carriers and catcallers were well-groomed women from the finest homes in the city. And yet, as the Johnsons waded into Commerce Street, the women in red, white, and blue began to curse them, and to spit. (Later, some members of the "Mink Coat Mob," as they came to be known, claimed that they were not spitting, exactly, they were frothing.)

Why? What accounted for the hostility—or to use her word, indignation—of the fashionable and affluent Dallas Woman? In part she was simply a prisoner of her age: a woman of unfocused ambition, intensely competitive but unemployed (the working wife was still a signal of economic desperation), lonely at home and given to causes. She may have been financially secure, but she was deeply troubled by some unfathomable fear that her castle was built of sand and the coming tide would wash her away. She named the tide International Communism or Creeping Socialism. She worried about the "missile gap" and the spread of Communism. Moreover, people in her own country were talking enthusiastically about social change—Kennedy was already speaking of "the revolutionary sixties"—and the Dallas Woman knew those changes would come at her expense. She worried about the erosion of liberty caused by recent Supreme Court decisions (often delivered by Chief Justice Earl Warren, who was the Creeping Socialist personified). The Court was taking rights away from the Dallas Woman and awarding them to pornographers, criminals, atheists, Communists, and Negroes. The Dallas Woman felt herself to be under attack at home and abroad.

Now she was striking back.

Johnson made his way through the placards with his wife practically buried under his arm. Lyndon, of course, loomed over the tag girls, his huge hound-dog face visible even at the farthest reaches of the crowd, but Lady Bird was on their level, and she could see the rage in their faces. She started to answer one of the insults, but Johnson put his hand over her mouth and guided her into the lobby of the Adolphus. "Let's just let them do all the hollerin'," he said.

They were waiting there, the tag girls and the hangers-on, but also press photographers and television cameras. John Tower, Johnson's senatorial opponent, was lurking in the stairwell, waiting for a chance to spring into Johnson's path with a list of political charges; but Tower, despite his name, is a diminutive man and was easily shoved aside by the crush of women.

Even in that mob it would have been a short walk to the elevators if Johnson had bulled his way through. But instead of pressing ahead, Johnson did something quite surprising. He slowed down. He moved with excruciating slowness through the chanting mob and the rain of spit. For thirty minutes Johnson and his wife withstood the harangue of the crowd, as the senator stared into the television cameras with a martyr's embarrassed smile.

It was the most triumphant half hour of Johnson's career, because that evening on the television news millions of Americans met the new Lyndon Johnson. They suddenly understood him exactly as he understood himself. He was a liberal—in the Southern context. Overnight he became an acceptable candidate to big-city Northern Democrats who had automatically hated him and to traditional Democrats everywhere who had not (they now admitted) seen past the corn-pone mannerisms of LBJ to the winking FDR inside him.

That evening, watching the news, thousands of Texans and millions of Americans decided how to vote. Although Nixon carried Dallas by a larger margin than any other city in the country, Texas went for Kennedy-Johnson. (Johnson also beat Tower in the senatorial election, although Tower would win the subsequent special election.) It was the closest election in history, and it was decided that day in the lobby of the Adolphus Hotel. People said afterward that they were not voting for Kennedy so much as they were voting against Dallas.

Against us. Until then, Dallas had had very little national identity, but now we found ourselves with a new municipal image: a city of angry parvenus, smug, doctrinaire, belligerent—a city with a taste for political violence. We were shocked to see ourselves portrayed this way, but it had little effect on the way we thought of ourselves.

Until the Adolphus incident, my mother had been coy about how she was going to vote. We teased her that she was falling for the Kennedy sex appeal, but she insisted that it was his mind she admired. She had read *Profiles in Courage*, which had won Kennedy a Pulitzer prize. And yet the notion of voting for the Kennedy-Johnson ticket was a heresy in her circle, so Mother was, until that moment, undecided. She and I watched the news together that night—she with horror, because the faces in the mob were familiar to her. They were the same faces she saw at her luncheons and bridge clubs. These were the women she aspired to know and emulate, for they were all Dallas Women, all fashionable, sophisticated, and financially well off; but they were also, Mother saw now, terrified, uncertain, and filled with hate. I remember her cry as we watched the humiliation at the Adolphus: "Shame! Shame!"

3 / A MAN ON HORSEBACK

There was, in fact, a chip of defiance on the city's shoulder, encouraged by the *Dallas Morning News*. The *News* bills itself as the oldest business institution in the state, having been founded in 1842 when Texas was still a republic and Dallas little more than a presumption. Under George B. Dealey the *News* had been a progressive newspaper, leading the scourge that drove the Ku Klux Klan out of Dallas, at a time when that organization controlled nearly every elective office in town. The name Dealey would become famous because of the fan-shaped park directly across the street from the Texas School Book Depository known as Dealey Plaza, with a bronze statue of the publisher beholding the now magnificent skyline of downtown Dallas. Many citizens believe it is perfectly appropriate that Dealey's name should be tied so irrevocably to the assassination, even though it is his son they blame.

E. M. ("Ted") Dealey succeeded his father as publisher of the *News,* and in his hands it became the most strident, red-baiting daily paper in the country, excepting only occasionally William Loeb's *Union Leader* in Manchester, New Hampshire. Dealey was a crackpot on the subject of free enterprise; he even attributed the high rate of traffic fatalities in Texas to "the same human qualities that made America great—willingness to risk, driving energy, rugged individualism." Like many intensely conservative people, Dealey found his paragon in the movies and politics of John Wayne. Indeed, reading the *News* each morning was like watching a big-screen brawl in a saloon, in which the newspaper's editorials flattened the "socialists" (read: Democrats), the "Judicial Kremlin" (the U.S. Supreme Court), and virtually every representative of the federal government whose views differed from those of Ted Dealey. Immediately after the election, the *News*'s principal object of contempt became John Kennedy, whom the paper described on various occasions as a crook, a Communist sympathizer, a thief, and "fifty times a fool."

Ted Dealey went to the White House in the fall of 1961 with a group of Texas publishers to meet the man he had maligned so frequently in his newspaper. He used the occasion to attack Kennedy in person. He accused the President and his administration of being weak sisters (a favorite Dealey phrase, with its vaguely homosexual charge). "We can annihilate Russia and should make that clear to the Soviet government," Dealey advised. To the embarrassment of his colleagues in the room, he added, "We need a man on horseback to lead this nation, and many people in Texas and the Southwest think you are riding on Caroline's tricycle."

That was typical Dealey guff: abusive, personal, and absurd. Dealey reported in his paper on this exchange with the President (GRASSROOTS SENTIMENT TOLD), although he failed to include the President's response. "Wars are easier to talk about than they are to fight," Kennedy told him. "I'm just as tough as you are, and I didn't get elected president by arriving at soft judgments."

Afterward, the editor of the *Dallas Times Herald*, the evening paper, wrote to the President to say that Dealey was speaking only for himself, not for the other Texans in the room. Kennedy responded with a snap of wit: "I'm sure the people of Dallas are glad when afternoon comes."

Kennedy was still thinking of his encounter with Dealey when he spoke later that year of people who "call for a 'man on horseback' because they do not trust the people. They find treason in our churches, in our highest court, in our treatment of water. They equate the Democratic party with the welfare state, the welfare state with socialism, socialism with communism."

With his prescient political eye, Kennedy saw that a new and dangerous challenge was arising; indeed, it was a vast political culture in the South and West, and it stood opposed to everything he represented: East Coast liberalism, mainstream politics, Ivy League learning, the customary restraints of educated society. Although Kennedy was popularly understood as a man of his time, a thoroughly modern president, he was in many ways the last of the traditionalists. He called his administration the New Frontier, but his elected successors—Johnson, Nixon, Carter, Reagan—would show that the real frontier in American politics lay far away, in the new world.

Although we were filled with resentment toward the society Kennedy represented, it was a resentment born of envy and intense curiosity. We felt inferior. That Jacqueline Kennedy spoke French and Spanish was impressive to us. We admired her taste; we liked for her to be at home with the great artists of the world, and her breathy, seductive voice suggested she was not all white gloves and pillbox hats. The Kennedys invested the country with a self-conscious eroticism that was nicely balanced by the presence of children in the White House. We were reminded of the Lincolns, a parallel that became more closely drawn after little Patrick Kennedy died. It recalled the death of Willie Lincoln, and we looked at the Kennedys with a new sense of poignancy. My parents had lost a child as well.

The Kennedy celebrity was overpowering. There was nothing to compare with it, except perhaps the Lindbergh phenomenon in my parents' youth, and the rise of Elvis in my own. Celebrity itself was rather new to us. My parents did not speak in personal terms about public figures; certainly they never discussed Eisenhower's hair or Mamie's dresses. We didn't know them very well. However, by the time the Kennedys came onstage we were deeply into the television age. It was like adding a gene for vicarious living. We could see into people's lives. We could peek into the Oval Office and see Caroline and John-John crawling under the President's desk. There was Jack talking politics with Bobby (they didn't even notice us, we were invisible). Jackie took us on a tour of the White House and showed us her bedroom. We knew the Kennedys in the same way we knew the Nelsons, the Ricardos, the Cleavers.

Eisenhower was a hero, not a celebrity; he did not have "charisma"—a word we were still struggling to define. It had something to do with an excess of vitality, and it was powered by sex. Kennedy obviously had a larger life than the rest of us; he was not only President, he was a star. He threatened the natural balance. He suggested that a person could rise out of our ant-colony democracy and acquire a superlife. It's no wonder the young were drawn to such a man.

I can remember a photograph of the new President as he came out of the water on the beach at Santa Monica. In the picture he was being mobbed by women, and he was grinning. It was the photograph of a sexual idol, slim, muscular, potent. But it seemed strange and a little blasphemous to see a president's body.

Daddy had his own dark thoughts about Kennedy. As a younger man he had had political ambitions of his own. Like Kennedy, he was a war hero; like Kennedy, he hoped to trade his wartime glory for public office. Kennedy was a young congressman from Massachusetts when my father made arrangements for him to speak in Oklahoma, at the Ponca City Chamber of Commerce, which my father chaired. Clearly there were advantages in an alliance between my father and this young political star. My father was expected to supply whatever the congressman needed, and what he needed was an ample and varied supply of Oklahoma women—no, not dinner dates, my father was instructed, just sexual companions. It was the moment my father's own political aspirations died. He saw then the secret appetites of the public man, and he understood how his own appetite for power might lead him to violate his vows to God. He did not even go to hear Kennedy speak.

In Dallas, however, he had reached a grudging accommodation with Kennedy's presidency. He was a different man than he had been as a young Oklahoma banker. He had witnessed political power and the aggrandizement of wealth at closer quarters. He was not so easily shocked. He had come to understand men whose needs were greater than his own, men who made promises only to themselves.

He had voted for Nixon, because he believed Republicans were good for business and business was good for the country, and he stayed suspicious of Kennedy despite the tax cut, investment credits, and liberalized depreciation—all hallmarks of a conservative administration bent on pleasing businessmen like my father.

But like most Americans, my father was affected by Kennedy's youth and intense maleness. The world since the end of the war had been led by white-haired men—Adenauer, de Gaulle, Nehru, Macmillan, Khrushchev, Mao Zedong, Chiang Kai-shek—men of another time, born, as Kennedy reminded us, in another century. Kennedy made them all seem decrepit. His vitality became a national challenge. He didn't sit, he rocked, and rocking chairs became an instant fad. "He Eats Up News, Books at 1,200 Words a Minute," we read in *Life,* and soon I was taking a speed-reading course. My father refused to go on one of the fifty-mile hikes the Kennedys were popularizing—he'd had enough of hiking in the infantry—but he believed in the moral value of fitness. Kennedy phrases began to creep into his vocabulary. We did things "with vigor" now, and when I'd ask him a question he'd preface his response with "Let me say this about that." Kennedy hated wearing hats, so my father, like every other man in the country, gave up wearing them. Everything Kennedy did or thought or wore or didn't wear had immediate and penetrating effect on our lives.

People were stirred up. Like Roosevelt, Kennedy had reached into the symbolic regions of our brains, where fantasies play. Soon after his inauguration the mail to the White House increased by 50 percent, but the proportion of letters from lunatics increased 300 percent. He was a magnet for dangerous emotions. He was too strong, too attractive, too sexy, too potent as a father, too beguiling as a husband, too promising as a son, too many things to too many people. All lines of power concentrated in his hands. He was not only President, the leader of the free world, he was also Prince Jack of Hollywood, he held the reins of the Eastern Establishment, he was the darling of the intellectuals, he even (we later learned) shared a mistress with a Mafia godfather. He was simply the most powerful figure we had ever seen.

Our family was under the spell of Camelot like everyone else, and yet, like nearly everyone else, we felt ourselves to be outside its gates. Camelot was an American court where the rich, the glamorous, and the powerful congratulated each other. It was a pantheon of celebrity. In Kennedy's Camelot there was nothing surprising about having Marilyn Monroe sing "Happy Birthday, Mr. President" in Madison Square Garden—and also become his lover. Marilyn was the self-appointed prize of ultimate celebrity; she had already given herself in marriage to Arthur Miller, our most celebrated playwright, and Joe DiMaggio, our most famous sports hero, and given herself sexually to numerous other cultural icons, possibly including Albert Einstein. Fame was a great adventure for her, but she suffered the consequences. A few months after the President's birthday, Marilyn would be dead, ostensibly a suicide. "When you're famous you kind of run into human nature in a raw kind of way. It stirs up envy, fame does," Marilyn said shortly before her death. "You're always running into people's unconscious."

The best-selling record album in 1963 was *The First Family*, starring Vaughn Meader with his dead-on impersonation of Kennedy's halting Bostonian speech. My father thought it was disrespectful, but my mother and my two sisters and I would sit around the dining room table and listen to it over and over, until we were all doing Meaderesque imitations. The best cut on the album was the last one, when baby Caroline asks her daddy to tell her a favorite bedtime story. "The one about the tall man?" asks the President. "Yes," says Caroline, "the tall man with all the hair."

"Well, there was this uh tall man with a lot of hair, and he was a prince and a great wahriyah [warrior]. And the people of his uh country picked him to be their leader because he uh could protect them and lead them on to the uh new frontiers . . .

"Now one day the evil prince with the black beard from the island in the south, and the terrible fat bear from the cold north came and they tried to hurt the prince. But the prince was too smart and he uh chased them away. So the handsome prince and his people lived happily uh ever after."

Caroline thanks him for the story, and we hear footsteps and a door closing, then she says, "These sessions do him *sooo* much good!"

When my mother first heard the punch line she laughed until the tears flowed. It was not such a funny story as all that, but it told us something about how we saw the world, and how we saw Kennedy, and how Kennedy saw himself. We were all like Caroline; we were helping Kennedy through his presidency.

Our humor was edged with hysteria. It seemed to us then that the world was turning away from us, that our enemies were cleverer than we, more resourceful, more ruthless. We were losing ground in Europe, Africa, Southeast Asia, even in our own hemisphere. We watched the Berlin Wall go up on August 13, 1961, and saw the East German police, the Vopos, slaughtering citizens when they tried to escape. We were stunned when the Russians suddenly sent a man into orbit after our own failures in the space program. And we were frightened when they began to rattle the globe with immense atomic explosions, thirty in one month alone, culminating in a fifty-seven-megaton device that knocked the needle off the microbarograph at the Lamont Geological Observatory. It was 2,500 times greater than the bomb that destroyed Hiroshima, and according to one calculation five times greater than all the explosives of all the wars in history.

We resumed our own nuclear tests in spectacular fashion with a giant hydrogen bomb in space. Tourists lined up on Hawaiian beaches to get the best view of the blast. "The blue-black tropical night suddenly turned into a hot lime green," wrote *Life* reporter Thomas Thompson. "It was brighter than noon. The green changed into a lemonade pink . . . and finally, terribly, blood red. It was as if someone had poured a bucket of blood on the sky." We lived on the brink of apocalypse.

Our insecurity was compounded by the sight of our own society tearing apart. Since the lunch-counter sit-ins in Greensboro, North

Carolina, in 1960, we had seen the civil rights movement become more aggressive, attracting a violent reaction that was really a kind of war—a strange war that could be waged only in our violent democracy, a war fought in courtrooms and city councils and state-houses and PTAs and unions and fraternities and boardrooms, but also in the streets, the kitchens, and in the small details of human exchange between a woman and her maid, in the nuances of speech (Negro, nigra, nigger—my own family used the middle term), and always in the complications of etiquette, such as an adolescent white boy on a city bus wondering if he should surrender his seat to an elderly black woman loaded down with arthritis and shopping bags.

In the fall of 1962 President Kennedy and Mississippi governor Ross Barnett were facing off over that citadel of resistance to social change, the University of Mississippi. An Air Force veteran named James Meredith had applied for admission as "an American-Missis-sippi-Negro citizen," and was turned away on four occasions. The campus swelled up with angry segregationists, many of them carry-ing guns, some undergraduates wearing Confederate uniforms, ev-eryone giddy with excitement over the battle to come. In the middle of this riotous crowd was General Edwin Walker.

Five years before, when President Dwight Eisenhower sent fed-eral troops to desegregate Central High in Little Rock, Arkansas, he had placed General Walker in charge. It was the most distin-guished act of Walker's career. Later he was relieved of his com-mand in Germany when he was discovered to be proselytizing his troops with right-wing literature. Walker resigned his commission and moved to Dallas, where he expected his politics to be more welcome. *Newsweek* placed him on the cover in 1961 as a symbol of the emerging radical right. Like Bruce Alger, he became a darling of the conservative Dallas housewife. He drew many of them into the local chapter of the John Birch Society. In return they helped to make him one of the city's most prominent citi-zens—notable enough, at least in the mind of another citizen, Lee Harvey Oswald, to be worth assassinating.

Walker said he came to the Ole Miss campus to repent for Little Rock. "Now is the time to be heard," he cried out in a muddled radio speech. "Ten thousand strong from every state in the Union. Rally to the cause of freedom. The battle cry of the Republic. Barnett, yes; Castro, no. Bring your flags, your tents, and your skillets. . . . The last time in such a situation I was on the wrong side. . . . This time I am out of uniform and I am on the right side and I will be there."

The riot that followed was one of the bloodiest in the long history of civil rights struggles; two men were killed, hundreds were wounded. General Walker was charged with insurrection and seditious conspiracy and was sent to Springfield, Missouri, for psychiatric observation at the U.S. prison and medical center. He returned to Dallas on a $50,000 bond, a hero of the resistance. Soon after that he joined up with the anti-Communist radio evangelist Billy James Hargis for a coast-to-coast speaking tour entitled "Operation Midnight Ride."

Walker did have a certain appeal (his military rectitude and air of command recalled General Douglas MacArthur, and with his Southern dignity of manner he would have been well cast as a Confederate cavalry officer), but he played only a brief role in the events of the moment. In a few years he would be virtually forgotten—an eccentric but, to some newsmen, rather dear old biddy, who twice surfaced from obscurity in the 1970s when he was arrested on misdemeanor homosexual offenses.

On March 10, 1963, while Walker was out of town on Operation Midnight Ride, Lee Oswald went to the general's home on Turtle Creek Boulevard and snapped some photos. He also made sketches of the placement of the windows in the house. Two days later he sent a money order to a mail-order sporting goods company in Chicago for $21.45, along with a coupon he had clipped from *American Rifleman* magazine. It was payment for an antiquated Italian rifle known as a Mannlicher-Carcano. The weapon came with a four-power telescopic sight.

One month later Walker was back in town, seated at his desk, working on his income tax return. It was 9 P.M.; his head was in the sight of Oswald's rifle, 120 feet away.

Walker thought that a firecracker suddenly exploded directly above him. He turned and saw a hole in the window frame and realized that he was covered with bits of glass and a pale wash of plaster. The police hypothesized that Walker had moved his head at the last moment. Walker disagreed. In his opinion the light in the room had flooded out the window frame from the assassin's perspective. The bullet had struck the sash and been deflected. In the morning Walker showed the damaged window to newsmen and wryly remarked, "And the Kennedys say there is no internal threat to our freedom."

I've often wondered what scale in Oswald's mind would give General Walker and President Kennedy equal weight. To me this first assassination attempt is the strongest evidence against a conspiracy, although one could argue that by demonstrating his willingness to kill, Oswald certified himself as a real assassin to— whomever. But a person would have had to have been in Dallas, looking at the world through our own provincial lens, to have seen General Walker as anything other than a local crackpot. Oswald told his wife, Marina, that he shot at Walker because he was a fascist. "If someone had killed Hitler in time, many lives would have been saved." Only in Dallas could Walker have been seen as a figure of such importance. He wasn't even that notable in Texas. He had run for governor in 1962 and finished last in a field of six. To the world at large, Walker was just another right-wing Dallas fanatic, a curiosity.

Oswald did not make any further attempts on Walker's life, but he did follow the general's activities in the city. Walker was now partly martyred and riding high. When UN ambassador Adlai Stevenson announced that he would come to Dallas to speak on United Nations Day, October 24, 1963, it was a dare that Walker couldn't ignore.

Some right-wingers persuaded Governor John Connally to declare October 23 "U.S. Day," and they promoted it into a small event. Bumper stickers around town said U.S. DAY OR UNITED NATIONS DAY—THERE MUST BE A CHOICE and YOU CANNOT RIDE BOTH HORSES. The night before Stevenson was to speak there,

General Walker rented the Dallas Memorial Auditorium for a U.S. Day rally. Oswald went to hear Walker's talk.

There were twelve hundred of Dallas's most radical citizens in the auditorium that night—Birchers, Minute Men, Christian Crusaders, and members of the National Indignation Convention, which had been founded in Dallas to protest the training of Yugoslavian pilots at a nearby air force base. The NIC was at that point the fastest-growing right-wing organization in the country, according to *Newsweek*. Walker reminded his audience that the United Nations was an instrument of the worldwide Communist conspiracy, and that on the following night they would have the opportunity to make the rest of the world know that Dallas was one place where the people weren't fooled. Walker proposed to have a welcoming party for Adlai Stevenson.

Everyone knew that Stevenson was facing a hostile reception. The *Dallas Times Herald* published a cartoon on the eve of Stevenson's visit, showing Kennedy telling his quaking ambassador to "Be Brave." Stevenson stood hand in hand with the Kennedy boys and with Earl Warren as the most hated men in Dallas, with the difference that while the people who hated Warren and the Kennedys claimed to admire the institutions they represented, they simply couldn't tolerate the United Nations. It stood for one-worldism, which was nothing more than Communism. It stood for talk, not action. It was a forum for anti-American complaints, which we didn't care to hear. The Texas Legislature passed a bill that year making the display of the UN flag a crime. Nearly every car in the city with an IMPEACH EARL WARREN bumper sticker boasted its companion, GET US OUT OF THE UN.

There was, in addition, something intensely personal about the hatred of Stevenson. He was the last word in eggheads, Mr. Humpty-Dumpty himself. His urbanity didn't wash in Dallas, where intellectual charm was suspect (if you took the trouble to be witty, you probably didn't have it where it counted). Stevenson was the original weak sister.

He arrived to find the auditorium surrounded by pickets. Among them, perhaps, was Oswald, who claimed later that he had attended the speech (others thought they saw him holding a sign). Of the two thousand people inside, many of them were supporters of General Walker, and they had brought Halloween noisemakers and placards that had been stored in Walker's house overnight. When Stevenson stood to speak, the auditorium erupted with tooting, clanging, ratcheting sounds. Protesters paraded up and down the aisles carrying miniature American and Confederate flags. One man screamed, again and again, "Kennedy will get his reward in hell! And Stevenson is going to die! His heart will stop, stop, stop! And he will burn, burn, burn!"

For the majority of the audience, both the ardent Stevenson supporters and those uncommitted citizens who only wanted to hear him speak, it was the most embarrassing public display they had ever attended. Already Dallasites had begun to grow concerned with their city's image, and that night for the first time an aroused sense of civic protectiveness began to assert itself. The majority cheered Stevenson and several times gave him a standing ovation, despite the taunts and jeers. They did what they could to police the disrupters in the audience. When Frank McGeehee, a beefy garageman who was the founder of the National Indignation Convention, stood up and began a loud tirade, a small elderly man approached him and tried to push him back into his seat. Police officers finally ejected McGeehee. Above the ruckus, Stevenson coolly observed, "For my part, I believe in the forgiveness of sin and the redemption of ignorance."

The police formed a cordon around Stevenson when he left the auditorium, but outside were more than a hundred pickets waiting for him—a lynch mob, really—and Stevenson's sudden appearance set them off. They crowded toward him, waving placards and screaming his name. Stevenson found himself penned in, facing mass hysteria. This was an episode completely outside his experience. He was himself well known for his civility. He had a gentle belief in the power of reason. One woman caught his eye. He should have disregarded her. He must have wondered how his mere presence could send this lady into such a flight of frustrated despair. Who was Adlai Stevenson that he had such emotional power over strangers? His instinct was to talk sense to her, to exorcise the demon he was in her mind. He stepped toward her, out of the police line.

The mob swallowed him. While the police fought to retrieve him, the hysterical woman, who was the wife of an insurance executive, brought her placard down on the ambassador's head. (The sign said, IF YOU SEEK PEACE, ASK JESUS.) A college student spat on him. When the police finally pulled him into the waiting car, Stevenson wiped the spit from his face with a handkerchief and asked aloud, "Are these human beings or animals?" The crowd responded by rocking the car. At that moment it seemed likely that Stevenson would be murdered on the streets of Dallas, but the driver gunned the car and burst through to safety.

What effect must this have had on Oswald? If he was standing there, as he claimed he was, did he despise the mob? Or was he rocking the car as well? Did he, in this moment of hysteria, feel a sense of permission, a license for political violence?

Kennedy asked Arthur Schlesinger, Jr., to call Stevenson and congratulate him on his courage. It was the quality Kennedy admired above all others, what he called "that most admirable of human virtues." Stevenson joked about the incident, but he was shaken. "There was something very ugly and frightening in the atmosphere," he said. He urged Schlesinger to discourage the President's scheduled trip to Dallas the following month. That, unfortunately, Schlesinger decided not to do. How could Kennedy go to Texas and bypass Dallas? People might say he was afraid of Dallas. Even to suggest such a thing in the Kennedy White House was evidence of cowardice. "I was reluctant to pass on Stevenson's message lest it convict him of undue apprehensiveness in the President's eyes," Schlesinger recalls.

Yes, we were shocked by the Stevenson incident. The city's leaders wired an apology, the city council adopted an antiharassment ordinance, and the mayor spoke out against the far right. On the other hand, Bruce Alger contended that the city had no reason to feel disgraced; the protesters had only proved that Dallas was "proud, courageous, and truly the home of the brave." General

Walker hung the American flag upside down outside his Turtle Creek home, signaling distress at the city's apology to Stevenson. "Adlai got what was coming to him," he told reporters.

Since much of the world would hold the political atmosphere of Dallas responsible for the President's assassination, it is interesting to discover how closely attuned Oswald was to the events of the moment. He was everywhere, a political gadfly. He was incredibly exotic in Dallas—a man who called himself a Marxist, who actually had defected to the Soviet Union, but who lived now in Oak Cliff with a Russian wife. He thought of himself as a Communist spy. He wrote a letter to Communist party headquarters in New York describing General Walker's speech. "As you see, political friction between 'left' and 'right' is very great here." He proposed to infiltrate the American Civil Liberties Union. "Could you advise me as to the general view that we had on the A.C.L.U. and to what degree, if any, I should attempt to *highten* [sic] its progressive tendencies?"

The night after the Stevenson riot, the ACLU met at Southern Methodist University. It was a small meeting, as any gathering of Dallas liberals was bound to be. Someone made the statement in the flow of discussion that just because a man was a Bircher didn't mean he was an anti-Semite. "I disagree with that," said a voice, and Lee Harvey Oswald stood up. He explained that he had attended General Walker's rally and had heard a number of anti-Semitic as well as anti-Catholic remarks. People who heard Oswald speak that night had varying reactions to him. The Reverend Byrd Helligas, the associate pastor of the First Unitarian Church, thought Oswald "erudite." A woman found him too sarcastic. Michael Paine, a research engineer and a Quaker, who knew Oswald slightly and who had brought him to the meeting, thought his companion had spoken "loud and clear and coherently."

Afterward, a Dallas couple who had learned about Oswald's background cornered him and grilled him about politics. The man recalled: "I said to him, 'I know that you have communistic tendencies.' He interjected, 'I am a Marxist.' It left me with the impression that it was decidedly different. Of course, Stalinist, Communist, Marxist—to me he's a Commie."

Oswald was utterly out of place in Dallas. The biggest surprise of the assassination was the evidence that the President had been shot by a leftist. In *Dallas?* It was unusual to meet even a liberal Democrat. Oswald once related that he had become interested in Marxism when a woman on a street corner handed him a brochure protesting the recent execution of Julius and Ethel Rosenberg. That was in 1954, the year of the Army-McCarthy hearings, the peak of the Red Scare in America. The country was terrorizing itself with its obsessive fears of Communism. Congress was considering extending its witch-hunt into the classrooms and the churches. And yet Communism as a real political force was already extinct in America, a phantom. At that point fifteen-year-old Lee Oswald in New Orleans decided to give form to the fears: He would become a Communist, the national enemy. He would become a Rosenberg.

Psychologists would say he had joined a pseudocommunity, one that existed only in his mind. Oswald told acquaintances that he was looking everywhere for a Communist cell to join; he also wrote letters to the Socialist party. But even after he defected to Russia, he testified to the solitariness of his political beliefs in a letter to his brother, Robert: "I have been a pro-communist for years and yet I have never met a communist."

He had an admirable feeling for the underdog. In highly segregated New Orleans he once provoked a fight when he chose to sit in the Negro section of a city bus. A group of white boys attacked him. "People who saw the fight said that Lee seemed unafraid," Robert Oswald has written. "His fists flew in all directions, but he was outnumbered and thoroughly beaten up."

Oswald eventually fled to Russia, married a pharmacist, then returned to the United States and settled in the city where he was most likely to be feared, despised, and persecuted. Like many villains he fantasized about being widely loved. He told his wife, Marina, that he would be president himself in twenty years, when he would be forty-three, the same age as Kennedy was when he was elected. And yet few people loved Oswald. "Everybody hated him," Marina said after the assassination, "even in Russia." In Oswald's mind, hate was superior to indifference; he wanted people to feel strongly about him. In Dallas, they certainly would.

Like General Walker, Oswald was drawn to the volatile, violent politics of the new world. Such men always appear in the midst of social hysteria. Dallas would excuse itself because the assassin was not right-wing—we were enormously relieved when we heard about Oswald's Marxism—and yet the atmosphere of fanaticism beckoned to chaotic and suggestible individuals and drew them near.

In November 1963 the cover of *Life* magazine showed Senator Barry Goldwater with his horse, Sunny. THE ARIZONAN RIDES EAST, said the headline. The month before, *Time* magazine conducted a state-by-state survey and predicted a "breathlessly close contest" between Kennedy and Goldwater in 1964. It would be Ted Dealey's dream come true, a political showdown between the old America and the new. Was Barry Goldwater the man on horseback who would ride out of the West and take control—in our name?

Goldwater was idolized in Dallas. He would come to town and preach against welfare, Social Security, collective bargaining, and public housing. "The inescapable by-product of such operations," he said, "has been the weakening of the individual personality and of self-reliance." That was the creed of the new world. He took our breath away by saying things in public that even reactionaries only muttered in private. Goldwater's solution to the war in Vietnam, which was suddenly becoming a nuisance, was to "drop a low-yield nuclear bomb on the Chinese supply lines." As for the Russians, "let's lob one into the men's room of the Kremlin." I was secretly thrilled when he said that "the country would be better off if we could just saw off the Eastern Seaboard and float it out to sea." It was the first time anyone had touched that nerve. We were just beginning to realize the depth of our resentment against the bureaucracy, the media, and the dominating institutions of that part of the country.

Goldwater would not have won the 1964 election, even if

Kennedy had been alive to contest it. The new world was not yet strong enough, but it was growing, expanding, extending itself. What was happening in Dallas was spreading throughout the South and the West. New forces were arising. Ronald Reagan, whose political career began with his nomination of Goldwater at the 1964 convention, would capture the California governor's office by a million-vote majority two years later. George Wallace electrified the South in the spring of 1963, when he stood on the steps of the Alabama statehouse to take the oath for his first term as governor, and cried out, "Segregation now! Segregation tomorrow! Segregation forever!"

In Texas the ancient coalition that constituted the Democratic party was being pulled apart. John Tower had become the first modern Republican to win statewide office, which he did with the help of the liberals. (They thought he'd be easier to beat next time around than his conservative-Democrat opponent.) The state's other senator, the liberal Ralph Yarborough, was engaged in a quarrel with conservative governor John Connally, which was splitting the party into warring factions. Connally himself was having second thoughts about supporting the national Democratic ticket in 1964, even though his mentor, Lyndon Johnson, was on it. But perhaps Kennedy could hold them all together through one more election if he would just come to Texas. And bring his wife, Yarborough advised.

Crowds in San Antonio, Houston, and Fort Worth met the President with enthusiasm, but those receptions were eclipsed in the press by the rift between the party leaders. In Fort Worth, Kennedy had to order Yarborough to ride in the motorcade with the Vice President. In every other respect the trip was a big success. Kennedy was in great form, the audiences were enchanted, and his wife's presence gave the trip an air of glamour and high occasion. The President joked in Fort Worth on the morning of his death, "A few years ago I introduced myself as the man who accompanied Mrs. Kennedy to Paris. I'm getting somewhat the same sensation as I travel around Texas. Nobody wonders what Lyndon and I wear . . ." He was irresistible, completely winning.

He left behind him an administration that was nearly paralyzed. His thousand days in power had been a complete failure in domestic matters. Spending for social welfare had risen less rapidly than it had during the Eisenhower years. His social agenda was blocked in Congress by Southern committee chairmen who were willing to bring all government to a halt over the single issue of civil rights. The signal accomplishments of his presidency were a tax cut, the test-ban treaty, and a military buildup that was proportionally larger than the one Ronald Reagan would initiate two decades later. "In the past three years we have increased the defense budget of the United States by over twenty per cent," Kennedy boasted in Fort Worth, "increased the program of acquisition for Polaris submarines from twenty-four to forty-one; increased our Minuteman missile purchase program by more than seventy-five per cent; doubled the number of strategic bombers and missiles on alert; doubled the number of nuclear weapons available in the strategic alert forces; increased the tactical nuclear forces deployed in Western Europe by over sixty per cent; added five combat ready divisions to the Army of the United States, and five tactical fighter wings to the Air Force of the United States; increased our strategic airlift capability by seventy-five per cent; and increased our special counter-insurgency forces which are now engaged in South Vietnam by six hundred per cent."

Despite his reputation as a liberal, even in Texas we were beginning to understand that Kennedy was a conservative president. "The business record of this President," Lyndon Johnson planned to say that afternoon, "is written in the terms of our highest gross national product, highest personal income, highest employment, highest corporate profits in history. If that record—plus the tax cut, plus liberalized depreciation, plus investment credits, plus trade expansion—is 'anti-business,' then it is time we rewrote the dictionary."

Dallas was next. Although crowds everywhere else in Texas had been large and responsive, there was still concern on the part of the Texas politicians with the Kennedy entourage about what might happen there. After Dallas, the Kennedys would fly on to Austin.

According to Stanley Marcus, Lyndon Johnson was going to conclude his welcoming speech the following night with the remark "And thank God, Mr. President, that you came out of Dallas alive."

After his breakfast speech in Fort Worth, Kennedy was given a copy of the *Dallas Morning News*, which contained front-page articles about the spats among the Texas Democrats, and a full-page, black-bordered advertisement inside the front section. "Welcome Mr. Kennedy to Dallas," it read. "A city so disgraced by a recent Liberal smear attempt that its citizens have just elected two more Conservative Americans to public office. . . . A city that will continue to grow and prosper despite efforts by you and your administration to penalize it for its non-conformity to 'New Frontierism.' " The ad included twelve rhetorical questions that accused the President of going soft on Communism and betraying American allies. It was signed by Bernard Weissman, chairman of the "American Fact-Finding Committee," a completely fictitious entity. Weissman turned out to be a member of a right-wing coterie formed by three American servicemen who had recently been stationed in Germany. Like Oswald and General Walker, the members of the group had gravitated to Dallas.

Kennedy read the advertisement and handed it to his wife. "Oh, you know," he told her, "we're headed into nut country today."

4 / GOD AND THE BOMB

An inventory of myself on the day the world changed:

I was sixteen, a hormonal volcano. Like all romantic virgins I was interested only in sex and death, but was untouched by either. I hated my innocence and viewed myself as unfortunate for having lived a happy life. I had felt neither grief nor ecstasy, only years of pubescent anxiety and shallow, unmerited happiness.

We were *middle class*—already that term sounded like a death sentence for the soul. I saw my life as being essentially frivolous. Insulated from need, unfamiliar with injustice, I longed for tragedy and consequence. I wanted something to happen. I think the fevered politics of Dallas was fueled partly by this same emotion, which was a type of fear. We were afraid something would happen. We were afraid nothing would happen.

My family lived in the largest house on a modest block in East Dallas. My father loved houses; he preferred them solid and roomy, and always with a fireplace. There were five of us, counting my parents, me, and my sisters, Kathleen and Rosalind, both younger than I. We owned a 1959 Chevrolet station wagon and, until that summer, a 1956 Ford sedan, solid black, standard transmission, which I had nearly destroyed in drag races on Gaston Avenue. After I ruined the clutch, my father sold the Ford and bought a secondhand six-cylinder Dodge Dart with a push-button automatic transmission, which could barely gain enough speed to navigate in traffic.

My high school was named after Woodrow Wilson, a devout internationalist who would have been held in the same regard as Adlai Stevenson were he not long and safely dead. If you walked down the hallway of Woodrow Wilson High School in November 1963, you would see kids dressed as they were nearly everywhere in the United States at that time—boys in madras shirts, slacks (blue jeans were forbidden), girls in woolen shifts or pleated skirts, both sexes wearing white socks and penny loafers. To dress differently would invite comment, which no one cared to do. The constituency of my school was middle- to lower-class whites. The only Negroes were the kitchen help. One of the few notable alumni (he didn't graduate) was Richard Speck, who would soon inaugurate a new age of mass murder by killing nine nursing students in Chicago. We still began each morning with the Pledge of Allegiance, but this was the first year that we no longer prayed before class. The Supreme Court declared prayer in public schools unconstitutional in the summer of 1963, a decision that infuriated the zealots in the community. We were often reminded that no one could prevent us from praying secretly, and that silent prayer was a small but worthwhile rebellion.

I spent my summers working, first as a busboy in a hamburger joint, and then as a loader on the dock of East Texas Motor Freight, on the midnight-to-eight shift. I grew to hate sunrises. What I liked about the night was the absence of time. At four in the morning when the night surrounded the loading platform and filled the empty bays with pitch, I might have been working on a space station; nothing else was alive at that hour beyond the glow of the floodlights and the drone of the "line"—an oval track embedded in the concrete floor, which ferried flatbed dollies around the dock. Most of the men who worked the midnight shift had this same predilection for darkness. I imagined that many of them were on the run from some darkness in themselves, and this was appealing to me; they carried an air of defeat and hidden pasts. We were overseen by a scowling ex-marine who lived in a raised, glassed-in office, which was like a guard tower in the center of the dock. He was Management, we were Labor.

I belonged to the notoriously corrupt Teamsters Union. In Texas, unions were widely distrusted and despised, not only because they were an impediment to free enterprise but also because they were thought to be controlled by mobsters or Communists or both. Once, when I was late paying my dues, two men came into my truck and asked if I'd ever heard of the Black Glove. "That's what they stick on your door when you forget your union. They use a stiletto." The other man added, "It don't happen a second time." It was a measure of my mental state that this threat was thrilling to me.

We went to church twice on Sundays and sometimes on week nights for chautauquas. Like everyone I knew, I accepted Jesus Christ as my personal savior, but I never really felt the Spirit come over me. Once, when my dog ran away from home, I prayed for God to bring him back and promised I would never doubt Him again if He would only bring Beau back to me. Thirty seconds later Beau came shambling up the sidewalk, expecting forgiveness. I thanked God, but I felt tricked.

Much of my high-school social life in 1963 revolved around a Christian youth group called Young Life. We met once a week in the evening with our Bibles to talk about God and adolescence. Our leaders were a former all-American football player and a former stewardess—Roy and Johnnie, husband and wife, a pair of sexual magnets who kept the wires humming in the teenage imagination. They seemed to be machine-tooled to appeal to the football hero–cheerleader set, of which I was conspicuously not a part. Roy was a muscled cube with a Rose Bowl ring and a nose that had been pounded flat. Once, a couple of girls jokingly asked him to flex his muscles, and when, jokingly, he did, the room went dead quiet. Johnnie was an ironic brunette, part Indian, with black eyes and Cherokee cheekbones. She had a high tolerance for moony adolescent boys. For those of us who fell into that category, Johnnie was an object of reverence, the only grown-up, full-blown woman we knew who laughed at our nervous jokes and treated us with an unexpected sexy forbearance.

I was drafted into the spiritual leadership, a special study group called Campaigners, which dwelt on the eternal problem of bringing new souls to the Lord. One of the souls I recruited was my sister Kathleen, who is eighteen months younger than I am. I took on her faith as my own special assignment, nurtured it, prayed for it, and reported on it in our inner council. We were gearing up for a Young Life ski trip over New Year's, and Roy suggested that Kathy should come—her salvation was at stake. He expected me to be there as a matter of course; I was one of his lieutenants.

Imagine a hundred horny teenagers crowded into a meeting room, red-faced and windburned from two days of skiing in subzero weather, bright-eyed with faith, singing at the top of their lungs:

> *V! is for Victory!*
> *Victory in Christ our Lord!*

It was New Year's Eve, a night of salvation. We were girding ourselves against the disbelievers, the Doubting Thomases, the godless intellects of the universities. Roy picked me to play the role of an intellectual agnostic, whose argument was that God was like a watchmaker, who wound up his timepiece (life) and then died. I hadn't thought of myself in that role before; in fact I pretended to a piety I didn't really own. But as I argued for the heresy of God's death I found a new voice inside me, honest, skeptical, and horribly persuasive. Where had this voice come from? Was this really me, uncorked? Or was I merely performing for Roy? I could see him smiling at my cynical responses to the anxious questions of the Christians before me. I was crushing their faith with irresistible logic. "Now," said Roy, "refute yourself."

I surveyed those blithe, windburned faces in front of me. Time passed. Roy glowered in my direction, but the thoughts wouldn't come.

"I guess," I said weakly, "you just have to believe."

That seemed to satisfy the audience; they were prepared for belief, not for doubt. They were Saved. Tears were falling now as the testimonials began. One of Kathleen's best friends put her arms around her and told her she loved her and asked her to forgive her.

"What have you done?" Kathy asked warily.

"I slept with your boyfriend."

I had my own sexual confession to make. I told Roy about my overpowering lust, which he assured me was nothing out of the ordinary. But when would it be over, I wanted to know; it was a fever that wouldn't break. Roy grinned and put a fatherly hand (the one with the Rose Bowl ring) on my shoulder. "It never stops," he confided. "I'm still struggling with it myself."

I was scandalized. Married to Johnnie, the female paragon, Roy wanted more!

Suddenly the lights went out, and the voice of Johnnie herself cried out, "Happy New Year, everybody! We will now have three minutes of darkness!"

We stumbled around in a sanctioned Christian orgy of anonymous kisses and felt breasts. I sorted through the girls, looking for Johnnie. But she would not be found.

Roy made his final appeal the next day. "I want everyone who loves the Lord to follow Johnnie into the next room," he said. "Anyone else, I want to have a word with in here."

I wanted to love the Lord, and I wanted to follow Johnnie, but there was that stubborn new voice inside me that wouldn't allow it. A moment later, Kathy and I were staring at each other: we were the only people left in the room.

It was a long train ride back to Dallas. Roy had been shocked; he said he would pray for us, but he scarcely spoke to me after that. The other Christians were on us like bees all the way home—it wasn't Dallas we were headed toward, it was hell itself.

Why had I lost my faith? That was a question I couldn't answer, even to myself. The new voice inside me—the voice Roy had permitted to speak—said that God was dead, man was in control. Where was God when we bombed Hiroshima? When Hitler exterminated the Jews? We lived on the edge of extinction in a world where comfortable morality had given way to fallout shelters and survival ethics. Were we supposed to turn the other cheek when the Russians launched an ICBM? I wasn't aware that these pessimistic thoughts of mine were a part of a larger national impulse, a disillusionment with old values that would be characteristic of my generation. I only knew that in Dallas, Texas, in 1963, the voice inside me was the voice of apostasy, and I should do what I could to shut it up.

The Bomb always had been a part of my life; it was arguably the reason I was even alive. The first atomic bomb fell on Hiroshima on August 6, 1945, almost exactly two years before I was born. My father was a captain in the infantry then. When the war ended in Europe he prepared for the invasion of Japan. It would have been the bloodiest invasion in history; the Army calculated as many as two million casualties. Later, my father went to Japan with the Occupation, and when he learned of the impregnable defenses of Tokyo harbor, he became convinced that the atomic bomb saved his life. That was an association he passed on to me. When I was old enough to see the films of the horrors of Hiroshima and Nagasaki, the thought that never left my mind was: three hundred thousand Japanese dead, but I am alive.

And so whenever the civil defense sirens interrupted my school-days with their apocalyptic howls, I folded my papers neatly and filed into the hallway and squatted in front of the lockers with my head between my knees and my hands on the back of my neck, like everyone else, but my thoughts were complex and vaguely guilty. Three hundred thousand Japanese—had they ever really existed? Or was life nothing more than a dream played out in the theater of my mind, which invented details of reality—the smell of wax in the hallway, the scuff marks on my shoes, the discomfort of en-forced silence, the presence of "others"? There is really no end to the rationalizing power of the teenaged solipsist.

But suppose I really was only an assemblage of atoms in a vast real universe, practicing to be annihilated in the hallway of Woo-drow Wilson High? Suppose that the weight of history had crushed three hundred thousand Japanese for the single reason that I might be conceived and grow to adolescence in order to die in Dallas while staring at my shoes? Was this divine? Was this the organiz-ing principle in the real universe—not God but absurdity?

In those days we did not know if we would survive from month to month. We spoke about "brinkmanship," and the metaphor buried in that term was that we were a crew of Spanish explorers who feared we might finally sail off the end of the earth. The difference between us and the Spaniards was that our atomic brink really existed. The chances of a nuclear exchange were increasing every year, so that growing old, or even growing up, seemed unlikely. Even if we missed the apocalypse, our bones were already saturated with radioactivity from all the testing in the atmosphere; we might be doomed already to ugly deaths from cancer. The most popular book in the country in 1961 was a Defense Department publication titled *The Family Fallout Shelter*. Kennedy wrote a letter to the readers of *Life* magazine urging us to build shelters in our homes to supplement the government shelters already under construction. Everyone was thinking about large questions and What Is to Be Done? Did we really want to survive in a postnuclear world? An opera singer at the Met (a mezzosoprano) had her Social Security number tattooed on her abdomen in case of disaster and boasted that she would never seek refuge in a fallout shelter. What if she did? Our usual ethical solutions lost their snap when we faced the moral puzzles posed by nuclear catastrophe. Should you shoot a person who seeks safety in your shelter? That was a question we debated in church, without satisfaction. Our pastor recalled the parable of the Good Samaritan, but it didn't seem appropriate to the occasion. "I can see letting one or two guys in," said a member of the congregation, "but what about ten? fifty? You've got to draw a line somewhere." Another woman, slightly ecstatic, said we were all going to die in the blast and meet Jesus, so what's the problem?

As in every other town in the country, we imagined our city was on the Kremlin's first-strike list. It was a strange kind of civic pride that would not permit a nuclear war without our immediate destruction. The only people assured of survival were the President and certain government officials. They would be spirited off in high-altitude jets or buried in a hardened bunker under the Catoctin Mountains in Maryland—with their secretaries, not their spouses. Kennedy appointed a secret group of 1,300 people, called the X Squad, who were supposed to run the country after the war.

I appreciated the need for contingency planning, but it worried me that the people most likely to trigger a nuclear encounter were the ones most likely to survive it. Properly prepared, we were told, the rest of us could expect a 97 percent chance of survival—a figure universally recognized as a lie. Nonetheless, we kept an extra supply of canned goods in our house, and Mother stored bottled water in the closet. We had a small store of candles, flashlight batteries, and a transistor radio with the Conelrad stations marked with the nuclear triangles. Parents were told not to try to rescue their children from school; presumably we were safe in the hallways. The mother of a friend of mine told him if she *ever* came to school to get him, he was to go with her and never mind what the teachers or the principal might say. One day he was gazing out the window of his classroom and saw his mother drive up, and he jumped right out the window and ran to her car. She was bringing his lunch money.

During the Cuban missile crisis, I wrote to an Italian pen pal that by the time he received my letter the world might be destroyed. I wonder what that teenaged Neapolitan must have thought about me and my country. I had written with a certain cold-bloodedness characteristic of the moment. We were verging on apocalypse, but we faced it proudly. All we asked was to defend our principles by blowing up the world. It's no wonder the rest of the world began to distrust us, and to worry about our terrible resolve.

We still believed that God was on our side—it wasn't a joke then. We believed in the forces of light and the forces of darkness. My parents' generation had seen America rise out of the Depression to become the liberator of Europe and the dominant power in the world. The sins of the Nazi empire reinforced our own belief that we were the defender of the faith. We saved civilization. As our reward, God gave us the Bomb.

But by 1963 we had the feeling that God had turned away from us. The idea of a magic nation that ruled the earth died in 1957, when the Russians sent up *Sputnik*. Suddenly America was second-best and in decline. Kennedy was supposed to change that with his breathless challenges. He said we would meet any burden, pay any price to secure liberty, but the Bay of Pigs had made him look incompetent and even morally wrong. Were we really the same nation that had liberated Europe? He said we would put a man on the moon by the end of the decade, but we couldn't get our own rockets off the pad. Was this the same country that built the Bomb? Where was American know-how? Now the only scientists we believed in were the Germans we had rounded up after the war. We thought of ourselves as a people that believed in justice, but in our own country we had just begun to notice poverty and institutional racism. Abroad, we were squandering the great asset of our history, our revolutionary heritage; now our corporate conglomerates dominated the world markets and represented repression and the status quo. Before, we could count on our luck and industry and our infallible conscience; these were divine trusts. Somewhere, somehow, we must have betrayed them in God's eyes—in Hiroshima, perhaps. We had lost faith in ourselves, and why not? Hadn't God?

Now we had to fend for ourselves. We were learning what it was like to live in the world of men, without God's blessing. There was a spirit of panic in the press and in Congress. What to do, what to do? Work harder. Americans were too soft, especially the young. We had to be firmed up, educated, made tough and vigorous—like Kennedy.

I admired Kennedy's education and polish, his fabulous reading speed, his war record, his fitness—although sometimes his qualities seemed too good, either fake or superhuman. There were always rumors about his health. During the 1960 campaign, John Connally claimed that Kennedy was suffering from Addison's disease and might not survive his presidency, if elected. We all knew about his bad back, but there were rumors that he was a virtual cripple, another FDR. And yet there he was, playing touch football in Hyannis Port and swimming in the White House pool.

My father wondered about Kennedy's war record. He didn't

question the President's courage, but his judgment. It was true Kennedy had saved the life of one of his men on PT-109, on a mission in which Kennedy was supposed to torpedo a Japanese destroyer. Instead, the lumbering destroyer managed to slice the speedy PT boat in half, killing two crewmen. Apparently, Kennedy had failed to notice the ship until it was bearing down on top of him. "Our reaction to the 109 thing had always been that we were kind of ashamed of our performance," admitted one of the crew, Barney Ross. "I had always thought it was a disaster."

Was this heroism? Or just luck—that Kennedy was still alive and not brought before a court-martial? The Navy rejected his application for a Silver Star, and it wasn't until a friend of the Kennedy family, James Forrestal, became secretary of the Navy, that Kennedy received a life-saving award. To my father, it seemed that Kennedy's vaunted war record was neither heroic nor lucky, it was just a function of privilege. I later came to feel the same way about Kennedy's Pulitzer prize for *Profiles in Courage*, which actually was written by Kennedy's speechwriters and Jacqueline Kennedy's former history professor.

Kennedy had spent thirteen years in the House and Senate without passing a single important piece of legislation. And yet even before his election to the presidency, people were comparing him with Franklin Roosevelt, with the young Churchill, with various movie stars, with Lindbergh. I felt the heat of his glamour; you couldn't miss it—he was so smart, so polished, he was blessed. But there was something else about him, something about his *type*, that put me off. Everything was too easy for him.

The archetype behind Kennedy in my mind was Charles Van Doren, who had also impressed me with his Eastern style and grace, his offhanded elegance, and his apparently easy access to all worlds of knowledge. During the prime-time game show era of the late fifties, my family would watch "The $64,000 Question" and "Twenty-one." We were in awe of the erudition of the contestants sweating it out in the isolation booths. I remember the actor Vincent Price matched against a twelve-year-old genius on the subject of art history, and another child prodigy who scribbled fantastic mathematical equations on the glass face of the booth. The most exciting contestant of all, however, was Charles Van Doren, who held the nation in thrall for fourteen weeks on "Twenty-one." He was clean-cut, graceful, apparently omniscient. He was thought to be a counterweight to the sinister influence of Elvis Presley on the minds of the young. His family was scholarly; his father, Mark Van Doren, a Shakespeare scholar and a Pulitzer prize–winning poet, had written one of my literature textbooks. I remember the tension as Van Doren struggled for his answers. Who sings the aria "Sempre libera" in *La Traviata*? "She sings it right at the end of the party given by . . . What's her name? Soprano. Her name is—Violetta!" Mother often knew the answers; she had a vast amount of erudition she never gave herself credit for (as if, being who she was, she didn't deserve her intelligence); and she would agonize as Van Doren appeared to search for answers she had already guessed. The only answer I knew was the names of the seven dwarfs in *Snow White*. "Bashful! Bashful!" my sisters and I cried, the dwarf Van Doren nearly forgot.

He was a fraud, of course; the contestants had been given their answers in advance. After Van Doren was indicted he loudly insisted on his innocence, as if innocence were his birthright. In that way he finally reminded my parents of Alger Hiss, another elevated Easterner who defended himself by pointing to his honorableness. We gave Van Doren more than the benefit of the doubt; even when he fled his indictment we imagined he'd been kidnapped, and when, ultimately, he confessed, three out of four Americans said they would have done as he had done.

It was the system, he said, that made him do it. Corruption was built into the system—he was just going along. Until then, I believed what I heard on the radio, what I saw on TV, what I read in the papers. But on the edge of the sixties the system cracked like an egg on a bowl. "Payola" was the new word for bribery, applied now to disc jockeys who were paid to play particular records, to cultivate hits. Even Dick Clark admitted taking payola on "American Bandstand." Dick Clark!? I knew Dick Clark!—in the same way I knew Charles Van Doren. They had become part of my life. I had believed them, I had accepted them entirely.

Television was still new enough that we hadn't learned to distrust it, but now we were learning, and fast. The special quality of television was that it could create false heroes. Van Doren was just the first to drop his mask. That was the question I had about Kennedy. I couldn't decide if he was truly heroic, or one of those simulated heroes of television, whose real appeal was his heroic "image."

The final question we all hated to ask was whether Kennedy was rightfully President. Immediately after the 1960 election there were charges it had been stolen. The Republican National Committee received 135,000 complaints of voting irregularities, such as the South Texas county with 86 registered voters, which cast 24 votes for Nixon and 147 for Kennedy. Around Lyndon Johnson there had always hung charges of voting theft, going back to his 1948 election against former governor Coke Stevenson, which Johnson won in a runoff by 87 votes. By 1960 Johnson controlled the Democratic party apparatus in Texas as no one ever had. In the presidential election, according to the *New York Herald Tribune,* there were 100,000 votes counted in Texas for the Kennedy-Johnson ticket that had never been cast in the first place (the Democrats carried the state by only 46,000 votes). In Illinois, Mayor Richard Daley held back the vote tallies for his machine-controlled city of Chicago until the downstate Republican vote had come in. At that point, according to Theodore White, who was watching the vote in Hyannis Port with Kennedy's campaign aides, the election was over—Daley would make sure of that. In fact, Richard Daley was the first person to call Kennedy "Mr. President," which he had done several hours before.

Illinois and Texas—it was enough to throw the election. The *Chicago Tribune* complained that the election was "characterized by such gross and palpable fraud as to justify the conclusion that [Nixon] was deprived of victory." And yet Nixon refused to contest the result. He went so far as to ask the *Herald Tribune* to stop its investigation of the election and to persuade the editors of the Chicago papers not to demand a recount of the vote in Cook County. Why? Why would any man surrender the greatest political prize in the world? Would an investigation reveal that enough votes were stolen by Republicans to make the issue moot? There was never any evidence of that. Nixon said he didn't want the country plunged into a constitutional crisis like the Hayes-Tilden dispute a century before. America's place in the world was too insecure. What if he demanded a recount and won? The nation would be divided by partisan bitterness; the act of governing would be almost impossible. Nixon admitted he would not like to show the American people that the presidency can be bought. And if a recount showed Nixon had really lost? Texas governor Allan Shivers reminded Nixon that voters never forgive a sorry loser.

I have wondered at times how the country might have been different if Nixon had won the election—which, fairly counted, he probably would have. So much sadness is buried in Kennedy's presidency. He led us into the Bay of Pigs. He got us into Vietnam. Nixon might have made the same mistakes as Kennedy; it was Nixon, after all, who originally proposed the invasion of Cuba. One future mistake of his own Nixon would not have made was Watergate, which was partly motivated, in my view, by his paranoia that the stolen election of 1960 might happen again.

And, of course, Kennedy would be alive. It seems to me that almost anything would be worth that single fact. What I have come to hate about Kennedy is the myth that replaced him, a myth he largely created, and yet it is the man himself, full of grace and humor, I love and miss. What a different country we might have had. What a different person I might have been.

5 / SOMETHING HAPPENS

In the morning I went out to get the *News* and found on our doorstep a flier that looked like a wanted poster in the post office. It was John Kennedy, full face and profile, and the flier said he was WANTED FOR TREASON. Below that his crimes were listed:

1. Betraying the Constitution (which he swore to uphold): He is turning the sovereignty of the U.S. over to the Communist controlled United Nations.

   He is betraying our friends (Cuba, Katanga, Portugal) and befriending our enemies (Russia, Yugoslavia, Poland).

2. He has been WRONG on innumerable issues affecting the security of the U.S. (United Nations—Berlin Wall—Missile Removal—Cuba—Wheat Deals—Test Ban Treaty, etc.).

3. He has been lax in enforcing Communist registration laws.

4. He has given support and encouragement to the Communist inspired racial riots.

5. He has illegally invaded a sovereign state with Federal troops.

6. He has consistently appointed anti-Christians to Federal office; Upholds the Supreme Court in its anti-Christian rulings.

Aliens and known Communists abound in Federal offices.

7. He has been caught in fantastic LIES to the American people (including personal ones, like his previous marriage and divorce).

I brought the flier in with the paper and read it on the way to the breakfast table. I had heard most of it before—who hadn't? It was the same old right-wing tirade, except for the charge of Kennedy's "previous marraige and divorce," which was new to me. I was already running late to school, so I didn't read the *News* that morning, but later in the day one of my first instincts would be to save the paper (as did many other people in Dallas, including eight-year-old John Hinckley, Jr.). It was November 22, 1963.

My sister Kathleen recalls seeing that date written on a blackboard several days before—she had a school assignment due that day—and feeling an instantaneous surge of horror, a buzz, almost an electrical shock. There were other premonitory currents in the city. Later, the guilt we felt for Kennedy's death would have less to do with his assassination by a man only slightly associated with our city than it would have to do with our own feelings of anticipation. Something would happen—*something*. We expected to be disgraced. It had happened with Lyndon Johnson, it had happened with Stevenson, it would happen again. There was a low-grade thrill in the city such as there might be in a movie audience when a gunfight is about to occur—it was that kind of secondary excitement, not the fear that someone would really die, but an expectation that something dramatic would appear to happen, that we would see it or hear about it, certainly talk about it later, but that it would pass with no harm done. Political theater, in other words.

My father was one of the city leaders invited to the Trade Mart for Kennedy's luncheon speech. He had gone there with his friend Jack Evans, who would later serve as mayor. As they were driving down Irving Boulevard they saw *Air Force One* just above them, approaching Love Field. It was 11:40 a.m. They remarked on the close timing of these presidential occasions, and how brief they were; Kennedy would be here and gone in a couple of hours.

Although schools were let out in Houston and San Antonio when the President's motorcade passed through, in Dallas we could be excused only in the custody of a parent. So like most of my classmates I was in school when it happened. It was right after lunch. I was in Algebra. Mr. Irvin Hill was describing a parabola on the blackboard when the three tones came over the public-address system and the principal started to speak. We knew something was wrong before he said a word. There was a choked pause. We could hear a radio playing in the background.

"The President has been shot."

It was only a fraction of a moment before he gave us details and then played the radio commentary into the PA for the remainder of the hour. But in that instant the world we knew shattered and collapsed. *It happened*—the something we had been waiting for. *It happened!* We were dazed and excited. We turned in our chairs and looked into each other's faces, finding grins of astonishment. Later, when reports appeared about Dallas schoolchildren laughing at the news, I wondered if I hadn't laughed myself. It was such a release of anxiety. At that point in my life I knew no more about the nature of tragedy than a blind man knows about the color blue. All I knew was that life could change, it had changed at last. Hadn't we known? Hadn't we been scared of exactly this? We asked ourselves these questions with our eyes, looking for some fixed response to this new flood of circumstance. We were giddy and frightened, and as for me I was grateful for the loss of innocence.

Meanwhile, in the Trade Mart, my father and the other guests waited and waited and began to grow impatient. Finally the first course was served. Then Eric Jonsson, president of the Citizens Council, arose and said in a quavering voice that there had been an "accident"—he wasn't more specific. "The President has been hit," someone reported. My father supposed there had been a rowdy demonstration of some sort. Another friend of mine stayed in the Trade Mart until the nature of the tragedy was revealed. Kennedy was his hero, but in the fumbling moments that followed the announcement, my friend, aged fifteen, went boldly to the dais and stole the salt and pepper shakers from Kennedy's place setting.

". . . shot in the head, Governor Connally wounded . . ."

My father overheard these words on a police radio as he passed by a motorcycle outside the Trade Mart. It was the first time he ever heard the term "grassy knoll." Shocked, confused, he drove back to the bank and watched television with his tellers.

Some of the details were off base. We heard that Vice President Johnson was shot too, that he was seen entering Parkland Hospital holding his arm. Who else? Were they killing everybody? I never paused to think who *they* were. It was Dallas, of course—faceless assassins but essentially Dallas pulling the many triggers. I supposed we were in the middle of a right-wing coup.

As we sat there, gazing crazily at each other and at the PA box on the wall, I finally noticed Mr. Hill and saw tears streaming down his wrinkled cheeks. His chest began to heave, then he sobbed in great barks. Everyone was watching him now, studying him as if he had some simple formula for this new hypothesis, but his grief was a private thing, and he picked it up like the greatest burden he had ever lifted and carried it out of the room. As he left, I felt the first prodding overture of shame.

"The President is dead."

It was a shock how much the world hated us—and why? Oswald was only dimly a Dallasite—he was a Marxist and an atheist—you could scarcely call him a product of the city. He was, if anything, the Anti-Dallas, the summation of all we hated and feared. How could we be held responsible for him? And yet the world decided that Kennedy had died in enemy territory, that no matter who had killed him, we had *willed* him dead.

The truth is we had drawn closer to Kennedy even as the rest of the country grew disenchanted. The disgrace of the Bay of Pigs actually helped Kennedy in Dallas. My father admired the way the President shouldered the blame. The missile crisis in Cuba showed Dallas that Kennedy had learned the use of power; it also showed us the danger of Ted Dealey's bluster. Kennedy was tough after all. We liked him. We wanted him to like us. When he came to Dallas we gave him the warmest reception he received in Texas. It was the perfect confrontation between Kennedy's vaunted courage (walking into crowds, stopping the motorcade to shake hands) and our new willingness to make friends with him.

The crowds and the cheering were real responses. In fact the last words Kennedy heard in life were spoken by Nellie Connally, the governor's wife, who turned and said, "Mr. President, you can't say Dallas doesn't love you." It was a true observation, but also history's damnedest irony, for an instant later Jacqueline Kennedy had to respond, "They've killed my husband. I have his brains in my hand."

She said *they*—meaning Dallas, an assumption the whole world shared.

Dallas killed Kennedy; we heard it again and again. Dallas was "a city of hate, the only city in which the President could have been shot"—this from our own Judge Sarah Hughes, who swore in Lyndon Johnson as president aboard *Air Force One*.

But Dallas had nothing to do with Kennedy's death. The hatred directed at our city was retaliation for many previous grievances. The East hated us because we were part of the usurping West, liberals hated us because we were conservative, labor because we were antiunion, intellectuals because we were raw, minorities because we were predominantly and conspicuously white, atheists and agnostics because we were strident believers, the poor because we were rich, the old because we were new. There were few of the world's constituencies we had failed to offend before the President came to our city, and hadn't we compounded the offense again and again by boasting of these very qualities? In any case we were well silenced now.

Oh, we felt sorry for ourselves, all right. The city's display of self-pity was another reason to hate us. The impression we gave was that Oswald's real crime was not murder but libel—of our reputation, our good name. We were not penitent, we were outraged. We were the victims.

The final words of the speech the President would have delivered in the Trade Mart were the Psalmist's injunction: "Except that the

Lord keep the city, the watchman waketh but in vain." He had meant to be speaking of his generation of Americans, who were charged with keeping peace in the world. But, as my father thought, Kennedy might have been speaking of Dallas as well, because all the watchmen of our city had not been able to protect him from one fey killer. It seemed an awful prophecy for Dallas that, despite our piety, God had let it happen here.

In church that Sunday, November 24, my father, Kathy, and I heard our minister preach a sermon entitled "Let's Change the Climate." The word "climate" already had acquired a supercharged meaning in Dallas. Where it once had been used only to describe the abundant opportunities for business growth, now it was appropriated by the newscasters and magazine writers as a sort of net that could be tossed over the entire city, implicating everyone in the crime. Yes, there were fanatics in Dallas, but weren't we all responsible for creating a climate in which fanaticism could take root? a climate of hate? a climate of intolerance? a climate of bigotry? It was an unanswerable charge. My father's jaw set as we heard the minister accepting the blame on behalf of the city—his sermon was being broadcast nationally on ABC radio—the blame for the climate that was responsible for Kennedy's death. At the end of the sermon, when we had sung the doxology and were standing to leave, someone walked to the pulpit and handed the minister a message.

"Oswald's been shot!"

The congregation slumped back into the pews. The police were telling us to leave downtown, to evacuate the area. What now? What was going on?

It was simply too much—a psychological breaking point for many of us, who, like my father, had held out against the insinuations of the press, who had refused to accept blame for the climate in Dallas. But the more we learned about the circumstances of Oswald's death and the background of his killer, the more we had to acknowledge our responsibility. A local nightclub operator named Jack Ruby had wandered upon Oswald being transferred from the city jail, and shot him down in front of the whole world.

Unlike Oswald, Jack Ruby was one of ours, he did his deed in the very bowels of our own city hall, and he did it in a spirit of horrified civic-mindedness. Our incompetent police force let him do it. The defense we had established for our city in the death of the President didn't apply in the death of the President's killer. Dallas didn't kill Kennedy, but in an awful, undeniable fashion it did kill Oswald.

A phenomenon remarked on by psychiatrists after the assassination was the dearth of dreams. The normal functions of the unconscious mind seemed to have been displaced by unending hours of television viewing. Commercials disappeared—that was itself a weird and ominous phenomenon. From the moment of the President's death at noon on Friday until after midnight the following Tuesday, the broadcasts virtually never stopped, and as they are played back in my mind now—the death march, the half-stepping troops, the riderless horse, John-John's salute—they have the quality of a remembered dream, haunting, full of meaning, experienced but unlived.

Americans have always had a secret love of pageantry, unfulfilled because of the absence of royalty, and this massive grandeur was new to us and thrilling. I remember being struck by the vocabulary of the occasion, words like "bier" and "caisson" and "catafalque," which had a sound of such solemn importance that they could be used only a few times in one's life—like rare china dishes one sets out only for the king.

My mother and Rosalind stayed home on Sunday morning to watch the Mass for the dead President. Cardinal Spellman called him "the martyr of this century," a designation we accepted without questioning what cause he had died for. Kennedy was lying in the East Room of the White House, where Lincoln had lain nearly a hundred years before. This was a parallel, Lincoln and Kennedy, we would never quite shake off, although the assassination of President McKinley might have drawn a closer analogy. McKinley had been a popular president, but he was not a martyr like Lincoln—

except perhaps to the cause of laissez-faire capitalism. Kennedy's claim to martyrdom was based on the belief that Dallas had killed him. But even I wanted to believe that his death had meaning, and so I allowed myself to think that he was a martyr to something—perhaps to my own evil desire for something to happen.

After Mass, the procession to the Capitol began to form, and the networks switched their coverage to the Dallas City Hall. It was a scene of confusion and anticipation. Before now we had had only a brief glimpse of the accused assassin. He had spoken briefly to the press in a wild, impromptu press conference. He didn't sound like a Dallasite; despite his years in Russia he retained his gumbo New Orleans accent—he said "axed" instead of "asked." He had a spooky composure about him, although according to our district attorney he was as good as convicted, so few of us doubted his guilt.

Finally Oswald appeared in the doorway, dwarfed by the beefy detectives on either side of him but still looking cool and at peace, while all around him chaos raged. I suppose this was the supreme moment in Oswald's unhappy life. He had always been the outsider, unaccepted, unloved, but he had turned the tables on us. He was suddenly the man with the answers, his secrets were locked in his skull, and we were all outsiders now.

And as he entered the basement of the city hall, Oswald's defiant glare fell directly on Jack Ruby. Was it an illusion, or was there the surprised look of recognition between conspirators at that moment, replayed a million times by now, when Ruby stepped into Oswald's path and gunned him down?

Since Oswald's death we have learned very little more about that or the event of the assassination, but we have learned unimaginable things about our country. The assassination sent a shaft through our society, throwing unexpected light on creatures used to the dark—spies, mobsters, informers, mistresses, all of them surprised in strange alliances. It was not the assassination itself but this vivid exposure that would forever change our understanding of how our country worked. We would become ashamed of our naïveté. Simple explanations would never satisfy us again.

It is odd that a single moment of reality—Oswald's assassination of John Kennedy—can be folded and refolded into infinite origami constructions. Was it a plot on the part of H. L. Hunt to protect the oil-depletion allowance? Was Oswald a secret agent for the Russians? for the Cubans? for us? Was he a part of a larger conspiracy? Was there really only one Oswald? Some theories suppose there were three, perhaps even five. Not a single assumption goes unchallenged; perhaps Kennedy is not even dead. (For years we heard the rumor that he was still alive in some vegetable state in Parkland Hospital, that another body had been smuggled out and buried at Arlington.) It is a way of explaining everything, of giving meaning to events. Reality is twisted into art. Is there such a thing finally as truth? (If there is not, there must be a God.)

I think what each of us believes about the assassination says something about the kind of person we are, what we are willing to believe about our country and ourselves. I believe Oswald acted alone. Perhaps it is easier for me to locate evil inside the single human heart than it is to believe in broad conspiracies. Also, killing has come easy for me. I once took a potshot at a red-tailed hawk that was circling below the clouds, and to my astonishment he folded his wings and fell out of the sky like a sack of mail. The year of the President's death I went hunting with my father and some of his business friends on a South Texas deer lease. I had experienced, I thought, enough of killing by then, but as I was walking across an open field carrying one of the hunters' guns, a stag broke out of the brush, nearly 175 yards away. I knelt and fired, then watched him cartwheel and fall on his side, his feet pointed at me. I've always had good luck in killing.

Why did I shoot the deer when I told myself I wouldn't? For one thing, I was licensed to kill (my father had taken that precaution). My action had been approved in advance. At the heart of the Dallas-killed-Kennedy argument is a similar presumption about Oswald: the community hated Kennedy so much that Oswald felt licensed to act out our fantasy.

There is another reason I killed the deer. I was there, I had a gun, the deer appeared. *He came to me.* It sounds mindless, I suppose, but I don't believe that thinking has very much to do with instinctive responses. Oswald must have felt something like this when he read in the newspaper that Kennedy's motorcade would pass directly in front of the School Book Depository, where Oswald was a warehouseman. *He's coming to me.* "He" who? Did it matter—any more than the identity of the deer in the field? Oswald had already tried to shoot General Walker. On another occasion he told Marina that Richard Nixon was in town, and he was "going to have a look" at him; Marina locked her husband in the bathroom and hid his pistol until she was certain Nixon was safe. However, Oswald never stalked Kennedy; Kennedy came to him. He said on several occasions how much he admired the President. After his arrest he told police "My wife and I like the President's family. They are interesting people" and "I am not a malcontent; nothing irritated me about the President." I don't think Oswald would have chosen to shoot Kennedy if the President had made different arrangements, if he had not come to Dallas, if he had not ridden in an open limousine, if he had not passed by the School Book Depository. In a similar way I don't think Jack Ruby would have shot Oswald if he had not been carrying a gun anyway (because he had gone to the Western Union with a wad of money to wire to one of his strippers), if he had not been downtown at that moment and seen a commotion at city hall, if he had not wandered down into the basement to see what was going on ("Curiosity got the best of me"), if he had not stumbled at that very moment into the presence of Lee Harvey Oswald. Conspiracists sneer at coincidences such as these, but I think coincidence can be a powerful, irrational spur to violent response. One opportunity—*act now or else!*

The paradox of Jack Ruby's life is that he would be the one to stop forever Oswald's answers to our many questions, for Ruby was himself both a lone nut (in my opinion) and a conspiracy buff. He came to the same conclusion many other conspiracists reached when he looked at the White House and saw Lyndon Johnson. "If Adlai Stevenson had been vice president," he told a reporter, "there would have been no assassination." Ruby was a shady character with mob connections, associations with anti-Castro Cubans, and a brief, ineffective history as an FBI informer. And yet he found it bizarre that people included him in a conspiracy—especially a conspiracy with Oswald. He did what he did "for Jackie and the kids."

Ruby was a compulsive glad-hander, a Big D booster who prided himself on knowing everybody in town—and on being known, especially to reporters and cops. He was always reminding them, "You know me, I'm Jack Ruby!" and giving them free passes to his strip joint, the Carousel Club. Psychiatrists at Ruby's trial would testify to his "voracious need to be accepted and admired . . . particularly by individuals in positions of authority and great social prestige." He knew the mayor. He knew the disc jockeys and sportswriters and entertainers in town. He once talked himself into a club sandwich with actress Rhonda Fleming at the Dallas airport. He longed to be well known.

When Ruby fired his gun, he was taking celebrity away from Oswald and giving it to himself. Hadn't Oswald done the same to Kennedy? Oswald had been nothing only a day before, now he was universally known and recognized; he already had that aura of fame. Ruby's first impression of Oswald was that "he looked like Paul Newman." Another irony of Ruby's sad life is that people would later say he looked like Lee Harvey Oswald.

Oswald was television's first real death. Until then TV had been almost exclusively a medium of fantasy, so that part of the shock of Ruby's action was simply that it was real. It was as if one had touched a statue and found it made of flesh. Suddenly we understood television in an entirely new way, in a manner that prepared us for the many murders to come, for the "living room war" of Vietnam, for the constitutional lessons of Watergate, and finally, monotonously, for the local murders of the ten o'clock news. To my father, television had been a most incidental piece of furniture, something one turned to in idle moments, which he seldom had. With Kennedy's death, the completely new realization came over people like my father that the thing to do was to turn on TV. By itself, the assassination and the televised ritual that followed would have signaled a new age. Television gave us our first universally shared experience. From now on, rich and poor, black and white, Northerner and Southerner, would live a portion of their lives in common. But it was Oswald's death on television that galvanized the country. We could not leave the set after that—it was too powerful, anything might happen now!

They buried Kennedy on Monday. The drum corps was at the lead, and then came the bagpipers, and six gray horses drawing the caisson; then the riderless horse, a brilliant black animal who pranced and skittered and who seemed, at that moment, the only really alive creature on the planet. The Kennedys came next, a family that had only begun to live out its tragedies. And then, en masse, the princes of the earth, a mob of presidents and premiers and sheiks and kings. At the head of the line I recognized Charles de Gaulle towering over Haile Selassie—de Gaulle dressed plainly as usual, Selassie burdened under the many medals he had awarded himself—and it made me wonder about the conceit of men who would live important lives. What kind of person was John Kennedy that his death could bring the world to a stop? Was his life so important? It was as if a god had died.

Everyone was superior to us now. In those days Texas plates on your car were an invitation to rudeness, or worse. When news of the assassination came over the radio, one Texas driver was paying for gas off the Pennsylvania Turnpike; the attendant threw his change in his face. That reaction endured, in less spontaneous fashion, for years, even after Los Angeles and Memphis suffered their tragedies. Dallasites have always begrudged the fact that those cities were never taken down the way Dallas was, and made to feel at one with Birmingham and Selma.

That year the University of Texas football team went unbeaten and played Navy in the Cotton Bowl. Texas won, 28–6, but the New York Touchdown Club voted Navy the 1963 collegiate champion. A friend of Rosalind's became Miss Teenage Dallas, but the pageant officials told her there was no chance she would be chosen as the national queen. We were outcasts, and we knew it. We stopped singing "Big D."

Our family made a trip to Florida the next summer. We had
been there once before, and what distinguished that previous trip
was a confrontation between Kathleen, then no more than seven,
and a hatchet-faced waitress at a truck stop on Highway 90. Kathy
had been to the rest room marked WHITES ONLY, and she asked the
waitress where it was that colored folks went. "Why, darlin'," said
the waitress, "they don't go 'round here *at all.*" Kathy, who has all
of her life suffered from an inability to bite her tongue, said, "You
ought to be ashamed."

Now we were back in Florida with Texas plates, and even Kathy
understood we had been morally neutered, that we had no standing. We stopped at a service station for gas and Cokes. It was
blisteringly hot. We sat in a sweat with the windows down while
Daddy paid for the gas. The attendant took the money and looked
in the car.

"Where from in Texas?" he demanded.

"Dallas," my father admitted.

The attendant nodded as if he already knew that, then he stuck
his face in the window to get a closer look at us. His face was deeply
tanned and cracked, like a dried-up creek bed. What frightened me
was the liberty he felt he could take with us, staring at us like that;
I felt like a slave at auction. "Y'all killed our president," he said
in a wondering tone, as if he had surprised himself by catching us
red-handed.

Daddy hit the accelerator in disgust.

After that I seldom told people where I was from. Once, at a
restaurant in Mexico, some Americans at the adjoining table overheard us talking about Dallas and they just got up and left—left
their dinner sitting there.

Years later, when I thought the world might have forgotten, I
was riding on the Orient Express en route to Istanbul. With me
in the coach were two Greeks, two Turks, a Spaniard, and a
Frenchwoman. We were trying to fill out the Bulgarian transit
cards, which were written entirely in the Cyrillic alphabet. One of
the Turks claimed to have experience in the matter and was filling
out our cards. He interviewed each of us in Turkish while his
companion translated his questions into Greek. One of the Greeks

spoke Spanish, the other French. When they got to me, the Spaniard asked in English, "Where you from?"

"United States."

The Turk nodded and said something else, which passed through the chain of tongues and came out, "What city you?"

"Dallas, Texas."

I was immediately, universally, understood. The others in the coach looked at me, and one by one they pointed their index fingers at me and said, "Bang, bang, bang." It's the same word in every language.

Perhaps an outsider can understand how each new assassination was greeted with relief and resentment in Dallas—relief, of course, that it hadn't happened in our city, and resentment that no other town would ever know the opprobrium Dallas had endured. Political murder has been a feature of American life since 1835, when Richard Lawrence tried to shoot Andrew Jackson, and between that time and Oswald's murder of Kennedy, three presidents were killed and three others had been the objects of assassination attempts. And yet there was a common assumption, frequently stated, that it all started in Dallas. The Dallas-killed-Kennedy theory swelled into metaphysics, until Dallas became responsible for assassination itself. We were the motive force that toppled the first domino in the murderous chain; the trail of bodies that have since fallen all across the continent could be traced back to the School Book Depository. You could walk through the world announcing "I'm from Los Angeles," or "Laurel, Maryland," or "Memphis, Tennessee," and receive an occasional dim acknowledgment that something tragic had happened in your town, but even then you would not expect to be held responsible. Waiters would not be reluctant to give you service because of your origins. Telephone operators would not refuse to place your calls. But for years after President Kennedy's murder, saying you were from Dallas was like saying you were from Nazi Germany.

To be from Dallas meant, in the eyes of the world, that you were inherently more inclined toward murder than the next fellow. The assumption was unconscious, a stereotype, no different really from a racial prejudice. It's no wonder Dallasites were defensive and angry. And yet behind our anger was the fear that there must be a whisper of truth in the lies people were telling about our city.

In December 1963 Melvin Belli came to Dallas to defend Jack Ruby. His first order of business was to get a change of venue. He should have gotten it; eventually Ruby's conviction would be reversed because the local judge refused to surrender the case. Jack Ruby would die with his guilt unproven.

It's true we didn't want to let go of the trial. After the embarrassment of Oswald's death we wanted to show the world that we were competent, that we knew how to administer justice. We looked forward to the trial as we might a heavyweight fight. In our corner was Henry Wade, our district attorney, who was a legend in Dallas. He had asked for the death penalty twenty-four times and been denied only once. Wade was tough, cagey, pitiless. He chewed on unlit cigars and said "day-id" for "dead." Belli called him a "country bumpkin," which was exactly the impression Wade hoped to create.

Belli appeared in court as a small, flamboyant man with a polysyllabic vocabulary and elevator shoes. He was an easy mark for the hard-boiled prosecutors on the country side of the courtroom, who called him "Mr. Belly" and ridiculed his wardrobe. Dallas was plainspoken and suspicious of fancy outsiders. Its style was glassy, modern, utilitarian, whereas Belli's was rococo; they were bound to detest each other.

And Belli brought the accusing finger. He charged Dallas with killing Oswald. In particular he charged Henry Wade, who had made several prejudicial statements about Oswald's guilt soon after his arrest. "I am convinced that after the official chorus, Wade in the forefront, already proclaimed him a fit subject for execution, Oswald became fair game for any crank who wanted to kill him," Belli later wrote. His book was called *Dallas Justice,* and he wrote it (with Maurice C. Carroll) "to help Dallas face up to its failures."

At first Jack Ruby was delighted to have the slick and glamorous California attorney defending him; it certified his celebrity. "It made him feel good," Belli related, "that I not only knew my law but was a sharp dresser and a great cocksman." Ruby was making plans for his own public career, and he loved the way Belli talked. He began working on his diction and tried to improve his vocabulary by playing Scrabble with the guards. "He would sit there dreaming absentmindedly and comb his hair for hours," one of the guards remembered. His cell was filled with congratulatory letters and telegrams. "He didn't think we were going to do anything to him," said Bill Alexander, Wade's chief prosecutor on the case. "He believed we were just going through the motions, because we had to. He was enjoying all that attention, just like a pig in slop."

Belli's defense, however, was to depict his client as a village idiot, a latent homosexual, an epileptic with possible brain damage (here he was on the mark; Ruby's autopsy showed more than a dozen tumors in his brain). Belli produced a parade of psychiatrists who testified about his client's "psychomotor epilepsy," which they demonstrated in a six-hundred-foot chart of Ruby's brain waves. The jury was not interested. After hearing eight days of testimony they took less than two hours to decide Ruby's guilt.

"What was the key that turned those friendly and polite people into a jury that could impassively reject testimony by some of the nation's most brilliant medical men and, in an insultingly brief one hour and fifty minutes, decide that Ruby must die in the electric chair?" Belli wrote in retaliation. "The people in whatever passes for the Kremlin in Dallas could figuratively push a button and, as if it had signaled transistors in their brains, direct the thinking of this great city's people."

Ruby was devastated, not so much by the verdict as by Belli's defense. He was ruined in Dallas, the city he loved. "I'm so grateful for the opportunities I've had in Dallas," he had written. "I'm a Jew from the ghetto of Chicago. I came to Dallas and made a fine success." Now he was a laughingstock, a queer, a mental failure. The worst blow was delivered the day before the trial even began, when Mayor Earle Cabell, who had known Ruby for years, testified in a change-of-venue hearing that the defendant could not get a fair trial in Dallas because he had hurt the city too badly. Six weeks after the trial was over, Ruby backed up in his cell, lowered his head, and tried to brain himself against the concrete wall.

That was the day he met my cousin Don. My sisters and I had always loved Don best among our relatives. He already had been wounded by his mother's early death, and at the age of sixteen he lost his father as well. At the funeral, my father had noticed his nephew and namesake standing alone, without prospects, his hair blowing in the endless wind of the Kansas prairie. Don was so like himself at that age, stuck in Seward on the two-lane blacktop that led to Hudson, Stafford, Turon, Penalosa, Kingman, Murdock, Cheney, Garden Plain, Goddard, and at long last, Wichita. After the funeral my father brought Don home with him, to the new world. Don was grateful but also independent. He got a job as an apprentice mortician in a funeral parlor on Harry Hines Boulevard. I used to visit him there, and he would take me into the viewing rooms to see death. Don also served as an ambulance attendant, and it was in this capacity that he rode to the county jail to ferry Jack Ruby to Parkland Hospital.

They became friends, after a fashion, because Ruby would make many trips to Parkland once his illness was diagnosed. "They're killing me, Don," he confided. "They're feeding me cancer." Soon he began to deteriorate, becoming markedly thinner, more Oswald-like. Don watched him waste away with every successive ambulance ride. It was sad, but Don had an orphan's attitude toward death and wouldn't waste his sentiment on a man he couldn't save.

In the end Jack Ruby was swallowed up by the numerous conspiracy theories linking him to the man he had killed. He demanded lie-detector tests and truth serum, and told his story again and again, but he was also, by now, struggling with conspiracies of his own imagining. He heard them torturing Jews in the basement. He believed the country had been overthrown by Nazis. He knew. They knew he knew. They knew he knew they knew.

Jack Ruby, defender of our city's honor, died on January 3, 1967. He is buried in Chicago.

6 / ESCAPE

I left Dallas on the afternoon train, bound for Tulane University in the city most unlike Dallas that I knew of: New Orleans. My hair was cut short and I wore a black suit. I had the idea from reading magazines that college students were carefully dressed nearly all the time.

There was a feeling I had whenever I traveled from Texas to Louisiana that I was moving back in time. Trains throw you off time anyway, since you are always passing the rear of things—people's backyards, the back ends of buildings, nothing ever faces onto the tracks—and the rear of things is timeless. Louisiana has a starkly uncharming antebellum quality about the tarpaper shacks in the countryside and the skinny black children waving at the train that never stops for them. It is the South, the Deep South, which doesn't begin, as far as Texans are concerned, until you cross the Sabine River. There is an air of prehistory about this country of mossy trees and dark water. From the train window it would be easy to imagine the Louisiana landscape as a Disneyland cyclorama in which some gigantic mechanical sauropod would lurch out of the swamp and we would all scream.

Outside of Berkeley, American campuses were very much under control in 1965. For the freshman on the train, the word "collegiate" was still a fashion statement. I had never heard anyone speak of "relevance" concerning my studies, or "imperialism" in connection with my own country. "Oppression" and "Third World" were ideas so freshly coined that I hadn't tested their worth. The events that were going to change my life and my country had already been set in motion, however. Watts had burned. Operation Rolling Thunder—the bombing of North Vietnam—was under way. Betty Friedan had published *The Feminine Mystique* two years earlier, although as yet there were very few women aware of feminism as a movement. The Pill had made its debut in 1960, and it was beginning to find its way into the hands of unmarried coeds, most of whom, in my experience, obtained prescriptions through dermatologists who were willing to support the conceit that it cleared up acne. The student revolt, prompted by the war, had not yet been announced, although something momentous was bound to happen, given the extraordinary numbers of students entering the nation's universities. I had never heard of Haight-Ashbury. I had never smelled the sweet, acrid odor of marijuana. The Gulf of Tonkin was a headline, but I seldom read the news. Why should I? Wasn't college a sanctuary where the gates closed on daily life? I should turn my attention now to the eternal, not the ephemeral, to Latin grammar and the Wife of Bath and the complexities of cell division, not Western movies and baseball box scores and news of the world.

I shared a cabinette on the train with another Tulane freshman named John Scurry, who was going to study architecture. I envied him his resolution. I was still trying on professions, hoping to discover myself among the infinite possibilities. I wanted to be a writer, but in my mind writers were a chosen race, like the Jews, with whom they frequently coincided. Over the summer I had endured a battery of aptitude tests, with inconclusive results. "Just don't go into medicine," the counselor advised me. I showed no talent for it and, until then, no interest. But the thought of losing an option was unbearable. Immediately after the test I contacted a family friend who was a doctor and began making rounds with him. He took me on a tour of his charity cancer patients, condemned men and women in shuttered rooms, and although I knew from the first glance of their incurious eyes that I would never make a doctor, I held on to the option. I told my cabin mate that I was going to study pre-med.

Hurricane Betsy struck us in Alexandria, Louisiana. By the time she reached us she had already devastated New Orleans and flooded the lower Mississippi valley. The train came to a dead stop on a blank stretch of track fifteen miles beyond the city and sat there, all systems shut down, for eighteen hours. At first it was thrilling— the thrashing winds, the incredible pounding rain—but there was too much security on the train even in the face of a hurricane to believe in danger, so we began to think of other things, such as the absence of air-conditioning, the loss of the dining car in Alexandria, the odor of the other passengers. At first we were all in it together. Gradually we fell into cliques. We began snapping at each other; it was easy to see cannibalism lurking ahead. A honeymooning couple grew alarmed after ten hours of this and decided to flee the train. I recall them disappearing into the sheets of the storm, carrying their suitcases back up the track toward civilization.

When we arrived in New Orleans it was as if the Bomb had fallen. Oak trees were ripped up by their roots; automobiles had been tossed about like toys. The cabbie who picked me up at the station was in a state of exhilaration. He pointed out the ironic symbols of destruction. We passed a Conoco station with all the consonants blown off the sign, and a Shell station with no S. The health department was in a panic, the cabbie told me excitedly, because Betsy had washed the cadavers out of the raised cemetery vaults, and old bodies mingled in the flood with the freshly dead. On the streets I noticed people picking their way through shards of glass and broken tree limbs, staring at each other with dazzled smiles.

New Orleans was old and rotten, corrupt, depraved, licentious, a grand old whore who had enjoyed herself too much but was still generous enough to give pleasure to someone else, someone new. It was a Catholic town and indifferent to progress. After the charmlessness of Dallas I fell in love with the overripe splendor of New Orleans: the great homes of the Garden District, with their huge trees and ivied yards, and the long verandahs where the plutocrats sat in rocking chairs and drank gin fizzes; the rows of pastel shotgun cottages (ordered out of the Sears catalog), which filled the Irish Channel district and ran down Magazine Street in front of the wharves; the glorious depravity of the French Quarter, deeply anchored in history—but a history of pirates and voodoo and jazz. I walked the streets of New Orleans in a state of aesthetic liberation, every bit as much of an émigré as Hemingway in Paris, and feeling at one with him and with all the great American writers. For hadn't they all stopped in New Orleans on their way to immortality—Whitman, Twain, Faulkner, Anderson, Williams, Capote—and which of them had ever passed a night in Dallas?

I was impressed right away that they sold beer in the five-and-dime and French wine in drugstores. Also, that I could buy it, a legal right I exercised with enthusiasm. In Dallas, when we teenagers wanted a drink, we would loiter outside a liquor store until we spotted some old black man in the parking lot. We'd give him five dollars for a case of beer and let him keep the change. In New Orleans liquor of all sorts was freely available and only marginally more expensive than tap water. A mixed drink at Larry & Katz's, which was a half-finished shack where the clientele sat on upturned liquor boxes and the bartenders wore revolvers, cost twenty-five cents. It was a fine place to start the evening.

From there a person might wander over to Felix's for oysters. In the too-bright fluorescent light, the oysters looked like puddles of mercury. Here in Felix's you could see the classes converge, however briefly. There were handsomely barbered men and women in evening clothes, truck drivers in poplin uniforms with their names embroidered above their breast pockets, Tulane literature professors in tweed jackets with elbow patches, lawyers and criminals, doctors and patients, professional bowlers—all of them engaged in the singularly barbaric act of eating living animals by the dozen. You could close your eyes and place a person in his class by the sound of his language. The rich Orleanian has a slowed-down, muffled tone like a record played at three-quarter speed; I have heard the word "mayonnaise" delivered with so much nuance that it occupied the space of a sentence and arrived with its own internal marks of punctuation, rather like "My, uh . . . *Nay!* uzzz?" The most characteristic speech of the city is an urban dialect otherwise associated with Brooklyn and Hoboken, a "dems" and "dose" kind of talk that originated with the Irish laborers who were brought in to build the levees. When city people greeted each other they'd cry "Where y'at, ya muddah?" so college kids referred to townies as "where-y'ats" or just "yats."

I became a food romantic. In 1965 New Orleans was one of the few American cities that took food seriously. Now, when there is scarcely a middle-sized town in the country without a representative sampling of international cuisine, as well as health food stores, specialty gourmet shops, fresh pasta, excellent bakeries, wonderful coffee, it is hard to remember how boring and desolate the American diet was. The only cookbooks on my mother's shelf were Miz Rombauer's *The Joy of Cooking* and Fannie Farmer's *The Boston Cooking School Cookbook*—both of them wedding gifts received by nearly every war bride in America. I grew up on meat loaf and mashed potatoes. When I was a child in Abilene, Texas, in the fifties, we would drive out to the local Air Force base after church to eat Sunday dinner—it was practically the only decent kitchen in West Texas. One of the great days of my childhood was when the first franchised restaurant came into my life: It was Kentucky Fried Chicken, and it caused a sensation. Now this was cooking! We went there every week and felt grateful, positively blessed, that Colonel Sanders would grant a concession to such a podunk town as Abilene. Even in Dallas in the sixties, Italian and Chinese restaurants were novelties. Pizza parlors were just catching on. The only exotic restaurant was La Tunisia, and its principal attraction was the seven-foot Negro who opened the door.

I spent part of my college career as a busboy and then as a waiter in one of the handsome small restaurants in the Quarter. My promotion was due entirely to my being the only busboy who owned a tuxedo. It gave me incredible pleasure to present the menus and watch the flushed, candlelit faces puzzle over the snapper versus the veal, taking those little internal soundings ("Do I feel like crabmeat tonight?"). I learned my way around the alleyways and kitchen doors that led to the secret chambers of Brennan's or Antoine's, where I might be dispatched to borrow a gallon of remoulade sauce. In the kitchens of those great restaurants were corpulent black men assembling dishes out of great troughs of condiments. I would dash back down the alley with the remoulade, up the rear stairs, into the kitchen, where I would pick up my entrées and walk slowly, with a sense of composure and purpose, into the dining room.

I had a hunger for bohemia. I wanted to see life raw and unpredictable. Later I recognized this as the Private School Syndrome— this idealization of the hard life, this romancing of the proletariat— but then it was all new and entirely original. I began to haunt the waterfront bars: the Acropolis, the Seven Seas, and particularly La Casa de los Marinos, a wonderful dive in the Quarter across from the Toulouse Street wharf, where sailors came to dance to Latin music and pick up college girls. French sailors were usually the most successful in this pursuit, owing to their tasseled berets, which were prized by the undergraduates of Sophie Newcomb College. For the most part, however, the students and the sailors didn't mix; they crowded together in an uneasy emulsion of culture, language, and class.

Until I came to New Orleans I had never met an acknowledged homosexual. In Dallas we had spoken of queers, but no one I knew had ever spotted one—they were like Communists, an unseen menace. I was always hearing about the practice of "rolling queers" in Lee Park; in fact, I had the idea that homosexuals existed (if at all) only to sit on park benches and wait to be mugged by indignant teenaged boys. In New Orleans, however, there was an active, aboveground homosexual culture (the word "gay" had not yet been bent to this purpose), which was wildly dramatic and self-consciously humorous. The center of the scene was deep in the Quarter at a bar called Dixie's. During Mardi Gras I would go there, safely ensconced in a phalanx of fraternity brothers, to watch the transvestite beauty contest at the corner of Bourbon and St. Ann. Some of the contestants were disconcertingly beautiful, despite the telltale Adam's apples and powdered whiskers. One year a contingent of Marines from the USS *Forrestal* came swaggering past. They were all drinking Hurricanes—those giant tumblers of liquor from Pat O'Brien's that usually signaled the drunken tourist. A moment later the Marines were on the stage with the contestants, hugging, kissing, groping, and quickly being hustled off into cabs. I wonder what they had to say to each other on the *Forrestal* the next morning.

It never occurred to me not to join a fraternity. Being a student was not yet the serious business it would become, and besides, I had an affinity for mystic societies and secret handshakes. By the time I graduated, fraternities had become passé, a redoubt for social reactionaries, but in 1965 we still believed, with Barry Goldwater, that "wherever fraternities are not allowed, Communism flourishes." My lodge, Delta Tau Delta, was housed in two condemned buildings on Broadway, with no air-conditioning and with a plumbing system that backed up under the foundations. Our housemother was a fat, elderly woman who walked around with a dachshund tucked under her arm. She was as ribald as any of the brothers, but she always dressed for dinner, and we were supposed to mind our manners around her. One of the conceits of fraternity life, despite all evidence, is that it gives a man polish. I had to remind myself, when I was stepping over unconscious upperclassmen in order to throw up in the community toilet, that I was gaining advantages.

Your fraternity was supposed to say something about the kind of person you were. Indeed, there seemed to be an intuitive truth about this association of man and lodge that was not bound to a single campus. It was like a horoscope in that respect. The SAEs were campus leaders, politicians, snobs who spent their spare time buying golf sweaters. The Dekes were good-natured drunks. The Sigma Chis were serious, dull, marginal nerds. The KAs were unreconstructed Confederates. Once they planted cotton in their front yard and sent their black porter out with a gunnysack to pick it. During homecoming one year, when our football team was playing the University of Alabama, the KAs built a two-story papier-mâché Kotex box in front of their house, with the legend STOP THE CRIMSON TIDE. The Delts were known, universally and accurately, as party boys.

The biggest party of all was Mardi Gras. The carnival season lasted from Twelfth Night (January 6) until Fat Tuesday, the night before Ash Wednesday. In that space of time, which was sometimes as long as two months, depending on the date of Easter, the city rollicked in one long bacchanal. New Orleans society divided itself into krewes—Comus, Rex, Momus, and Proteus were the big ones, and the Zulus for the blacks—and they put on spectacular parades. First came the flambeaux dancers, black teenagers twirling flaming batons, doing a shuffle-step dance to the music of the brass band that followed; then came the floats sailing through the Quarter like galleons. On the last day of carnival the streets filled with a million drunks in makeup and costumes, searching for sin on the eve of the season of repentance.

One of my fraternity brothers, Arthur Wright, who was also from Dallas (but no relation of mine), rented an apartment on Royal Street for carnival. It was a cheap efficiency in an old Creole house with a single large bed and a bricked-up fireplace. Arthur and I came to furnish it one night before the big parades began, and we were surprised to find someone else living there. As a matter of fact, Arthur learned, the apartment had been rented to three different people during the past week. He received this information from the landlord in an angry phone call. The landlord said he'd be right over.

He screeched up to the curb on a motorcycle, with his wife sitting in a sidecar. She wore a white plastic overcoat and a turquoise hairnet. Her husband was a paunchy little Cajun with a leather jacket and curly black hair. "I ain't gon' 'pologize," he told Arthur, " 'cause I got you one far better dan dis on Bourbon Street. You gon lak it fine."

We followed the landlord's motorcycle down to lower Bourbon, well past the tourist zone into a darkened stretch of tenements. For two Dallas boys it was a little darker and more menacing than we were prepared for. I noticed right away, when we came into the courtyard, that there were no windows or doors on the apartments, just gauzy curtains and beaded portieres, through which we could see fleshy women and men in undershirts smoking cigarettes. In a pale orange room a naked man was playing the saxophone.

Now this is the demimonde, I was thinking to myself, as an adolescent Mexican girl came down the stairs wearing a sarong. "My mistress," the landlord acknowledged. "Rita, bring me my blades."

She nodded and went into a room, returning with a carved wooden box. Inside, encased in green felt, were a dozen throwing knives. The landlord's wife stood against a wall fifteen feet away, with her arms spread in the crucifix position.

Whoomp! The first blade struck in the niche below her armpit. The mistress handed the landlord another knife and stood back to watch. Her mouth was partly open, and her tongue moved slowly across the edge of her upper incisors.

"I'm having second thoughts about this apartment," I whispered to Arthur.

Whoomp! Other armpit.

"They certainly have a trusting relationship," Arthur observed.

Whoomp, whoomp, whoomp! The wife stared unblinkingly as the knives tumbled toward her. Her husband finished with a nice flourish, placing the last blade an inch above her forehead. Arthur and I watched with maniac grins.

As the wife came away, leaving her outline pinned against the wall, I happened to see through her turquoise hair net. Half an ear was missing.

At last—real life!

There was a brief time in my life when my parents and I agreed on the music; it was the middle fifties, when Gisele MacKienzie and Dorothy Collins sang the popular songs on "Your Hit Parade." Snooky Lanson sang "Davy Crockett" week after week, and I knew every verse. At night, when I was supposed to be asleep, I would tune into WWL from New Orleans and listen to the smart sounds of the big bands playing the Blue Room of the Roosevelt Hotel. Then Elvis Presley sang "Hound Dog," and I began to give way to the tidal pull of rock and roll.

There was in my mind a certain suspicion that the music of my time would never be as sophisticated as that of my parents. Perhaps it was because their generation regarded rock and roll with contempt and bewilderment that the music became defiant. I remember being absolutely thrilled by the rumor that Gene Vincent had said "fuckin' " in "Woman Love"—although what he actually said was unintelligible. That the churches and the politicians were scandalized gave the music a political importance it had never aspired to have. I identified with the music, but I held back, too; it wasn't all I wanted it to be. Even when the Beatles came to America in February 1964, singing "I Want to Hold Your Hand" and "She Loves You," I didn't surrender to them. They were okay, I thought, but I didn't understand why the girls were screaming and the boys were suddenly growing their hair long.

The music hit me in 1966. I was walking into the University Center as Simon and Garfunkel were singing "Sounds of Silence" on the jukebox. The ambience was specific to me. The Mamas and the Papas sang "Monday, Monday." It was the year when everything I heard seemed to be drawn from some generational oversoul, and I resonated without thinking or resisting. I had the feeling of being in a movie and every song I heard was part of my own soundtrack. It was a year when soul music broke through, at least for me. Percy Sledge sang "When a Man Loves a Woman" and Ray Charles sang "Cryin' Time." I had just discovered the great soul singers of New Orleans, Irma Thomas and Benny Spellman. How odd it seems, when I reflect on the music of 1966, that the number one song that year was "The Ballad of the Green Berets."

In the fall of 1967 my roommate, Allan Denchfield, rigged his record player to a timer, so that every morning of the semester we awakened to the Beatles' *Sgt. Pepper* album. We couldn't get enough of it. We listened to Leonard Cohen singing "Suzanne." In the spring of 1968 the radio never stopped playing Otis Redding singing "(Sittin' on) The Dock of the Bay." Otis was already dead when that record came out, which seemed eerie then, although we soon got used to death being a feature of the music. I was eating crawfish in Eddie Price's bar the first time I heard Janis Joplin growl the opening of "Turtle Blues," and after that I always listened for the spot where her bottle of Southern Comfort shattered on the beat. Her sound was raw, insinuating, and powerfully ambiguous—neither black nor white, male nor female, but some revolutionary middle note between the races and the sexes. She was, it seemed to me, the Siren of our generation, beckoning us to the dangerous margins where death awaited.

The great object of college was not learning but sex. The sexual revolution may have been under way, but it was still unnamed and unacknowledged, and like all revolutions it started far away, on the sophisticated seacoasts, not in the Deep South. Here, one could only just now feel the moorings loosening on the Victorian Age. The girls of Newcomb College, Tulane's sister school, were highly proper ladies. They were also as closely guarded as convicts after ten o'clock on weeknights.

There is something feral about the needs of young men, something well outside the boundaries of civilized behavior. We had all heard about the sophomore geologist so cramped from desire ("blue balls" it was called) that it required three men to carry him to the infirmary. Many nights I would stand outside the women's dorm and find myself close to baying. Once, when I was standing there with a fraternity brother, and we had just returned our dates to the custody of their rooms, we decided to break into the dorm. I stood on my friend's shoulders and was just able to knock on my date's window, which she opened, quite obligingly. I crawled in and reached down for my friend, but as I was hauling him up a security patrolman grabbed his ankle. There was an awkward tug-of-war, which I lost. Then I heard the alarms.

It is a stupid feeling to be fleeing down a corridor to the screams of coeds, searching for an exit. All the doors were chained. I heard a commotion behind me, which I took to be the security patrol. I dove into a stairwell and nearly trompled a girl in curlers and a nightgown, whose mouth made a little *o* as I went flying past. I was in the basement, trapped, I realized, in the darkened laundry room.

How was I to know, as my pulse beat out a drumroll between the washers and dryers, that I was the last victim of the Age of Innocence? Liberation was riding to the rescue, but it would not reach me in time. I would be captured and returned to Dallas in disgrace (me, the once-promising student, led astray by boiling hormones). Or else—jail! Breaking and entering! My life in tatters! I heard the boots clumping down the stairs. I edged back into the shadows, and felt—a door. I hit it with everything I had. As I burst outside and fled through the shrubbery, I heard the sound of women cheering.

There was a constant search for private places. The college acted, in the phrase of the day, in loco parentis, and consequently unlocked empty spaces were rarely found and highly valued. Practically the only such places were the practice rooms in the music building; I spent several dates hugging and kissing under the legs of a studio piano. Sometimes, I discovered, the very most public places had privacy hidden inside them—the Newcomb auditorium, for instance, which was usually dark, lent an interesting theatrical setting to my frustrated sexual pursuits. Once, when the auditorium was locked, my girlfriend and I were drifting around campus and came upon Tulane's famous stadium, where the Sugar Bowl is played. The fence was thirteen feet high, but we scaled it and wandered into the vast black space. There was a murmurous, echoing sound like a seashell held against the ear. Small slivers of light reflected around the elliptical tiers, ring after expanding ring. We felt ourselves to be in the center of the universe, we were all that existed, we were life itself. It is a memory that is recaptured for me every New Year's Day when I watch the Sugar Bowl game and see the fifty-yard line, where I finally scored.

At Tulane we began to hear about the student movement against the war, but we were buried in the Confederacy, and the idea of protest seemed foreign and rather crackpot. Nonetheless, it happened that the first mass student protest in the South took place one midnight at Tulane in 1968, when 350 students marched on

President Longenecker's home to protest the censorship of two "pornographic" photographs in the school literary journal (one of the pictures was of a naked art instructor). We had no idea what to expect, or even how to go about staging a protest. A graduate student, a woman who had gone to Berkeley, stood up and told us what to do when the police came. "Link arms, then lie down like you're dead," she said. Of course, the police never came; in fact, no one noticed us at all.

That march was a small act of repentance on my part. The year before, I had encountered the first demonstration I had ever seen: a group of about fifteen students protesting the decision to hold the homecoming dance on board the *President,* the paddle-wheel steamboat that ported conventioneers up and down the Mississippi to the sound of white Dixieland jazz. It was a segregated boat. The management was making an exception to accommodate the Tulane student body, which included a very small number of blacks, and Dionne Warwick, who was going to perform. That seemed like progress to me—hadn't we forced a change in the policy? The protesters wanted another site for the dance. They were standing outside the University Center with signs saying DO NOT SUPPORT RACIST INSTITUTIONS and NO STUDENT MONEY FOR SEGREGATION. I was walking from class with a friend, and we both thought of the same hilarious idea. We would protest the protest. We made a couple of signs, BAN THE BOMB and PREPARE TO MEET THY GOD, then we sidled up to the demonstration and stood there, trying to keep straight faces.

Some fraternity brothers came by and applauded. My picture was published in the student newspaper. There I am, with a smirk, in the last half of the sixties, on the cusp of the seismic changes that would characterize that era. All around the country protest was making itself heard, in the causes of peace, brotherhood, racial justice, but at that moment I thought it was something to ridicule.

The next week I went to pick up Dionne Warwick at the airport. I was the welcoming committee. I gave her a dozen roses and drove her downtown to one of the grand old hotels. She was the first black woman, other than my maid, that I had ever driven anywhere. She

was charming and glamorous. I was completely enchanted. We talked about football. She followed the Philadelphia Eagles, who were playing the Dallas Cowboys that Sunday, and we made a twenty-dollar bet on the game.

When we got to the hotel there was a flurry at the desk. Suddenly they couldn't find her reservation. It took me more than a minute to realize that the hotel was segregated too. Not legally, of course—the Civil Rights Act of 1964 had been passed—but in that insolent, closed-face fashion that says we never have a vacancy for black people. The bellmen hadn't even bothered to pick up her luggage. Miss Warwick was standing there with her roses, and I saw for the first time that look—an ancient look of burned-out anger and humiliated pride. I suddenly felt sick about my idiocy of the week before. I had made fun of something I clearly hadn't understood. That was the force of the repression for which I, being white, was responsible. The manager of the hotel came to the desk to deliver the excuse, but I cut him off. "You are about to make a terrible mistake," I told him. "This is Dionne Warwick. Don't you know who she is?" He looked blank. "She's one of the most popular singers in the world. If you don't give her a room, and a really good one, you're going to be in every newspaper in the country tomorrow morning."

He suddenly discovered a room key.

This was my only triumph for right and decency in my four years of undergraduate life. I never paid Dionne Warwick her twenty dollars, however (the Cowboys lost on Sunday).

I had come to New Orleans to escape Dallas, but I had not left the assassination behind me. The madness followed. New Orleans was Oswald's city, his birthplace, and his spirit hung over the place like an evil spell. Soon New Orleans would be lit up in one of those queer American binges of lunacy, a paranoia of conspiracy that has been part of the national psyche since the Salem witch trials.

On Bourbon Street one day near the end of my freshman year I met Delilah, who would play a small but fatal part in the craziness to come. She was a stripper who did an Egyptian belly dance to "Hava Nagila," the Hebrew song of celebration. She was clearly not reading the latest news from the Middle East. I introduced myself as a representative of Tulane's Cosmopolitan Committee. One of the committee's purposes, I explained, was to bring interesting cultural acts—such as hers—to the university. I had the idea of billing her as a "Jewish-Egyptian ethnic dancer" and letting her take off her clothes in McAlister Auditorium.

Delilah agreed to meet me at the club the following Tuesday, and at the appointed time I appeared. There was a Grayline bus tour parked outside, and the place was filled with Iowa chiropractors who were nursing their four-dollar drinks and watching Lynda Bridgette, the World's Largest Stripper, shake her 378 pounds as the stage creaked and moaned.

"Delilah's expecting me," I told the barmaid in my best Peter Gunn style (I was eighteen years old).

"Oh sure."

"No, really."

She gave me a look that said this better be real, and went back to the dressing room. I took a seat. In a moment Delilah came out and shimmied through her big number. She had a shiny appendectomy scar that I hadn't noticed before, but in the stage lights it seemed phosphorescent. Then, to the admiring astonishment of the Iowans, Delilah came to my table and ordered a Dr Pepper. She was in her mid-thirties, I calculated, or a little older—twice my age, in any case. She had black hair and olive-toned skin, which was probably the inspiration for casting herself as an Egyptian. However, she affected a Zsa Zsa Gabor accent along the lines of "Vere are you from, dahlink?" She was a walking cultural malaprop.

I admitted I was from Dallas.

"No kidding? *Dallas?*"

Her Hungarian accent fell aside and was replaced by the more familiar nasal tones of North Texas. I asked if she knew Dallas. "Yeah," she said, "I know that goddamn town too well." We sat quietly for a moment. Being from Dallas was an awkward bond to share.

"I used to work for Jack Ruby," she volunteered.

She seemed to want to talk about him. He was a nice man, she remembered, but "a little crazy." It was Ruby, the Jewish impresario, who put her together with "Hava Nagila." Delilah gave me her telephone number, and I told her I would call next semester concerning her performance at Tulane. She said I could come to her apartment for "coffee."

All summer long I thought about that invitation.

I was already alarmed at the direction my life was taking. When I fled Dallas for the university, I left behind a sweet Christian girlfriend. She had given me a Bible for my eighteenth birthday. "Cherish this book always, Larry, and diligently read it," she admonished on the flyleaf, but I had fallen into the hands of the Sybarites and the existentialists, and when I returned to Dallas that summer I felt like a moral double agent. Half of me was sitting with my girlfriend in church, underlining Scripture with a yellow marker, and half (more than half) was scheming of ways to lead my little Christian exemplar into one of life's dark passageways.

I was lying on her lap, with that thought in mind, watching the ten o'clock news, when a photograph of a black-haired woman in a belly dancing costume flashed on the screen.

"That's Delilah!" I said, sitting up.

"*What?*"

"Shh. I know her."

Her name, it turned out, was Marilyn Magyar Walle. She had just been murdered in Omaha, shot eight times by a man she had been married to for a month. Her association with Jack Ruby was noted. My girlfriend looked at me with an expression of confounded decency.

"Do you have something you want to tell me, Larry?"

I wasn't the only one who marked Delilah's death. The conspiracists were keeping a list of "witnesses" who had died since the assassination, a list that grew and grew. By February 1967 seventeen others had died, including two more strippers who had worked for Ruby (one was shot to death, the other was found hanging by her toreador pants in a Dallas jail cell). Most of these deaths were from natural causes or explainable under other circumstances, but in the aggregate they had a weight they wouldn't have had by themselves. Seven of the victims had given testimony to the Warren Commission, six others had been interviewed by the Dallas police or the FBI. What are the chances, one might wonder, that so many people connected with the assassination would be dead in three and a half years? An actuary in London said the odds against all of them being dead in that time were 100,000 trillion to one—a figure that throws mysterious shadows across the otherwise unmysterious fates of car wrecks, failing hearts, jealous husbands, and disappointed suicides.

Like the majority of Americans, I wondered if the whole story had been told. Was there only one assassin on November 22, 1963? What about the Zapruder film, which seemed to show the President being shot from the front, not from Oswald's angle in the upper rear? Were there other assassins on the grassy knoll? Was Oswald framed? There were enough unexplained questions in my mind that I was prepared to believe the New Orleans district attorney, Jim Garrison, when he announced on March 1, 1967, that he had solved the case.

"Big Jim" Garrison was already a heroic presence in the city. He was a reformer with a New Orleanian sense of ethical balance. He had cleaned up Bourbon Street, which meant keeping the G-strings on the dancers and getting rid of the streetwalkers. He cracked down on gambling operations in Orleans Parish but left intact the sacrosanct pinball machines, which paid off at the rate of a nickel a game (I had several friends who went to school on a "pinball scholarship"). The big gambling syndicates fled next door, to Jefferson Parish, out of Big Jim's grasp. Garrison had the reputation of a man who feared neither the moral zealots nor the local mob; he was tough, unbribable, cagey, unorthodox. Plus he had the power to issue subpoenas. He seemed to be the perfect man to solve the crime of the century.

What his investigation did, however, was to dip a ladle into the bizarre society of the New Orleans underworld, which was filled with mercenaries and mobsters, CIA agents, disaffected priests, and YMCA homosexuals. Somehow all of these creatures combined themselves in a single person, a man the district attorney called "one of history's most important individuals." Unfortunately, David W. Ferrie had already joined the list of the mysteriously dead.

Eastern Airlines had fired Ferrie as a pilot after he was arrested for a "crime against nature" with a sixteen-year-old boy. He had been a leader of the local Civil Air Patrol, which Lee Harvey Oswald joined in 1954. Robert Oswald suspected Ferrie of introducing his brother to Communism, but Ferrie's politics seem to have been oriented in another direction. He once wrote a letter to the secretary of defense asking for an opportunity to "train killers." "There is nothing I would enjoy better than blowing the hell out of every damn Russian, Communist, Red or what-have-you." He may have been given his chance when the CIA drilled anti-Castro Cubans in the backwaters of Lake Pontchartrain. Ferrie later claimed to have taken part in the Bay of Pigs invasion.

On the day of Kennedy's assassination, Ferrie was in a courtroom with his boss, Carlos Marcello, the godfather of the New Orleans Mafia, a man who had his own good reasons for wanting the President dead. The President's brother, Attorney General Robert Kennedy, had deported Marcello to Guatemala. (According to legend, Guatemalan authorities transported him to El Salvador, where he was dropped into the jungle wearing a silk suit and alligator shoes.) Ferrie supposedly rescued Marcello from the tropics and smuggled him back to the United States.

By any standards Ferrie was a peculiar person. He had a disease that rendered him completely hairless, a condition he tried to disguise by gluing orange tufts of hair, and sometimes even carpet scraps, to his scalp and to the place where his eyebrows would have been. He filled his apartment with thousands of white mice, on which he tested various cancer cures. He was also a pianist and a pornographer, and a bishop in a church in which he was the only member.

Garrison had developed information linking Oswald with Ferrie and a third man, known as either Clem or Clay Bertrand. However, on February 22, 1967, Ferrie's nude, bald body was discovered in his apartment, some eight hours after he had been interviewed by a reporter for the *Washington Post*. An autopsy showed he died from a cerebral hemorrhage resulting from an aneurysm—natural causes, in other words—a diagnosis that was complicated by the fact that Ferrie left behind two handwritten suicide notes.

Ferrie's death left Clay or Clem Bertrand as the only living member of Garrison's assassination triangle. This person had been described to the county investigators as being a young homosexual, about five feet eight inches tall, with sandy hair. The man Garrison eventually indicted was a wealthy and aristocratic New Orleans businessman in his mid-fifties, six feet four inches tall, with stark white hair. His only real link to the case was that he was a homosexual and his name was Clay. Clay Shaw.

Shaw would spend the next two years of his life trying to clear his name. During that time New Orleans was Assassination Central. Every buff in the country came to town. There was an awestruck feeling that Garrison was peeling the lid off American society; it was as if he had discovered some further dimension of reality, as if he had found the point where parallel lines really did converge, where Ruby and Oswald and Ferrie and Shaw met the Cubans, the Russians, the Pentagon, and the CIA. And Garrison was amazingly self-assured. He gave long interviews in *Playboy* magazine and on the Johnny Carson show detailing the massive conspiracy. He confirmed every suspicion. "My staff and I solved the case months ago," he said breezily. "I wouldn't say this if we didn't have evidence beyond a shadow of a doubt. We know the key individuals, the cities involved, and how it was done."

At the heart of Garrison's theory was the unoriginal notion that Dallas killed Kennedy; the city's millionaire right-wingers financed the plot with the collusion of the Dallas police force and the technical advice of the CIA. These were the witches Garrison hunted. There was also the fashionable idea, added later, that Kennedy was murdered by the military establishment so that it could wage unrestrained war in Vietnam. What made Garrison's investigation so appealing is that he satisfied the profound paranoia of the moment by saying yes, it's true, and it's worse than you thought. Somehow that news came as a relief.

Many of the assassination buffs came to speak at Tulane. New York attorney Mark Lane entangled the Warren Commission in lawyerly webs of contradiction and intrigue. Comedian and activist Dick Gregory spun spooky scenarios of universal government control. He invited us to give a round of applause to the federal agents in the audience tonight, and we cheered ironically, glad to throw aside our naïveté. That was the first time anyone had ever suggested to me that the government thought students were worth keeping an eye on.

When Clay Shaw finally came to trial, one of the witnesses against him was a Baton Rouge insurance salesman, who said in advance he planned to lie on the stand (because he didn't like Shaw's attorney). Another witness was a heroin addict who said he was sitting on the banks of Lake Pontchartrain, shooting up, when he saw Clay Shaw talking to Lee Harvey Oswald. My favorite prosecution witness was a New York City accountant who had heard Shaw planning the execution of the President. The accountant also admitted that he had been hypnotized frequently— against his will—usually by New York City police officers who were engaged in a Communist conspiracy against him. Part of their scheme was to substitute "dead ringers" for his children during the night, a plot he foiled by fingerprinting his kids every morning at the breakfast table.

New Orleans was the laughingstock of the nation. The conspiracy movement had been gathering energy for years; lightning was bound to strike somewhere, and New Orleans was a natural target. There was a feeling that this travesty could only have happened here, in Oswald's hometown, with a cast of characters only New Orleans could offer. Like Dallas, the entire city was made to feel responsible, an unfair charge that was still too appropriate to deny.

Clay Shaw, who distinguished this episode with grace and humor, died of cancer soon after his acquittal. He had been one of New Orleans's most respected citizens, the managing director of the International Trade Mart, the author of many plays, an expert on Restoration period architecture, whose hobby was rehabilitating French Quarter homes. In World War II he had won the Legion of Merit and the Croix de Guerre. He was a political liberal who had voted for John F. Kennedy. He died, vindicated but ruined, a victim of conspiracy paranoia, queer baiting, and the political ambition of an unscrupulous, and perhaps insane, prosecutor.

For a while it seemed that every conspiracy theorist in the country was working out of Garrison's office. Afterward they scattered in disgrace, with Clay Shaw's reputation, and possibly his death, on their consciences. Of course they later realized that Garrison's investigation had been just another clever scheme to discredit them. It was all part of the great conspiracy, all evidence of witchcraft.

In my sophomore year I fell in love with a redheaded girl who smoked a pipe. I was snaring freshmen for my Cosmopolitan Committee at an open house when Tamzon Feeney walked into my life (as they say in the romantic novels), wearing black stockings and a beige jersey dress. She was as tall as I and more strongly built; I found out later, to my faint disgust, that she had put the shot for a Catholic girls' school in San Diego. Her hair was cut short and combed into bangs, to disguise an unusually long forehead. Her eyes were hazel, and too large; her nose was pug, and too small. She had the usual freckled pallor that accompanies red hair. She was the most beautiful girl I'd ever seen.

There was always about Tamzon an alluring innocence, a part of her nature that the nuns had nearly trapped into a convent, but there was another part that was ready for anything. I never knew anyone who was less afraid of life. While other freshman girls stood about properly cowed and demure, Tamzon entered the room with a look in her eye that suggested she had just gotten shore leave. She watched me for a moment—I was surrounded, for once, by women—then she walked out of the room.

When people say they fell in love at first sight, they usually mean that they saw themselves in another person. What I recognized in Tamzon was a romantic attachment to life that was even greater than mine. We had both suffered restraint in our backgrounds—she by Catholicism, I by growing up in Dallas—but in us that restraint had acted like a drawn bow; when we met we were both in the full flight of release. That was what I saw in her eyes: that there was no dare she would not take, that her life would be lived all the way through—and to hell with convention! On the other hand, I knew from the moment she walked into the room that her hunger was greater than mine, and when she walked away I must have known that she was going to have to break my heart.

She was seventeen. Like many people with excess brains who have raced ahead of their peers, she was oddly immature, and got by largely on bluff and humor. Her most profound secret was that she believed she was called to greatness. She was going to be another Albert Schweitzer or Dr. Tom Dooley. As a result she saw her time in school as a last fling before she disappeared into the jungles and surrendered herself to good works.

On our first date I took her to the French Quarter. Although I had been in New Orleans for only a year myself, I presented the Quarter to Tamzon Feeney as if it were a living thing and mine to give. I took her to Preservation Hall to hear the old black jazzmen; we paid a dollar at the door and sat on the floor, and we could feel the music pounding right through the floorboards and up our spines. This was an obligatory stop for me, although the jazz was fossilized and I felt, as I sat inside the ring of white people in the audience, all of us grinning and tapping our toes, that we were attending a Negro zoo. Afterward, Tamzon and I walked down Chartres Street, to the Napoleon House, the bar of my dreams, a dim old place with dark stains on the wallpaper like Rorschach blots, and a phonograph at which customers picked through the records and played, let's say, "Bolero" or "L'Elsire d'Amore," but the volume was only just loud enough to draw a curtain of sound between the tables, and every table floated in its own isolated pool of candlelight. Redheads are always more beautiful at night, especially in candlelight. A hard look at noon and the colors are all wrong—the hair's gone orangish, the skin is vividly freckled but also translucent and veiny, a kind of 3-D skin—but night brings out the redness and the complexion falls into focus. Here in this atmosphere of excessive romance we told each other about ourselves.

"I am surrounded by hypocrites."

"I know, I know."

"Life is too valuable to be wasted on fools."

"I'm going to change the world."

"I'm going to save it."

Then we laughed a little at our pretension, but the terms were stated. We had been alone forever. We had cultivated our alienation, but we had believed that no one would ever understand us, or even care to. Until now. We looked at each other with relief, and fear.

"Let's get out of here."

I decided to test her. We went for a drive on the levee, where I often went in marginally suicidal moments when I wanted to peer over the edge of life. I owned a 1955 MG roadster, and because it was red, and because the model number, TF 1500, had her initials in it, Tamzon saw it as a kind of chariot for her personality. We put down the top and then lowered the windshield, and the breeze hit us smack in the face. I had never taken a girl riding on the levee before. I turned off the headlights and navigated by moonlight. It was dangerous and famously illegal, but Tamzon was whooping as we flew over dips and bumps. The filthy Mississippi snaked along beside us, filled with gleaming chemicals and the slow commerce of freighters. Then we parked and lay on the grass and listened to the tugboats blast. I was afraid to touch her. Male and female suddenly felt like animals living in different elements, I in the water and she in the air. I thought how strong she was, and how avid. I was already terribly afraid of losing her.

A cop stopped me on the way home. I had forgotten the time—Tamzon was late, she would be punished—but instead of giving me a ticket for speeding, the cop took pity on our predicament and gave us an escort all the way back to Tamzon's dorm. When I walked her to the door and asked for a kiss, she burst into tears.

* * *

I entered college at a time when the tide of revolution was just beginning to break across the campuses of the nation. I did not picture myself as a part of that tide. I knew that I was part of the Baby Boom, but I had not understood how my generation, by force of numbers, would change the political and cultural life of our nation. I had not seen how society was already arranging itself to accommodate youth. It was part of the solipsism of my own youth to believe that my teenaged taste for hamburgers, for instance, would naturally find expression in the rise of fast-food outlets all over the country, just as my sexual desires would batter down barriers of conduct, and my political beliefs, aimlessly acquired, would change the course of historical events. All of my interests and needs and whims and predilections had enormous conse-quences, because they were characteristic of millions like me. But I didn't yet understand myself as part of this mass. I didn't foresee our power. I was pleasantly cloistered among the great stone build-ings, eager to shut out the world of adults and the world of children, and happy to live among my peers, aged eighteen to twenty-two, in a sort of sexual rhapsody of serious talk and giddy uncoverings and long dizzy afternoons of Kierkegaard and Jax beer.

News reached us nonetheless. Richard Speck, the failed scholar of Woodrow Wilson High School, murdered eight nursing stu-dents in Chicago. Charles Whitman, the nation's youngest Eagle Scout, climbed into the tower at the University of Texas and shot forty-four people, killing fourteen. One of the injured students was a high-school classmate of mine. I watched a ceremony on the Quadrangle for the widow of the first Tulane graduate killed in Vietnam. It reminded me that university life was a parenthesis, enclosed on either side by the draft.

But I was in love, and enjoying four years of deferment, and it seemed absurd to worry that this "brushfire war" would be waiting for me on graduation day.

7 / FATHER AND SON

One of the most powerful memories of my childhood is standing on the edge of the bed, at the age of three, and pinning my father's ribbons to his chest after he was called up to fight in Korea. He had already spent five years in uniform in World War II, and the record of his Army career was told in the ribbons and medals that he had, until now, stored away. He tried to explain to me the color-coding of the service ribbons, which represented different campaigns or acts of heroism. One of them, a red ribbon with yellow trim and a thin blue stripe, stood for the Bronze Star, which he had won on the battlefield in Germany. The blue stripe represented the infantry, as did the blue badge with the silver wreath and the crossed rifles on his collar. On his shoulders were his division patches, the trident of the 97th Infantry, with which he had served in Europe, and the thunderbird of the 45th, the Oklahoma infantry division he had joined in the National Guard. On his right collar was a gold oak leaf signifying his rank: major. I had never before seen my father in uniform, and this transformation from his banker's blue suit into the warrior's splendid vestment left me thunderstruck.

From then on soldiering became a basic part of manhood in my mind. I believed I had been initiated into secrets only men could know. I would lie in the grass imagining combat, and idealizing death—not my father's but my own.

My father was less romantic about war, having fought in one of them already. He had spent too many years in foxholes, huddled together with his own mortality. His object had been to survive, not to win glory. He had won his Bronze Star on the Sieg River when he resupplied his forward machine-gun positions by carrying boxes of ammunition through a minefield. He never thought he deserved the award, because he hadn't known the riverbanks were mined. The closest he came to death, in his opinion, was when the commissary truck ran over his tent in the middle of the night—a night when he happened to be sleeping in the colonel's staff tent. He decided then that God had spared him for a higher purpose. When he came home, he had a driven need for peace. He sailed into New York harbor with the European war behind him, and when he saw the Statue of Liberty he began to cry. He hid behind a post to keep his men from seeing his tears.

But now he was being snatched out of civilian life again and sent back to battle. Korea was far away and mysterious. My father resented fighting in that undeclared war: He hadn't known it could happen; it seemed un-American. On my third birthday, the day I pinned the medals to his chest, he took me and several of my new toys with him to the armory in Oklahoma City, where the division was receiving its instructions. I sat on his lap, and as he recalls it, every time the colonel issued an order, I blew a noisemaker, the kind that unrolls and makes a sound like a Bronx cheer. It was my first antiwar demonstration. Back then, my father and I were on the same side.

Fifteen years later I became a soldier of sorts when I joined the Army Reserve Officers Training Corps. This was before soldiering was held in disgrace on campuses around the country, before the ROTC buildings were bombed, before young men would stop wearing their uniforms to class. I took ROTC because what I feared most about military life was not being an officer. For me, soldiering still had a gentleman's aura about it. I was too much of a snob to be a part of the ranks. What mattered to me was the adventure of war—and, to a lesser extent, the uniform. I gave some thought to transferring to the Navy because of its dress whites.

Even in ROTC I was less of a soldier than I had expected to be.

For one thing, I couldn't keep cadence, and when the drill was given to me, I had the entire company stepping on each other's shoes. Also, the academic course that accompanied the program was supposed to be a snap, and yet it wasn't for me, as I discovered one semester when I made A's in every other subject and a C in ROTC.

There was another consideration that was just now beginning to trouble me. I wanted to see combat, but I wasn't certain that I wanted to kill. It was a niggling distinction at first. Killing, and risking death, were the objects of war, at least from the point of view of the warrior. I thought I was willing to kill for my country, in fact I was already being trained for it, but now that I stood on the threshold of military service I was flooded with doubt. I saw the news. I saw the enemy in his black pajamas, racing through the rice paddies. I saw Buddhist priests burning themselves alive and robust Americans wearing necklaces of Vietcong ears. I found myself suspended between two extreme emotions. On the one hand, I believed my country was wrong, and I thought it was immoral for me to contribute my service. On the other hand, there was a war going on and I might miss it. This was fundamentally at odds with my image of myself as a man.

In the summer of 1967, between my junior and senior years in college, I suddenly announced at the dinner table that I was going to join the Marines. My sisters and my mother were alarmed. "Why?" they cried. I was going to be a medical corpsman. That way I could avoid having to kill. If I stayed in ROTC and waited until graduation, I'd have no control over my assignment. Rosalind began to cry. Kathleen became sarcastic. "No one," she said, "has ever joined the Marines to avoid killing." My father said nothing; he only smiled.

Rosalind got a letter from our cousin Don, who was already in Vietnam. His helicopter had crashed. He was all right, he assured us, but he was injured and being sent home. That seemed to me the best luck in the world.

I thought about my decision for the next several days. I knew why I wanted to join the Marines: I didn't want to miss the war.

During that time my father was queerly elated. He would go to the head of the stairs and jokingly call "Medic! Medic!" Mother pleaded with him to stop; it wasn't funny.

I finally went to see the recruiters in the federal building in downtown Dallas. The following morning I went to the induction center to take the examinations. There were two hundred boys my age. I was the only volunteer. Most of them were black or Hispanic. The white boys had come into the city on buses from the farm towns of East Texas. I was the only one with any college education. For the first time I saw the faces of the young men who would fight this war. They were not like me; they had had no advantages. Some of them were excited—they were cutting up in line, pretending to spill their urine samples, making wisecracks to the doctors. But most of them were anxious. They looked about with wide eyes and thin lips and startled movements. When it came time to take the pledge, I did not step forward. It was humiliating, but I was free to go. I still had my deferment.

That night I drove out to Cox Cemetery. It sits on a dark hill behind White Rock Lake, looking like a set in a horror movie. An arched wrought-iron gate creaked in the breeze. I sat on a tombstone all through the night, waiting for God to speak to me. I was scaring myself for His benefit. I thought that in the graveyard I might find a seam between life and death, where my prayers might be heard. I wanted to know what to do. But when dawn came I was still confused, angry, and without revelation. I had come to a line in my life that I had always expected to cross. One step forward: it was a powerful symbolic act. On the near side was civilianhood, safety, and in some respects youth; on the far side was uniformed service, danger, and the awful maturity of war. Every schoolboy in Texas knows the name of Moses Rose, the only man who refused to cross the line Colonel Travis drew in the dust at the Alamo. I had always believed about myself that I would have died with Travis and Crockett at the Alamo rather than have risked dishonor, even in a war I now suspected was little more than a racist land grab. But I was not the person I thought I was.

And the line was still waiting for me.

* * *

My parents had gloried in the Second World War. Mother would speak about the sacrifices, the rationing, the anxiety, but her voice was unmistakably thrilled. It was a great time to be alive. The music was new and swinging, you had never heard music like that before. The fashions, the hairstyles—women were newly created, they practically had the country to themselves. And the men—all the men in uniform, everyone you knew—they looked so dashing, and yet what? Vulnerable. A little uncertain. But eager, intense, burning with life.

The Japanese had bombed Pearl Harbor—we had no choice in that war. In Europe a madman was overrunning civilization, conquering entire nations in a matter of days. Our enemies were formidable and clearly evil. Rommel—my God! what a genius. But we had Patton. We had Eisenhower, Bradley, Ridgway. In the Pacific we had MacArthur and Nimitz. There were heroes everywhere. Newspapers were full of them: hometown boys returning with medals and promotions, or else not returning but dying brilliantly, for a cause everyone endorsed. Freedom.

By contrast, my war seemed puny and vague. Until the late sixties I scarcely knew it was going on at all. I certainly had no previous emotional investment in Vietnam. I doubt that I could have found it on the map when I entered college. I had been a stamp collector as a teenager, but I never owned a single Vietnamese stamp, so in that sense the country was less familiar to me than Togo or Somaliland.

Eisenhower, my father's hero, had kept us out of Vietnam when the French begged us to save them at Dien Bien Phu. "I am convinced the French could not win the war because the internal situation in Viet Nam, weak and confused, badly weakened the military situation," Eisenhower wrote in the spring of 1963, only two years before Lyndon Johnson began his massive draft calls, in a passage that was excised from his memoirs.

"But this factor was in itself not overriding. Had the circumstances lent themselves to a reasonable chance for victory or a

chance to avert a defeat for freedom, then the task of explaining
to the American public the necessity for sacrifice would have been
an acceptable one. The jungles of Indochina, however, would have
swallowed up division after division of United States troops. . . .
Furthermore, the presence of ever more numbers of white men in
uniform probably would have aggravated rather than assuaged
Asiatic resentments. Thus, even had all of Indochina been physically occupied by United States troops, their eventual removal
would have resulted only in a reversion to the situation which had
existed before."

Eisenhower goes on to explain that unilateral involvement of
American troops in a foreign war is a violation of our fundamental
defense policy, which is that because America does not have the
manpower to police the world, its proper role must be that of an
ally: "Unless our allies were willing to participate along with us—
which they were not—action by the United States alone would
have been a violation of our firm and wise defense policy.

"But the strongest reason of all for the United States refusal to
respond to French pleas is the fact that among all the powerful
nations of the world the United States is the only one with a
tradition of anti-colonialism. . . . The standing of the United States
as the most powerful of the anti-colonial powers is an asset of
incalculable value to the Free World. It means that our counsel is
trusted where that of others may not be. It is essential to our
position of leadership in a world wherein the majority of nations
have at some time or another felt the yoke of colonialism.

"Thus it is that the moral position of the United States was more
to be guarded than the Tonkin Delta, indeed than all of Indochina."

It's heartbreaking to read those words now, after all of Eisenhower's premonitions proved true. And yet it was Eisenhower who
backed the French war in Vietnam with a billion dollars in aid,
accounting for 78 percent of the total cost of that war. Knowing
the popularity of Communist leader Ho Chi Minh after the fall of
the French, Eisenhower spurned the Geneva accords, which called
for national elections and reunification in Vietnam; in fact, it was

Eisenhower who fabricated the nation of South Vietnam itself—a wholly arbitrary and untenable creation—and then installed a corrupt Catholic aristocrat named Ngo Dinh Diem, who recently had been living in Lakewood, New Jersey, as the prime minister of this American-made country of Buddhist peasants.

It was Kennedy who led us into the war. In his first year in office he had suffered the humiliation of the Bay of Pigs, the erection of the Berlin Wall, an accommodation with the Communists in Laos, and an intimidating encounter with Khrushchev in Vienna. "Now we have a problem in trying to make our power credible," he admitted to James Reston, "and Vietnam looks like the place." By the time of his death there were 16,900 American soldiers in Vietnam, and 109 were already dead. Now we were fighting for the "independence of South Vietnam," while most of that country's population was struggling against the oppression of Diem.

As a soldier, my father understood the logistical problems of fighting a land war in Asia. He was appalled by the casual spread of American commitments during the Kennedy administration, especially to South Vietnam, where the supply line would extend halfway around the globe. History taught us that a large power should never fight a guerrilla war: you forfeit your advantages. The Redcoats had learned this lesson in the American Revolution; had we forgotten it ourselves? Moreover, China loomed over Vietnam like a balancing rock. My father had fought the Chinese in Korea, and he believed we were lucky to gain a standoff. And there was confusion about our mission. Was it to win the war? to contain Communism? or just to tread water until the South Vietnamese could snap to life? Kennedy had said of Vietnam two months before his death, "We are not there to see a war lost." Was that all we wanted from the war—to not lose? All of these factors, to a man who had commanded infantry for seven years in two wars, persuaded my father that Vietnam was a bad cause on a poorly chosen ground.

Wars were expensive, but my parents' generation had learned to trust war; war had pulled the country out of the Depression, war had made America into the dominant economic force in the world. When my father returned from World War II, America was the most expansive and powerful economy history had ever seen. It held $35 billion of the world's $40-billion-plus supply of monetary gold. This was the corpus of his generation's inheritance. And yet by 1961, when Kennedy began to involve American troops in the Vietnam War, the supply of gold, weakened by the Korean War and the European revival, was down to $17 billion. As a banker, my father should have foreseen the disastrous economics of the war, but like everyone else he was enjoying the false bloom of wartime deficits. As the war grew, so did the economy. But the balance of trade began to shift, gold reserves diminished, productivity declined. Most of the apparent growth in the gross national product during the sixties was inflation. Wages shot up, along with prices, but the real income of the American worker stayed flat. We were paying for the war by making America smaller, in terms of its economic importance in the world. The America my generation would inherit would be complexly indebted and confounded by its failures to compete with the rising world economies.

There were also psychic expenses of staying in the war, which were extracted from my father in the forms of anger, misgiving, frustration; and these costs were not small because they had to do with his own worth. What did he stand for after all? What did his son stand for? Everything American was becoming cheaper, less worthy, like the baser metals that were now sandwiched inside American coins.

My own doubts about the war had to do with the idea of America, which was special in the world. Every great power has an idea of itself, an animating myth that gives meaning to the national culture. It is partly nonsense, just gross stereotypes—the French are cultured, the Russians soulful, the English civilized, the Germans efficient, and so on. In America we believed that we had hold of a sacred truth about individual freedom. When my father went off to war I understood that he was going to make the world safe for democracy and that that was what the world wanted. America had a mission—we thought it was a divine mission—to spread freedom, and freedom meant democracy, and democracy meant capitalism, and all that meant the American way of life.

It came as a surprise to me to learn that much of the world lived in terror of America and that the qualities we appreciated about ourselves and wished to share with others—our ideals of progress, for instance, or our friendly feeling for the common man, or our famous "know-how"—were often the very qualities other peoples feared. We threatened the qualities they most valued in themselves. To the French we were uncultured, to the Russians we were soulless, and so on. Hating America was a way of confirming one's identity.

In a way, that same hatred of America expressed the identity of my generation. This was not something my father could understand. In the world he had grown up in, America was the reluctant knight, not the menacing dragon. One of his earliest memories is a fireworks display in St. John, Kansas, on a bitterly cold Armistice Day. He was three years old when news came of the end of the war. He remembers his father rubbing whiskers on his face and showing him a newspaper photo of the kaiser. My father grew up in that interlude of peace between the world wars. His own life was hard, deprived, at times brutal, but he believed with most Americans that his country was virtuous. He was fortunate to become a man at a time when America was historically correct. I will always envy him that. He matured in a magic age, the 1940s, when great evil and great good faced each other. In that splendid moment he knew which side he was on. He was an American farm boy doing what God and his country had designed for him. How heady this was, for after all he must have spent many lonely, anxious moments in the wheat fields wondering whether life would ever offer him direction or even escape. And yet here he was, saving the world.

I grew up expecting to inherit his certainty. Since America was on the side of freedom, I wouldn't have to worry about my conscience. Duty would take care of me. When I pledged allegiance to the flag, as I did every school day and every Scout meeting and every week at Sunday school, I believed in its promise of liberty and justice for all. I longed for the chance to exercise what seemed to be a profound right of an American man: to fight for my country, to fight for what was right, to do my duty.

It is easy to understand my anger, and the anger of my generation, when we realized that our country had taken a wrong turn. Eisenhower was right; we had forfeited our moral position. We had surrendered our anticolonial past. Now that we were compromised, the world did not divide so neatly between good and evil—that was my opinion. In my father's mind, however, America could never be wrong. Even in Korea, in a war he hated, we had stopped the advance of Communism, and that was finally worth the sacrifice. He was briskly confident still that the values of democracy, progress, capitalism—America, in short—were good and that other forms of government or economy were un-American or bad. I grew to hate his conviction. That American bullheadedness of his, coupled with a smug and pious attitude toward the rest of the world, with which he had had some small experience (and I, none), began to anger me, and we started to spar, as you might expect, since I was also bullheaded, pious, and smug about conclusions of my own.

In my father's college days he became an acolyte of Franklin Roosevelt and the New Deal. He had been taught from childhood to value independence and self-sufficiency; he loathed the idea of welfare, and yet it was the make-work programs of the Depression that put him through school. One year, working for the National Youth Administration, he helped build a football stadium by scraping dirt out of a hillside and hauling it away in burlap bags. Many of his professors, even at the small state teachers college he went to in Oklahoma, were socialists, and although my father never swallowed their philosophy, he had seen capitalism fail. He would describe himself as a New Deal liberal then, since he relied upon the federal government to rescue him and the millions like him who had no other ladder of escape. He went to Washington one summer to work in the mailroom at the Department of Agriculture, and he read the scribbled notes of desperation from farm families whose only mule had died or whose land had been seized, and he understood that without government assistance many thousands of citizens would have starved. His own family back in Seward, Kansas, was scarcely any better off. Even later in life, when his politics began to change, my father never forgot what the federal government had done for him, and he never lost his emotional feeling for Roosevelt. Once, when my father was in Officer Candidate School, Roosevelt himself came to Fort Benning to see his detachment perform in a war game, and afterward the President complimented the young lieutenant who had idolized him since adolescence. "That was a clever young man," Roosevelt was reported to have said, as he rode off with the base commander; "What's his name?" "I've got no idea," the general replied.

However, the shame of watching his own father fail would shape my father profoundly. He developed instincts of caution and a powerful need to accumulate security. These are conservative instincts, and they became more pronounced in him as he grew older and assumed responsibility for a family of his own. Another man might have come to different conclusions about his experiences. For instance, I have often wondered about my father's choice of banking as a profession, which he turned to after the war instead of practicing law. If I had been a farmer in the Dust Bowl and had seen the banks foreclosing on my neighbors' farms, I wonder what my attitude toward bankers might have been. And if I had fought in two wars and seen many friends die, I don't know how eager I would have been to see my own son fight in another.

My father had been strongly affected by the folly of appeasement, such as Chamberlain had tried to effect with Hitler in Munich. Compromise was an indication of weakness, and weakness an invitation to disaster. In 1939, my father would often say, the entire U.S. Army could have fit into the Rose Bowl. When he was drafted in the spring of 1940, men in his outfit were issued toy rifles and World War I uniforms. If we had been more alert and better prepared, he believed, Pearl Harbor would not have happened. This was a lesson we should never forget. America must always be the arsenal of democracy, no matter what the cost.

Other than Roosevelt, the political figure who most influenced my father was Winston Churchill. It is characteristic of my father's politics that he was suspended between two ideologues, Roosevelt the liberal and Churchill the conservative. My father thought

Churchill was a prophet. He had been right before the war when he urged his country to prepare itself, and he was right again after the war when he foretold the Iron Curtain's falling across the European continent. In the postwar world, however, my father began to reconsider Churchill's wartime wisdom—his demands, for instance, for unconditional surrender and no separate peace, which had kept the Germans from establishing internal opposition to Hitler and turning their forces entirely against the Soviet advance.

Since then, my father has come to rue the decision that his heroes, Roosevelt and Churchill, crafted at Yalta with Joseph Stalin. He saw for himself the arrival of Communism at the end of the war. He was with Patton's Third Army, moving rapidly into Czechoslovakia. In another few days the Allies would have liberated most of Eastern Europe. Instead, he was stopped in his tracks at Marienbad, as the Soviets fought their way to Prague. All of his life he would remember the faces of the Czechs urging the Americans into their country before the Russians came.

These were the major experiences of my father's time: the Depression and the War. They were bound to stamp him with certain attitudes and political beliefs, and in this respect my father was representative of his generation. He was basically conservative. He was cautious about his own finances as well as the nation's; he was ready to help the needy but suspicious of the dole; he worried about Communism and was determined to keep the country strong. In addition he had a positive feeling about progress. He had seen the country transformed from the isolated rural nation of his own father's time into the dominant power of the world. He saw cities grow. He saw wealth spreading across the land. He saw highways and airports and shipyards and skyscrapers and immense factories arise, liberating the poor, bringing jobs and a "standard of living" whereas before there had been only scarcity. He believed that free enterprise was the key to personal freedom and that freedom itself was the object of man's long march.

After Roosevelt and Truman, he voted Republican in presidential contests, with the exception of his choice of Lyndon Johnson in 1964. And yet he continued to think of himself as a Democrat, largely because Texas was still a one-party state. Not until 1968, the year I would be eligible to vote in my first election, did my father identify himself as a thoroughgoing, unapologetic Republican. No doubt it was a wrenching decision, because in the 150-year history of Wrights in America there had never been a registered Republican. Although it seems a long and perhaps peculiar political odyssey from Franklin Roosevelt to Richard Nixon and eventually to Ronald Reagan, it was a journey my father made, along with a steady majority of his contemporaries.

I grew up in another world, the suburban Southwest, a new world invented by people like my father to give form to their need for order, security, prosperity, and peace. This was America's promised land, a gridwork of tract homes and two-car garages, schools and country clubs, and lawns more caringly cultivated than the wheat fields of Kansas. We lived in a series of such neighborhoods, each of them somewhat better than the place we left. We were "upwardly mobile," a term that could not have been employed in my father's youth, when the object was survival.

There was a dazzled sense that all the important problems were solved, or would soon fall away. The economy had been figured out. With the postwar boom, whole new industries appeared, and entirely new branches of science. The economy wasn't just growing, it was bursting with life. Management was the present concern; one had only to allocate resources correctly, since abundance was guaranteed. We thought of the economy as a machine, with a monetary accelerator and fiscal brakes, and we had the confidence of a mechanic who has fiddled with the engine and made it hum. The environment was being tamed, not just the wilderness but the discomforts of nature—the heat, for instance. In Texas, civilization languished until the air conditioner made life endurable; it was virtually a man-made geologic era, an indoor ice age. One by one, diseases that had always plagued mankind were being outsmarted. Miracles seemed to happen nearly every day. There was always a new vaccine or wonder drug; I had the feeling as a child that all illness would be cured when I was old, and even death itself might soon be treated. Perhaps all children hope for immortality, but a long, if not permanent, life seemed to be a promise of my age.

We were moving into an era of no-iron shirts and no-wax floors, sitcoms and TV dinners, Formica and polyester, Brunswick and Evinrude, Huntley and Brinkley, Whirlpool and GE. It was an era of leisure and excess, of increased horsepower and better living through chemistry, where your fingers did the walking and pizzas came to your door; and the most amazing fact of this quite wonderful world was that it was within reach, it belonged increasingly to common Americans, people like us. If there were still poverty and injustice, we believed that progress inevitably would eliminate them, along with disease and even unhappiness.

To grow up in this heaven on earth was rather like living inside a plastic bag. There was a suffocating sense of confinement and of breathing one's own air. Too much order, too little risk, made life anxious and trivial, and yet this was supposed to be a world of freedom and opportunity. This would be the big surprise to my parents' generation. In their minds we were living in an idyll they had created for us, but instead of growing up grateful we grew up angry, confused, and rebellious. Couldn't we see that the middle-class suburb was the answered prayer and that it would spread like a salve across the land, and eventually across the entire globe, bringing serenity and prosperity and joy to mankind?

Although our childhoods were relatively free of disease and the immediate danger of war, we developed morbid notions of impending catastrophe and seemed to live always in fear. Moreover, we were impatient, despite the progress that seemed to be happening everywhere at such fantastic speed. Psychiatrists began to comment on the pessimism of my generation, and on a tendency toward nihilism. What was wrong with us?—that was the question our parents began to ask in the early sixties, in the coffeehouse days, when we were singing plaintive folk songs that had come, many of them, out of our parents' own youth, out of the hard life they had left behind, the life they had fled.

Our family was racing to satisfy our material desires with my father's well-earned income. We replaced the Chevrolet with an Oldsmobile and the Oldsmobile with a Cadillac. We joined the country club. We bought an A-frame cabin on a small lake in East Texas, with a garden for my father to pour himself into on the weekends, and a bass boat so that he and I could cast our Hula Poppers toward the lily pads on summer evenings. We traveled. My father invested, mainly in local over-the-counter stocks. Mother entertained. At Christmas our tree was surrounded with expensive and thoughtful gifts. And yet, having described all this, I must add that in the world we lived in, our standards were modest. Luxury was never important in my parents' house, comfort was. In fact they had an ingrained resistance to quality, which always seemed to cost more than it was worth. In the view of their children, our parents were cheapskates. Early on we determined to educate them about the relative values of material objects. By the time I was fourteen, my parents would not consider making a major purchase without consulting me, for I understood better than they what to look for in stereos and automobiles and even pedigreed pets. I was a teenaged connoisseur, and I had a poorly disguised disdain for my parents' choice of products. When they inquired about automobiles, I pointed them to the Mercedes-Benz, which was not only a superior car but a better investment than the Cadillac. My father looked at the price and remembered that he had bought houses for less than that. Yes, but—! There was no way to answer him. I wanted it more than he did. The point of life was to get ahead, of course, and to earn money, of course, but finally (and here is where my parents faltered) to spend it, to use your money as intelligently as you acquired it, to get the best. It's not surprising that the consumer movement would grow to maturity with my generation. We were natives in the new world of shopping malls and department stores; it was a world in which our parents were still only immigrants.

But what did I *really* want? This was the question of my youth, and the answer had always been: more. I wanted not only to travel farther, go out to finer restaurants, buy more fashionable clothes, but also to experience life more profoundly. Naturally I was in despair. Christianity had been the prop that sustained my materialism—in Dallas this was no contradiction. On Sunday mornings the church parking lots were filled with expensive new cars, the pastors were busy making real-estate deals and defending the oil-depletion allowance, especially wealthy churchgoers were said to be "blessed." Once I began to lose my grip on the Christian God, however, I found myself alone with the material world. I was falling, falling from grace, falling through an echoing chamber of brand names and back issues of *Consumer Reports,* alone and helpless in the long drop from birth to oblivion.

The thin ledge I found in college was existentialism. There was little comfort there except in the heroic personalities of the European existentialists, especially the French writers Sartre, Beauvoir, Malraux, Camus. It was not so much their philosophy as their courage I admired. They faced death without prayer. I was drawn also to the fatalistic but highly sensual life-style that existentialism seemed to endorse. What the Protestants called sin the existentialists called experience. One could no more be an existentialist and live in the suburbs than one could be a Methodist and live in the smoky demimonde of bebop and free love.

Above the simply bohemian attraction of existentialism was an open and welcoming recognition of absurdity. Absurdity was the devil of the rationally ordered Protestant suburban capitalist universe. To doubt that life made sense, or that history had an object, was to deny God, and yet as a teenager I had begun a secret affair with this heretical proposition. In his autobiography, *The Words,* Sartre wrote admiringly of the sculptor Giacometti who, being run down by a car in the Place d'Italie, fell into a "lucid faint" and experienced a feeling of joy that at last something was happening to him. "So," he said to himself, "I wasn't born to be a sculptor or even to live; I was born for nothing." "I admire this will to welcome everything," Sartre commented. "If you like surprises, you must like them to this extreme; even to those rare lightning-flashes which reveal to its lovers that the earth was not created for them." This passage was itself a kind of lightning flash to me, discharging heresies I had been afraid to pronounce. Life is absurd. Life is ordinary. Life is pointless. Even tragedy can be welcome. I thought at once of my guilty feeling of gratitude when I heard that Kennedy had been shot. Something had happened! Something absurd! In my hungry mind there was a shock of confirmation.

Existentialism was a mood, which had been born in the German occupation of France, a mood that was both defeated and defiant. It seems wildly presumptuous that American college students would adopt this same mood as their own. We were the children of the liberators, we were free, we had every apparent reason to hope. And yet our minds were preoccupied by the prospect of atomic death, the central absurdity of our lives. It was a direct replacement for faith. In the days when I knelt beside my bed and said my prayers, I could call up a bearded image of God: he was the Old Testament, Sistine Chapel God, and he resided in a quiet, central place inside me that I called my soul. Now that place was filled with a different image, the mushroom cloud. If you asked my soul what it believed in, it believed in the hydrogen bomb. It believed in man-made apocalypse, which had nothing to do with divine judgment. It believed in the end of the world, brought about by politics.

I knew who I wanted to be and what I wanted to think. My ideal me was a French intellectual, like Malraux or Camus, who had fought in the Resistance, who was accepting of death but who lived his own life intensely. My ideal me would look like Yves Montand, not beautiful in the glossy, cleft-chinned, wavy-haired American fashion, but ugly in a compelling, European-morose way, with cynical eyes and a wounded mouth, and a humorless expression that says I have seen hell. It would be easy to ridicule this imaginary self-portrait, and the hopelessly American boy who painted it; in fact, I cringe when I confess that I took up smoking largely to complete this image of myself. There was a photograph of Camus on a book jacket, against a black background, with gray cigarette smoke partly blotting out his face like some ectoplasmic eruption; when I saw that picture I knew I was going to have to smoke. And yet beyond the silliness of my desire to be a Left Bank intellectual was the simple and truly existential need to live a complete life, which meant a life without illusion or fear. A romantic life, in other words.

My break with my father began before the war fell between us. It began, I suppose, with the Kennedy assassination, which would mark my life in a way it would never affect his; compared with the Depression and combat, one man's death could hardly be expected to alter the course of my father's life or even profoundly change his thinking. However, my disillusionment began that day. Until then, I had thought that life would make sense. Kennedy's death was like a crack in the door, but instead of light, darkness rushed in.

Then the war came. Or rather, the war was already there; it was Kennedy's legacy and, in a way, his revenge. (Only Kennedy could have gotten us out of Vietnam, we said again and again, but Kennedy was gone, we had killed him.) Each year, as the war dragged on and I came closer to the end of my deferment, the arguments between my father and me became more heated. In part it was merely youth and age in their eternal grappling; we were acting out roles that fathers and sons have played forever. We were bound to struggle. What made this generational contest greater than any in our country's history was the lack of balance between the Baby Boomers of my generation and the Depression- and war-seared generation that gave birth to us. That balance was skewed not only by the vast number of young people but also by the extreme contrasts between our experiences and expectations and those of our parents.

It was not Vietnam we were arguing about, but America. In our polarized state, my father saw America as all good and I saw it as all bad. I think only Americans could be so arrogant, so naive, so moralistic about their country's place in the world. We would argue in the living room, after my father had several scotch and waters during the "social hour" before dinner. Mother would sense the

battle coming on and attempt some brave diversion. "Oh, let's not
talk about *that.*" For one thing, she never had an opinion. What
my father said, she supported; he was the family executive, he
brought home his boardroom manner, his abrupt decisiveness,
which became overbearing if the social hour lingered too long.
Mother's loyalty dismayed me, and I wondered what it cost her as,
one by one, her children lined up against her husband. She saw
herself as the matrix that held us all together, and when we fought
she was the one who was pulled apart. It was her loyalty, however,
that allowed my father to go too far. Certain of her support, he
permitted himself to bully and threaten us. "Oh, Don," she'd say
after he had handed down some injunction, which usually had to
do with cutting off our living expenses. Then she would retreat and
cry by herself. She had a dream of pleasant company. She wanted
us to sit around and tell great stories and discuss important but
noncontroversial matters. She liked to gossip and talk about movies
and art. But for years the war ruined everything, turning all conversation into angry debate, which she loathed.

And yet she had always loved soldiers. She had been a hostess
at Fort Benning when she met my father. Now, during the Vietnam War, she would go out to the USO at Love Field and spend
several afternoons a month playing gin rummy with the servicemen
who were passing through. At last she found companions who did
not wish to talk about the war.

The war was dividing the country along the lines of race and
class, as well as age. I knew that the weight of the war was falling
heaviest on the poor and the minorities—I had seen it for myself
in the induction center—and yet like most middle-class white boys
I hid behind my II-S deferment, which was out of reach of those
who couldn't afford a college education. Those who went, the kids
who couldn't avoid the draft or the patriots who wanted to fight,
came home talking about gooks and slopes, which added to the
image of a racist war. Lyndon Johnson always believed that the real
racists were people like me, who refused to sacrifice our white,
well-educated lives for less precious Asians.

My language became filled with the rhetoric of the time. In 1967 students were often speaking of revolution. If our use of that term meant anything, other than social reform, it was the overthrow of recognized authority—the Establishment, we called it. The Establishment we were speaking of was not just the Eastern Establishment that my father struggled against, it was all authority, from the phone company to the landlord, and any socially acceptable form of behavior, from marrying your sweetheart to going into business with dad. The Establishment believed in containing Communism while supporting dictatorships abroad and ignoring racism at home. We understood that the real interests of the Establishment were in promoting American imperialism, not freedom, and that profit was the real goal of our foreign policy, not democracy. Everything we had been taught up to now we recognized as false. All policy, all history, all convention, would be rounded up and brought in for questioning. Everything was to be thought through anew, fearlessly, radically.

My father became an embarrassment to me. I was no longer proud of his accomplishments or his position in the community— they were merely evidence of his involvement in the Establishment. Although he had never been a part of the right-wing politics of the city, I began to attribute them to him, and to hold him responsible for attitudes he didn't really have. He did the same to me. He saw the protests on the news, he read the accounts in the newspapers, and he thought of his angry son. Although I was never an active protester and was filled with misgivings, around my father I became strident and dead certain. We stopped knowing each other, and in some respects we even stopped knowing ourselves.

The war between my father and me was fought in other households all over the country, tearing the generations apart. We fought the war across the dining room table, or in angry letters, or sullen phone conversations. Every family gathering was bound to drown in the whirl of argument and insult. When we were not shouting at each other, we were stalking the perimeter, elaborately cautious, keeping everyone around us—especially Mother—in a state of apprehension and internal frenzy as the evening progressed and the two antagonists moved inevitably toward the vortex. There was no way to hold us back. We were too angry, not at each other but at what each represented. My hair grew long, and I became to my father one of the nihilistic unwashed barbarians, opposed to progress, naively longing for peace, excoriating my expensively educated mind with frightening drugs, at turns passive, simplistic, snobbish, unpatriotic, ungrateful, amoral, suspiciously feminine, and obnoxiously proud of myself. I watched my father's jaw set, and I saw in his reactions exactly what I expected to see: the entrenched resistance of the middle class and the middle-aged, who hated the young because of their youth, who was fighting old wars in new times, deaf to reason and blind to injustice, hung up and uptight, afraid of experience, terrified of change, materialistic while being tasteless, pious but spiritually dead, locked into an angry and un-happy life that he would gladly press upon his children. We stopped being father and son to each other and became types.

We no longer spoke to each other, except in the most perfunc-tory fashion about my education. We were too indignant to talk about ordinary subjects, so either we said nothing at all or one of us would discharge a broadside about the war, the country, or who we really were. What annoyed each of us most was the unspoken realization that we were behaving exactly alike. There was a power-ful sense of identity we would both have liked to deny. At some level this must have been maddeningly comic, almost slapstick, like two men trying to get through the same door. "After you." "No, after you." Then they collide in the doorway.

We had each glimpsed in the other the boundaries of our love. This was the cruelest revelation of the war. In my father's mind I was either dishonorable or cowardly. He could not love that part of me that refused to serve our country. As for me, as I listened to the words we threw at each other in our endless argument, I realized that my father was humiliated by me, and I began to think that he would rather see me dead in Vietnam than alive and shouting in his living room. Once we saw that our love for each other was limited and conditional, the war between the two of us found a temporary peace. We didn't care to fight an enemy who no longer loved us completely.

8 / EXISTENTIAL POLITICS

From the day Lyndon Johnson took office I had been grooming my accent to rid it of the Texas twang, that dead giveaway. The first time I heard myself on a tape recording was in language lab, and I felt a shock of dismay. To a Texan there was as much difference between my nasalized North Texas drawl and LBJ's Hill Country brogue as there was, to a Southerner, between the pinched vowels of the Tidewater and the diphthongs of Alabama. When Lyndon Johnson said "wire" it came out "war," as in a "bob-war fence." When I said "wire" it made a noise like a Civil Defense siren in my nose. But when I heard myself saying *"hablo muy bien el español,"* I sounded like Lyndon ordering a platter of tamales.

I could not help feeling a grudging kinship with Johnson. We were stained by the same brush. The same hatred directed at him—from the East, the liberals, the Ivy Leaguers, especially from the Kennedys themselves—reflected on me as well. It was a class hatred. When Johnson complained to Hugh Sidey of *Life*, "I don't believe that I'll ever get credit for anything I do in foreign affairs, no matter how successful, because I didn't go to Harvard," I knew what he meant. Harvard was a chord often sounded in the new world, which saw the country being controlled by academics in Cambridge and New Haven, and by New York newspaper barons and network executives ("the malevolent press of the Eastern Seaboard," Johnson bitterly labeled them), and by old-money lawyers and bankers in the Boston-to-Washington corridor. These people held the reins on the lobbyists and elevated bureaucrats who were themselves moneyed, privileged, and conditioned to represent the interests of their class. They were the Eastern Establishment. Outside their circle the rest of us stood about like orphans peering into shop windows. It was the classic and predictable confrontation of new money versus old, of a raw new breed trying to wrench respectability out of the hands of the effete old families, who were bound to deride our nose-picking manners and our undisguised ambitions. We were playing out the comic drama America itself had played for the amusement of Europe during the last two centuries. We were the new New World, and Lyndon Johnson was our innocent abroad.

Everything about Lyndon—his size, his earthy way of speaking, his legendary gaucherie—was a caricature of Texas qualities. He never seemed like a real person to me; he was not only larger than life, he was a sort of mythic Texas freak, like those jackelope postcards tourists bought when they drove through the state. His touch was more than common, it was coarse. He didn't pet his dog, he picked him up by the ears. His idea of entertaining foreign leaders was to take them to the ranch and speed about in his open Lincoln with a six-pack of beer. When he went around the world in 1966, he took along a planeload of plastic busts of himself, which an aide dispensed from a shopping cart—he even gave one to the pope. The Kennedy entourage detested him, largely because of the clash of styles between their elegant champion and his indomitably tacky successor. Their attitude toward him was sealed in Dallas, when Johnson abruptly took control. "We didn't like Johnson taking over *Air Force One* when his own vice-presidential plane, with identical facilities, was available," Kennedy aide Larry O'Brien remembered. "We didn't like his delaying the takeoff. We resented his calling Jackie 'honey.' " Bobby Kennedy never forgave Johnson's demand to be sworn in immediately; it was unseemly and constitutionally unnecessary. Despite Jackie's state of shock and the panic of the Kennedy aides to get the hell out of Dallas, Johnson held the plane on the ground until Judge Hughes arrived to administer the oath—not on a Bible, as Johnson believed, but on Kennedy's Catholic missal. In the sharp-eyed view of the Kennedy men, it was typical of Johnson to get even this historic moment just wrong.

Jackie wouldn't leave the White House. Of course Johnson wouldn't hurry her. She said she had "nowhere else to go." In Texas we felt that her reluctance to leave was a personal slight—against us. We felt her grief, but we also felt her resentment. She didn't want to relinquish her husband's bedroom to Lyndon, the archetypal Texan. She was in pain, but so were we, so were the Johnsons. Liz Carpenter, Mrs. Johnson's press secretary, expressed the sentiment of many guilty Texans when they faced the coincidence of Kennedy's murder in their state and his succession by Lyndon Johnson: "It's a terrible thing to say," Carpenter told Lady Bird, as they rode together to The Elms, where the new President resided, "but the salvation of the State of Texas is that the Governor was hit." And Mrs. Johnson replied, "I only wish it could have been me."

This was the bloody transfer of power between the new world and the old—a by-product of madness, an incidental coup. The new world was bound to come to power someday; the census was on our side; but the fact that it came too soon and that it came through murder made our accession illegitimate. Johnson believed that Bobby Kennedy actually considered preventing his presidency. "I thought that was on his mind every time I saw him the first few days, after I had already taken the oath. I think he was seriously calculating what steps to take. For several days he really kept me out of the president's office. I operated from the Executive Office Building because it was not made available to me."

Johnson understood that his presidency was premature, that he was acting as a regent for Kennedy's ghost. Kennedy had drawn around him a Cabinet of pedigreed intellectuals, exactly the sort of men who were most likely to add luster to Kennedy's own polish, but they would make his successor appear ignorant and crass, a Texas yokel. In their presence Johnson became intensely conscious of his background. He used to joke uncomfortably about how many men serving him were Rhodes scholars, how many had gone to

Harvard, how many to Yale, but there was only one man in the room who had gone to Southwest Texas State Teachers College in San Marcos, Texas. He seriously considered not running for his own term in 1964, he told *New York Times* columnist James Reston, because the country was "not far enough from Appomattox" to accept a president from his part of the country. "I was not thinking just of the derisive articles about my style, my clothes, my manner, my accent, and my family," Johnson recalled in his memoirs. "I was also thinking of a more deep-seated and far-reaching attitude—a disdain for the South that seems to be woven into the fabric of Northern experience."

But the choice that year was not between the new world and the old, it was between Johnson and Goldwater, the one running under the banner of the Kennedy legacy and the other sounding the trumpet of new world insurgency. Johnson's historic mandate in that contest was a repudiation of his own region and origins, and in a subtle way a slap at himself. If he had been running against Rockefeller, he might have understood more clearly how the nation was shaped, for him or against him.

I have wondered since then how much of the antiwar movement was actually an Eastern Establishment reaction to President Johnson. The same Establishment had drawn Kennedy into Vietnam in the first place and had steadily pulled Johnson in after him, until suddenly the Establishment changed its mind. Johnson watched them desert him and questioned what his critics would have said if Kennedy were alive and running the war. What would the students say, who loved Kennedy so? Johnson believed that if he had backed out of Vietnam, Robert Kennedy would be leading the pack against him, crying out at the betrayal of his dead brother's policies.

In fact, Robert Kennedy did that anyway. I watched, with complicated feelings of guilt, obligation, and suspicion, as Bobby entered the primaries in 1968. He had a tie on my loyalties that went back to the School Book Depository, and yet I had always distrusted him. I didn't understand how, exactly, a man who had worked for Joe McCarthy during the worst days of the anti-Communist witch-hunts, who had been a hawk all during the early days of our Vietnam involvement, could present himself as a liberal peace candidate. His appeal actually had little to do with the war. From the beginning his supporters were evenly divided between those who approved of the war and those who opposed it. He was a Kennedy—that was what mattered—and the hysteria that surrounded his campaign had more to do with celebrity than politics, more to do with myth than reality.

When John Kennedy was alive, we understood him as a political man. In death, however, he was wrapped in the myth of Camelot, a myth invented by an anxious widow as a way of forestalling the judgment of history. After the assassination Jacqueline Kennedy summoned Theodore White to Hyannis Port, and as *Life* magazine held the presses she sold him on her own version of John Kennedy, the creature of destiny. "All I keep thinking of is this line from a musical comedy, it's been an obsession with me," Mrs. Kennedy said, according to White's notes of the interview. "At night before we'd go to sleep . . . Jack liked to play some records . . . I'd get out of bed at night and play it for him . . . on a Victrola ten years old—and the song he loved most came at the very end of this record, the last side of *Camelot,* sad *Camelot:* . . . 'Don't let it be forgot, that once there was a spot, for one brief shining moment that was known as Camelot.' "

White dictated this story to his editor forty-five minutes later, with Jacqueline Kennedy standing over his shoulder, and the result of this collaboration was the most powerful myth of modern American politics. It ruined Johnson's presidency. Even after he received the greatest majority vote in history, Johnson was overshadowed by the vastly romanticized re-creation of his predecessor's brief term. Part of the message of Camelot was that the Kennedys were America's royal family, and the White House rightfully belonged to them, especially to Bobby. Columnist Murray Kempton compared the Kennedys to the Bonapartes: "They identify with the deprived, being the radical foes of all authority when they are out of power."

This is what the crowds were screaming about when Bobby's campaign wheeled through America five years after his brother's death. They were responding to the ideal of a golden age, an era of charm and sexiness that had been celebrated on television and in the fan magazines and then cut short by murder. Added to this nostalgic brew was a kind of spiritualism that saw Bobby as our link to his dead brother, and in a way to a dead America. And yet Bobby was not Jack. He was not elegant, he was not handsome; he was toothy, and his voice sometimes sounded as if it were floating on helium. In place of Jack's charm, Bobby offered a grim drive for power. He was "ruthless"—that tag placed on him by Jimmy Hoffa, the corrupt Teamsters Union boss whom Kennedy hounded during his years as attorney general. He was also an opportunist. He had won election as senator from New York on the barest excuse of residency. And in 1968 he was late coming into the primaries to challenge LBJ; he had waited for Eugene McCarthy to show it could be done.

Nineteen sixty-eight was the year the Baby Boom arrived at the voting booth. Before the general election I would turn twenty-one, which was still the legal age required to vote, and for the first time I heard the candidates speaking to me, a fully vested citizen. The voice that most appealed was dry, witty, haughtily intellectual, and politically alienated; it was the voice of Eugene McCarthy. Norman Mailer characterized him as looking and feeling "like the dean of the finest English department in the land"—no wonder students accepted his authority. What we admired was his intelligence and his courage. Everybody knew that it was impossible to topple Johnson, especially from within his own party. But McCarthy ignored conventional wisdom. He refused to kiss babies or flatter campaign contributors, and he always said what he thought with eloquence, though without drama. He was pointedly anticharismatic. To the frustration of the press, McCarthy never permitted himself the hollow gesture, the hypocritical statement, or the trumped-up pseudoevent, which had become the mainstays of the evening news. He refused, as the *New Republic* noted, "to respond in kind to ersatz seriousness and spurious conscientiousness." His genuineness was turned against him.

McCarthy came within 410 votes of beating Lyndon Johnson in the New Hampshire primary. His main appeal, beyond his pledge to end the war, was the fact that he wasn't supposed to run. Even my father admired him for that. McCarthy gathered support from unlikely quarters, including the Republicans and the Wallacites. (George Wallace was nominated in Dallas as the presidential candidate of the American Independent party.) Three fifths of the people who voted for McCarthy in New Hampshire actually supported American involvement in Vietnam and thought that Johnson wasn't pressing the war aggressively enough. McCarthy was bucking the system, that was what mattered. Although he arrogantly advertised himself as the most qualified man ever to have run for the presidency, he was actually an interloper, and it is easy to perceive in him the same outsider appeal that became the basis for the more successful candidacies of Jimmy Carter and Ronald Reagan.

On March 31, 1968, I stood in the lobby of my dormitory and watched Johnson declare a halt to the bombing of North Vietnam. As always with Johnson on television, there was a languid, underwater quality to his speech and movements, as if he were hypnotized by the TelePrompTer. I could never square that awkward figure on the tube with the legendary muscleman of the Senate cloakroom. Whenever he came on TV my instinct was to leave the room, in the same way that I might steer clear of some pathetic relative at a family reunion. "I call upon President Ho Chi Minh to respond positively and favorably to this new step of peace," Johnson said—a statement that was quietly and, I think, cynically received by the students around me. Then Johnson hesitated. He glanced away from the camera (he was looking at his wife) and continued: "There is division in the American house now. There is divisiveness among us all tonight. And holding the trust that is mine, as President of all the people, I cannot disregard the peril to the progress of the American people and the hope and prospect of peace for all people. . . . I do not believe that I should devote an hour or a day of my time to any personal partisan causes. . . . Accordingly, I shall not seek, and will not accept, the nomination of my party for another term as your President." There was an instant of shocked silence before the room erupted in cheers. "We did it!" someone cried, and I knew what he meant. We—the American student body—had brought down the President of the United States.

We had booed him off the stage, that miserable creature with his compulsive fibs and grotesque piety. But there was another part of me that felt repudiated—as a Texan once again—and that made my hatred of Johnson seem cheap and traitorous. In some non-political, purely human region of my soul I felt ashamed of what had been done to Johnson. No president had ever known the hounding mob that followed Johnson wherever he went, and finally kept him a prisoner inside the White House gates. What a relentless, formidable enemy we had become. In a way our persecution was a kind of assassination; at least Johnson thought so. "The only difference between the Kennedy assassination and mine," he later said, "is that I am alive and it has been more torturous."

Now that he was beaten I allowed myself to recognize him as a great man, in his own failed fashion. He had been trapped in the war, which he had no stomach for—although the war was the one issue that might have saved him. Until the Tet offensive that spring no more than 20 percent of the electorate favored withdrawal. When Johnson decided to bomb North Vietnam, his popularity rating immediately jumped 14 percent. If he had prosecuted the war more vigorously, he would very likely have been reelected, or else, if he had declared the war unwinnable and pulled out our troops, he would at least have been seen as a decisive leader. But Johnson was equally afraid of winning and losing. Finally the people who mattered to him, the liberals and the Eastern Establishment, turned against him and sent him off to the Siberia of permanent disgrace. He came home to Texas and let his hair grow down to his shoulders.

"It's narrowed down to Bobby and me," Eugene McCarthy said the day after his victory in the Wisconsin primary. At the time, neither Vice President Hubert Humphrey nor Richard Nixon appeared to be serious candidates. George Romney and Ronald Reagan were not giving Nixon much of a challenge in the Republican primaries, but Nixon had a reputation as a chronic loser; he was still trying to live down his tantrum before the press in 1962 when he was drubbed in the California governor's race. McCarthy ridiculed the Republicans for their characteristic blandness: "They're somewhat like the lowest forms of plant and animal life. Even at their highest point of vitality there is not much life in them; on the other hand, they don't die." As for Humphrey, he had lost his standing with the liberals during his hawkish years on Vietnam, and the moderates saw him as a hypocrite. He was trying to paint himself as a peace candidate, although he had advocated American troops in Vietnam as far back as the Eisenhower administration, and as Johnson's vice president he called the war "a great adventure, and a wonderful one it is." In the Senate, Humphrey had been a hero of the left because of his impassioned support for civil rights, but by 1968 he had become a buffoon, a tool of the Establishment. He launched his campaign bubbling about "the politics of happiness, the politics of purpose, the politics of joy." He never approached Kennedy or McCarthy in the polls, so he stood back from the primaries and let the party bosses quietly assure him of the nomination through secret pledges and old debts now called in. He might not have campaigned at all, but he raced around the country nonetheless, unloading an unmatchable torrent of verbal energy. "I don't know what kind of president Hubert would make," marveled Groucho Marx. "He'd make a hell of a wife."

McCarthy believed that Kennedy was his real opposition, and once he adjusted to Bobby's entry into the race, he affected a certain relish for the idea of running against Kennedy. "So far he's run *with* the ghost of his brother. Now we're going to make him run *against* it. It's purely Greek: he either has to kill him or be killed by him. We'll make him run against Jack." Then McCarthy added enigmatically, "And I'm Jack."

When Johnson withdrew, however, it took the war out of the campaign, and without the war McCarthy was lost. He was not Jack after all. I continued to support him, although perhaps, as Abbie Hoffman noted, it was easy to cheer for McCarthy now, knowing he would never win; it was like cheering for the Mets. It was different with Bobby.

More than anyone, Bobby Kennedy knew the dangers of public life. He saw the nearly hysterical adulation he excited, which left his hands bleeding and his clothing in shreds. His supporters, such as journalist Jack Newfield, spoke of his "existential dimension," acknowledging in that term the possibility of death that accompanied his candidacy. It was just such a possibility that sent the crowds into frenzies. Politics had become a blood sport for the Kennedys, and in that sense Bobby was playing a different game from that of the other candidates, and we were bound to notice him above the rest. "One of his possibilities was that he was always doomed," the poet Robert Lowell remembered. "It's very strange when you sort of anticipate something; then, when it happens, you're almost *more* astonished than if you hadn't anticipated it." Kennedy himself acknowledged, "I play Russian roulette every time I get up in the morning. I just don't care. There's nothing I can do about it anyway." That wasn't true; he could have protected himself better than he did, but he made a show of thrusting himself into crowds and disdaining security. He refused the assistance of local police everywhere he went. When Jimmy Breslin asked aloud, "Do you think this guy has the stuff to go all the way?" John J. Lindsay of *Newsweek* replied, "Of course he's got the stuff to go all the way, but he's not going to go all the way. The reason is that somebody is going to shoot him. I know it and you know it, just as sure as we are sitting here—somebody is going to shoot him. He's out there now waiting for him."

In fact Kennedy probably could not have gone all the way. McCarthy had the momentum in the primaries, and Humphrey had the party bosses in his pocket. Even if Kennedy had secured the nomination there was a scandal lurking that could have destroyed his candidacy, having to do with Marilyn Monroe. Rumor said that Bobby had been with her the night she died, trying to persuade her not to give a press conference detailing her relationships with him and with Jack. His brother-in-law, Peter Lawford, had spirited him out of town after Marilyn killed herself. This was all gossip; on the other hand, Bobby's nemesis, Jimmy Hoffa, had hired private detectives to bug Lawford's seaside villa and Marilyn Monroe's Hollywood bungalow. Hoffa supposedly had tapes of trysts between Marilyn and the Kennedy brothers, which he planned to distribute to newspapers.

Kennedy was in Indiana when news came of Martin Luther King's death. That afternoon Kennedy spoke to a shocked crowd in the Indianapolis ghetto. It was the finest moment of his career. More than any other politician, perhaps more than any other white person in America, Bobby Kennedy had an authority to speak on the subject of political violence to the black community, which would so soon explode. "In this difficult day, in this difficult time for the United States, it is perhaps well to ask what kind of a nation we are and what direction we want to move in. For those of you who are black—considering the evidence there evidently is that there were white people who were responsible—you can be filled with bitterness, with hatred, and a desire for revenge. We can move in that direction as a country, in great polarization—black people amongst black, white people amongst white, filled with hatred toward one another.

"Or we can make an effort, as Martin Luther King did, to understand and to comprehend, and to replace that violence, that stain of bloodshed that has spread across our land, with an effort to understand with compassion and love."

Privately he acknowledged the absurdity of events. He had lost patience with meaning. Perhaps that was his most existential quality. He told speechwriter Jeff Greenfield that King's death was not the worst thing that ever happened. Then he remarked, "You know that fellow Harvey Lee Oswald, whatever his name is, set something loose in this country." He knew that what was loose in the country was looking for him, and would find him, and when he was dead it would all have been pointless, for naught. "I am pretty sure there'll be an attempt on my life sooner or later," he admitted to French novelist Romain Gary. "Not so much for political reasons. . . . Plain nuttiness, that's all." As he walked in Martin Luther King's funeral, with his coat slung over his shoulder, he observed

how few white faces were in the crowd. Jimmy Breslin said that
you'd think a few would come out to look, even for curiosity.
Kennedy agreed. "Then maybe this won't change anything at all?"
Breslin asked. "Oh, I don't think this will mean anything," said
Kennedy, and then he turned to Charles Evers, brother of another
murdered civil rights leader, Medgar Evers, who was walking beside him. "Do you think this will change anything?" Kennedy
asked. "Nothing," said Evers. "Didn't mean nothing when my
brother was killed."

"I know," said Robert Kennedy.

In life, Martin Luther King had become a sad figure out of control
of his movement, derided by the young as an Uncle Tom, but in
death it was possible to believe he was a saint. He was not a perfect
man, as the FBI wiretaps would prove. He was an egotist and an
adulterer and something of a peacock. No doubt the minister of
my own church in Dallas had a higher set of personal morals.
Furthermore there was the problem of the Great Man—who is he
to presume on history? Why should I follow him? Isn't he flawed
after all? Toward the end of King's life people were turning away
from him everywhere; even his disciples were talking about his
naïveté and his irrelevance. King insisted on remaining nonviolent
as the power passed into the hands of the Black Panthers and the
hard-faced kids of SNCC (Student Non-Violent Coordinating
Committee). Black Power and the upraised fist were the appropriate responses now. The gospel of revolution was not the New
Testament but Fanon and Camus. The passive resistance of Christianity was pushed aside by the existentialist doctrine of "necessary
violence," which supposes that justice is more important than life.
King was written off by the white liberal intelligentsia as being
middle class and out of date. "Conventional commentators these
days like to speak of King's 'nobility' and the purity of his human-
ism, and they sigh that the world is not ready for him. But it is more
accurate to say that King is not ready for the world," wrote Andrew
Kopkind in an infamous issue of *The New York Review of Books*,

which had a diagram of a Molotov cocktail on the cover. Kopkind also wrote: "Morality, like politics, starts at the barrel of a gun." The younger black leaders, such as Stokeley Carmichael, believed that King deserved part of the blame for the riots in the summer of 1967, in Harlem, Chicago, Cleveland, and elsewhere, which indicated the impatience of the black community for change. "Those of us who advocate Black Power," Carmichael wrote, "are quite clear in our own minds that a 'non-violent' approach to civil rights is an approach black people cannot afford and a luxury white people do not deserve."

Of course it was ironic that the reaction to King's death was massive violence, but perhaps it was only the weight of his spiritual authority that had kept the ghettos unburned until then. In the final months of his life, King himself realized that the nonviolent tactics that had succeeded in the South were failing as the movement traveled North. One of his last marches in Memphis had turned into a riot over which he had no control. Now that he was safely martyred, the country just cracked in two, the black part and the white part. Everything King lived for seemed to be undone by his death, which sparked the worst eruption of civil disorders in the history of the nation. That night there were 711 cases of arson and ten people killed in Washington, D.C., alone. In Baltimore over the next four days there were more than a thousand fires, and it required 12,000 troops to subdue the riots. Before the convulsion subsided, more than 150 other cities in the country were in flames, more than 21,000 people were arrested, and 45 were killed, all but 5 of them black.

I had not loved John Kennedy until he was dead; then I fell guiltily in love with his legend, his promise—with Camelot, in short. With Martin Luther King my feelings were more confused. I thought I had moved beyond him. In 1968 *Soul on Ice* appeared, and I read it excitedly, because Eldridge Cleaver connected the black movement with the student movement and both with liberation movements throughout the world. The same connections had been made before—notably, by Martin Luther King—but they had not been made by a black rapist in a California prison, who was for me an American Camus. What appealed to me so strongly about *Soul on Ice* was the mood—romantic, existential, violent. I think those three adjectives described me and my generation as well. Reading Cleaver had persuaded me that Martin Luther King was beside the point. And yet if John Kennedy's death in Dallas had marked the end of my age of innocence—and perhaps the nation's as well—then Martin Luther King's death began another period for me, having to do with my role as a man and my place in the world. The question for me was violence.

The greatest hypocrisy of my childhood was the notion of Christian love—that is, the pacific brotherly love that Jesus preached. "Turn the other cheek" was a failed doctrine in Dallas. I grew up celebrating violence. It was not just the ritualized violence of sports, which have always been important in Texas. It was a matter of history. Hadn't my father's heroic violence contributed to the end of the war? What might have happened if America had stayed out of the fight, allowing the Axis to overrun the globe? What if Hitler ruled the world? You would never hear a word against the military from the pulpits of Big D. As an American boy I subscribed to the proposition that might makes right; after all, America had never lost a war, and hadn't we always been on the side of truth and justice?

My ideal American then was John Wayne. He was always setting people straight, with his fists or his gun, and he was invariably right. You could never imagine John Wayne turning the other cheek, but he did live by a code. Never back away from a fight, but don't go looking for trouble. Never draw first, but when you do, shoot to kill. In his humbler moments, when he was lying in his bedroll under a billion stars, John Wayne might gaze upward and realize what a small figure he was in the universal scheme of things, but that was a passing thought and he found no solace in it. The night was filled with bandits and Indians, so John Wayne never slept. In the morning the sun lit up the existential landscape and you knew there was no God, there was only John Wayne.

That was my image of America's role in the world. We lived by the code. In the real world the only certainty of justice came from our power, our willingness to use violence appropriately. It seemed to me then that strength and truth were welded together and that if one exercised power, justice would naturally follow.

Moreover, I *liked* violence. I liked the aesthetics of it—the beauty of the gunfight and the glory of the battlefield—it was noble action. My father brought home several weapons from the wars, including a samurai sword from the Occupation of Japan. When I drew it partly out of the black lacquered scabbard and tested the blade, it sliced my finger. I went light-headed at the sight of my blood running down the brilliant blade. Death, I thought, and I am its messenger.

In the sixties my faith in violence was shaken, first by the Freedom Riders and then by the assassinations. In Dallas we didn't know what to make of the Freedom Riders. On the one hand, the Supreme Court said black people had the right to use public accommodations involved in interstate commerce, the right to use public rest rooms, to eat in restaurants, to ride on buses, and in Dallas we were great respecters of the law. We desegregated our own public facilities—except for the schools—without a fight. On the other hand, there was custom to consider. Texas was never a part of the Deep South, but it had been a member of the Confederacy, and we were southern in our prejudices. When the first busload of Freedom Riders approached Anniston, Alabama, in 1961, a mob punctured the bus's tires and set it on fire. The next bus made it to Birmingham, where the police stood aside and let the white mob beat the riders nearly to death. The news reports never made it clear to me that the race riots we kept hearing about were actually white riots, often police riots. I didn't clearly understand that the Freedom Riders were not fighting back. Nonviolence was such a foreign idea to me that I assumed the blacks and several whites on the buses had provoked the mob and got what was coming to them. I didn't grasp the philosophy of nonresistance— but then nothing in my years of churchgoing had prepared me to understand the power of suffering, or redemptive love. The buses kept coming, and then the marches began, into the wall of fire hoses and mounted patrolmen and billy clubs and police dogs. I was

surprised by the violence at first, but I gradually began to realize
that these marchers and these Freedom Riders, who were always
singing, expected to be hurt. They had come for two reasons: to
be hurt, and for me to see it. They would not defend themselves.
They would keep coming. How would John Wayne handle this?
Which side of the line would he be on? You couldn't see him
charging his horse into the line of hot and frightened Negroes,
clubbing a teenaged girl who was crying "Freedom!" Still, you
wouldn't expect him to hold hands with her and march unarmed
into the face of the mob, or to stand still when some redneck spit
in his face. Not to fight back was cowardice—wasn't it? But in my
heart I knew the limits of my courage. I was brave enough to fight,
but I didn't think I would ever be brave enough not to.

It was unsettling to hear Martin Luther King, in those early days,
talking about Jesus. "I am still convinced Jesus was right," he said
in 1960 at the lunch-counter sit-ins in Durham, North Carolina.
"I can hear Him saying, 'He who lives by the sword will perish by
the sword.' I can hear him crying out, 'Love thy enemies.' " These
were injunctions I also heard nearly every Sunday, but didn't we,
as a nation, live by the sword? I never heard a sermon preached on
God's commandment Thou shalt not kill. And you couldn't say in
Dallas that we loved our enemies.

I remember the hypothetical game we used to play in Sunday
school: What would happen if Jesus came back? How would we
treat him? Would we recognize him? Would we acknowledge the
divinity of his message? Or would we ignore him, harass him, and
ultimately kill him again? The lesson of this game was that saints
are intolerable to society. We were supposed to be steeling ourselves for the return of the Redeemer, following that time when
brother would rise against brother, and children against their parents. Yes, we were soldiers of the Lord. Our doctrine was brotherly
love. And yet no one ever proposed that Jesus might return as a
Negro.

Perhaps if President Kennedy had not been assassinated the civil
rights movement would have remained nonviolent. It was strange,
because Kennedy never had the emotional commitment to civil
rights that Lyndon Johnson did—certainly Kennedy never in-

tended anything like the Great Society—but his murder shattered the idealists. After that, nonviolence seemed ineffectual and naive. With three shots Lee Harvey Oswald did more to change history than Martin Luther King, with all his talk about the beloved community, had done in a decade. After that, good no longer seemed certain to triumph over evil.

It may sound absurd to say that Oswald murdered my faith in God. Indeed I was never more pious than the year after Kennedy's death. Religion became a sanctuary for me, and I put my questioning aside. But it happened, slowly, that my faith was dissolving inside this shell of piety, and although the shell remained a while longer, the animal inside was dead. Martin Luther King had helped me see the hypocrisy of the religion I grew up in, but before I might have made the step across to join the ferocious Christians of the civil rights movement, Kennedy was dead, my faith was dying, and the movement was about to turn existential and begin its violent feast.

However, there were certain vestiges—religious ideals—that clung to me; it was all myth to me now, but even myth is a way of seeing things. In this sense I would always be a Christian. Once I had broken free of the church and declared myself agnostic, I found I had an unaccountable weakness for Jesus, or the idea of Jesus. I suspect this longing for Jesus may have been a part of the subconscious of my generation; suddenly there were quite a number of young men who looked like our idea of Jesus, with long hair and beards, preaching peace and brotherhood and stuffing flowers into the rifle barrels of the federal troops. They were trying to rescue Jesus from Christianity. I saw the beauty of their actions. I listened to the lyrics of the songs that called on us to *smile on your brother, to come together, to reach out, to love one another right now,* and I approved these sentiments just as I had in Sunday school. But I could never surrender entirely to the hippie mentality. There was too much anger inside me, too much turbulence and confusion. Also, the nonviolence of hippies seemed harmless and playful and passive; it could not be compared with the death-defying nonviolence of the Freedom Riders.

My attitude toward violence had not changed, except to this

extent: In a godless world, you had to fight for justice—even if it meant fighting John Wayne, the arrogant vigilante, the unloving reactionary, the swaggering bully of white America.

In the period between John Kennedy's death and his own, Martin Luther King tried to rebuild faith in nonviolence. He realized that he could not advocate nonviolence at home and continue to support a war abroad. One year to the day before his death, King spoke out against the Vietnam War at Riverside Church in New York City. I didn't hear the speech; it wasn't until after his death that I grew haunted by his words and his example and began to look to him for clues about how to conduct my life. King spoke about how Vietnam was a symptom of a deeper malady of the American spirit, and about the need to turn away from the militarism and violence inside ourselves. "This call," he said, "for a world-wide fellowship that lifts neighborly concern beyond one's tribe, race, class, and nation is in reality a call for an all-embracing and unconditional love of all men. This oft-misunderstood and misinterpreted concept so readily dismissed by the Nietzsches of the world as a weak and cowardly force—has now become an absolute necessity for the survival of man. When I speak of love I am not speaking of some sentimental and weak response. I am speaking of that force which all of the great religions have seen as the supreme unifying principle of life. Love is somehow the key that unlocks the door that leads to ultimate reality."

During King's first march in Memphis to support the garbage collectors' strike, a group of teenaged boys broke off from the march and went on a small rampage of brick throwing and window breaking. The *Memphis Commercial Appeal* described it as a "full-scale riot," although most of the violence was on the part of the police, who fired into the crowd and fatally wounded a sixteen-year-old boy. There were 120 arrests and 50 people injured. King and his colleague, the Reverend Ralph Abernathy, escaped by jumping into the backseat of a passing car. Nearly four thousand national guardsmen were rushed into town to impose a dusk-to-dawn curfew. That night King could not sleep. He wondered aloud, according to Abernathy, "if those of us who advocated nonviolence should not step back and let the violent forces run their course." He was suddenly quite desperate to get home.

None of his friends had ever seen him so pensive and depressed as he was in the following week. He knew he would have to go back to Memphis, but he put it off several days. When he finally did return, he closeted himself in the Lorraine Motel and sent Abernathy to speak in his place at the rally. The weather was awful—there were tornado warnings out—so the crowd in the auditorium was only a thousand people, but they were so enthusiastic that Abernathy called the motel and summoned Dr. King. He drove through a rainstorm to deliver his final speech.

Did he know he was about to die? As a casual scholar of assassination, I've wondered about the premonitions of men about to be murdered. Lincoln's personal aide, Ward Hill Lamon, recounted a dream the President had a few days before his death. In the dream the President heard a sobbing sound downstairs in the White House, and he arose and went searching for the source of the grieving. He entered the East Room. "There I met with a sickening surprise," he told Lamon. "Before me was a catafalque, on which rested a corpse wrapped in funeral vestments. Around it were stationed soldiers who were acting as guards; and there was a throng of people, some gazing mournfully upon the corpse, whose face was covered, others weeping pitifully. 'Who is dead in the White House?' I demanded of one of the soldiers. 'The President,' was his answer; 'he was killed by an assassin!' " Lincoln, of course, was notoriously melancholy; the thought of death was never far from his mind. Because of threats, he had to be smuggled into Washington for his first inauguration, and during his presidency he was several times the object of assassination attempts. Twice his stovepipe hat was shot off his head. However, that dream suggests to me that Lincoln knew his fate was at hand. John Kennedy also brooded about assassination. The day before his death he told an assistant, "Anyone perched above the crowd with a rifle could do it." Then, on the very morning he went to Dallas, he said to his wife, "You know, last night would have been a hell of a night to assassinate a president ..." He pointed his finger like a gun and fired twice.

In the last days of Martin Luther King's life, according to Andrew Young, one of his lieutenants, King developed a habit of looking about as if he might see an assassin stalking him. Like Lincoln, King had a preoccupation with death. He had twice attempted suicide as a child, by jumping out of windows, and in 1957 a crazed black domestic stuck an eight-inch letter opener into his chest while he was autographing copies of his book, *Stride Toward Freedom*, at a Harlem department store. After the Kennedy assassination he told his wife, "This is what is going to happen to me also." Moreover, given the depression he had fallen into after the Memphis riot, he may have felt doomed and helpless, so that thoughts of death, which were never far away, rushed upon him. And yet his speech that last evening of his life still seems to me a work of prophecy, in which he saw not only his own imminent death but the future of the movement as well. He compared himself with Moses, who had led his people to the Promised Land but would not be permitted to enter there himself. He talked about the threats of death that followed him. That very morning the flight from Atlanta had been delayed so that the luggage could be searched for bombs. "Well, I don't know what will happen now," King said. "But it really doesn't matter with me now. . . . Like anybody, I would like to live a long life. Longevity has its place. But I'm not concerned about that now. I just want to do God's will. And He's allowed me to go up to the mountain. And I've looked over, and I've seen the Promised Land." As he spoke, with that curiously impassive face of his, which was always like a mask of resignation, the congregation began to moan and cry out, and King's lieutenants looked at each other in alarm. Andy Young thought the speech was macabre. "I may not get there with you," King continued, "but I want you to know tonight that we as a people will get to the Promised Land. So I'm happy tonight. I'm not worried about anything. I'm not fearing any man. Mine eyes have seen the glory of the coming of the Lord."

I had grown up in a world that hated Bobby far more than it had hated Jack. Bobby had shown us the arrogance of power; he had a way of rubbing it in. He was always smarter, tougher, braver, meaner than everyone else. He had none of the easy glamour that made his brother attractive even to his opponents. In Texas he had almost no organized support at all. Partly, of course, this was because of the well-advertised loathing Kennedy had for Lyndon Johnson. One of the few old party men in the state to declare for Kennedy was Judge Woodrow Wilson Bean in El Paso, who said he was doing it "because if he's elected, anyone from Texas will need a pass to get to Washington, and I'm going to be the man handing out passes." But there was more to our fear of Bobby than that. The dread of change and revolt that had run through the new world in 1960 seemed far more palpable now. Bobby was drawing power from the disinvested, the underclass. What frightened people in Texas—and I think this apprehension was widespread around the country—was the subconscious intimation that Bobby was Samson and that he would bring the status quo crashing down in his vastly public death.

Of course, this may have been a miscalculation. Bobby Kennedy had been a liberal senator, but his politics were historically conservative, and in the end he was once again confounding traditional liberals by attacking the welfare system and proposing himself as the law-and-order candidate. "I get the feeling I've been writing some of his speeches," Governor Reagan said in California, and Richard Nixon pointed out, "Bobby and I have been sounding pretty much alike."

To be the existential hero, according to Jack Newfield, Kennedy's friend and biographer, was to define and create oneself through action, to learn everything from experience. The last several months of Kennedy's life are a legend of discovery and change. His candidacy was an extraordinary personal journey through the streets of the northern ghettos, the rural roads of the impoverished South, the oppressive world of migrant labor in California, the boiling campuses everywhere. No doubt he was deeply affected by the needs of the Indians and farmworkers and sharecroppers who became his special constituencies. And yet, as British journalist Henry Fairlie points out, "no constituencies can be bought more cheaply than the poor and the young." Kennedy was a powerful magnet, but his rivals already had nailed down the more significant Democratic franchises. McCarthy had the suburbs and the heart of the peace movement; Humphrey had the labor bosses, the civil rights leaders, and the party mechanics. What remained were the alienated and the dispossessed—people like Sirhan Sirhan.

Sirhan was born in Jerusalem in 1944. He had been traumatized early in life by Zionist terrorism, which left him with a lifelong hatred of Israel and its defenders. His family immigrated to Southern California when he was twelve.

Not long after that, bitterly unhappy in his adopted country, Sirhan may have heard the first soundings of his own destiny. In high school he underlined passages in two history books about assassination: one concerned the murder of Archduke Ferdinand, the event that precipitated World War I, the other was the death of President McKinley. One of the sentences in the history books read: "After a week of patient suffering the President died, the third victim of an assassin's bullet since the Civil War." Sirhan noted in the margin, "Many more will come."

He was already an assassin in spirit; what remained was to select his victim. Sirhan became a Rosicrucian. He wrote out his objectives in a notebook, a form of mind control practiced by that group. Robert Kennedy's name first appears in the notebook on January 31, 1968, shortly after the senator from New York proposed that the United States sell fifty Phantom jets to Israel to replace the aircraft lost in the Six-Day War. "RFK must die," Sirhan wrote. At that time Kennedy was not a presidential candidate, and the chances that he would cross Sirhan's path in California must have seemed remote. "Robert F. Kennedy must be sacrificed for the cause of poor exploited people," Sirhan noted. He also wrote, "I believe that the U.S. is ready to start declining, not that it hasn't— it began in Nov. 23, 63."

Just after midnight on the morning of June 5, 1968, Robert Kennedy stood on the podium in the Embassy Room in the Ambassador Hotel in Los Angeles to acknowledge his victories in both the California and the South Dakota primaries. "Here is the most urban state [California] of any of the states of our Union, South

Dakota the most rural of any of the states of our Union. We were able to win them both. I think that we can end the divisions within the United States." He made a pitch for McCarthy to capitulate. "What I think is quite clear is that we can work together in the last analysis, and that what has been going on within the United States over a period of the last three years—the division, the violence, the disenchantment with our society; the divisions, whether it's between blacks and whites, between the poor and the more affluent, or between age groups or on the war in Vietnam—is that we can start to work together. We are a great country, an unselfish country, and a compassionate country. I intend to make that the basis for running."

Sirhan shot Kennedy as the candidate walked through the food service corridor to escape the crowd. "Kennedy, you son of a bitch," Sirhan said as he fired a .22-caliber revolver an inch away from the senator's head. The hollow-point bullet exploded in the right hemisphere of Kennedy's brain. Sirhan fired seven more times, hitting Kennedy twice in the right armpit as he fell to the floor, and wounding five other persons.

Kennedy lay for a while on the floor, as confusion swarmed around him. He fingered rosary beads and asked people to stand back and give him air. The next day newspapers would carry a photograph of him splayed out there, among the shoes, with the puzzled look of a man falling through space. As they lifted Kennedy onto a stretcher, "The last thing I heard him say," recalled Charles Quinn, a television correspondent, "was 'No, no, no, no, no,' like that, in the voice of a rabbit at the end of his life."

Later Eugene McCarthy came to the hospital where Kennedy lay dead, and said to Ted Kennedy that he had heard the name "Sirhan Sirhan" on the radio, and he remarked how odd it was, and mysterious, and coincidental, that he had the same first and last names, like the hero in Camus's *The Stranger*. A man comes out of nowhere and kills.

This was the year of my political education. Nineteen sixty-eight.

9 / UN-AMERICA

Suppose there is some truth in Camus's proposition that a man could spend the rest of his life pondering the experiences of a single day. So few such moments are held back for study. In certain dramatic public events, such as the death of a president or the declaration of war, people take internal snapshots of themselves; they look around, they get their bearings, they check their watches. They are shocked, yes, and perhaps distraught, but they know that in certain respects the river of their lives has jumped its channel, and they automatically record their thoughts. Soon the comparisons will come. Where were you when ————? These moments are benchmarks. They unify generations.

But there are private benchmarks as well, and the furious, heart-broken boy who was flying across the Atlantic for the first time on July 21, 1968, was taking soundings of himself, because he believed his life would be different from now on. He felt quite distinctly that the curtain had closed on the first act of his life and was about to open on the second. The boy he was he had left behind, but the man he would become had not yet created himself.

I flew to Europe with the vague intention of never flying home. I thought I might be done with America. The country had gone wrong; it had slipped into a violent nightmare and couldn't wake up. I could feel the violence stirring inside me, boiling over—I was frightened of myself. And the war loomed closer: one last year of deferment, then what? It seemed to me that my destiny as an American was to become a murderer.

I was sick of America. I was sick of its billboards and bumper stickers, sick of its Chevys and Fords, sick of its freeways and rapacious suburbs, sick of the cold faces of its skyscrapers, sick of the naked spurning of beauty and art, sick of the war, and sick sick sick of the ugliness of spirit that had created all this. I felt a loathing for the creature who had grown up in this sterile American soil, for wouldn't he necessarily be stunted in intellect, and primitive in all the important respects? Wouldn't his mind and spirit be pot-bound? And wasn't that me, the dwarf of the new world, making a pilgrimage to the splendid home of his ancestors?

Of course I wanted to wander through the narrow cobblestoned streets and climb the Alpine paths of my imagined Europe, the Europe of travel posters and art history classes—but I was also drawn to the political morality that assumed the right to wag its finger at America over Vietnam. Everything I had believed America stood for only a few years earlier now seemed to be all lies and illusion. My American heroes were dead, my American ideals were turned upside down, and what remained that would give me the right or even the desire to call myself an American?

I was also done with love, I told myself. My hands were bandaged from cracking my knuckles against a brick wall. After two years of loving Tamzon, I learned the day I left that she was engaged to another man. It was the biggest shock of my life. I was in the same state of mind that causes men to join the Foreign Legion.

And yet, heartsick as I was, I felt a certain detachment, as if there were two of me, a me that was onstage exhibiting grief and a me in the audience who was appreciating the performance. It is odd how periods of extreme sensation awaken this theatergoer from his nap. "Something's happened at last!" he observes, and becomes immediately hopeful that the production will turn out to be interesting after all.

I am not making fun of my feelings, and yet an essential feature of my grief was that I couldn't surrender myself to it, I couldn't be swept away entirely by the tide of emotion. I was affected, I was devastated, but I was also alert and curious. Sartre spoke of this divided mentality as the for-itself and the in-itself. Even in moments of ecstasy I have felt my mind step out of itself and wander about, taking notes. I had this experience once with Tamzon on a field trip to Guatemala to see the Mayan ruins. At one of our stops we ate lunch in a coffee grove in Antigua, and after we ate I put my head in Tamzon's lap while she talked to a small naked child with black eyes and a peculiar Indian giggle. I was staring at the fronds in the high, arching trees that shaded the coffee shrubs, when a leaf snapped off in the breeze and began to spiral slowly down. As it fell I heard the child's laughter, I smelled the appealing odor of Tamzon's body, and I watched the flight of the leaf. This was happiness, I thought—and yet! Where was I? Who was compiling this inventory? I was outside the moment, not in it. I shifted a bit to get more comfortable and thought about nothing, and it was in that brief vacant space of nonthinking nothingness that the leaf landed on my nose. In that electric instant I was finally happy.

It is one thing to feel grief, and another to be aware of feeling grief. I suppose the difference defines the human condition; it is the difference between what a dog feels upon losing his master and what a master feels upon losing his dog. I could not pass a mirror without checking for visible changes, for gray hairs or facial lines, evidence of the maturity I thought pain must bring. When I was alone I caught myself striking poses—I was James Dean playing me. But for whom was I playing out this drama of my unhappiness? I had the feeling of being observed, not just by my theatergoing self but by a larger audience, the community of spirits, if there is such a thing.

This was my theology as I crossed the Atlantic. I was self-conscious and slightly spooked. I would not say that I believed in anything, only that I suspected the presence of Others, and I found myself playing for their sympathy.

When I landed in Luxembourg I was under the profound influence of two authors, Ernest Hemingway and Richard Halliburton, a travel writer of my mother's generation, whose fantastic life ended in 1939 in a typhoon in the China Sea. As his ship was sinking, he managed to get off a cable with his dying words: "Wish you were here." My mother introduced me to him when I was fifteen by giving me a book she had treasured from her own youth, *The Royal Road to Romance.* It is a manifesto for romantic personalities. Halliburton presents himself as a cheerful rich boy who graduates from Princeton and decides to have one great fling at life. "From childhood I had dreamed of climbing Fujiyama and the Matterhorn, and I had planned to charge Mount Olympus in order to visit the gods that dwelled there. I wanted to swim the Hellespont where Lord Byron swam, float down the Nile in a butterfly boat, make love to a pale Kashmiri maiden beside the Shalimar, dance to the castanets of Granada gypsies, commune in solitude with the moonlit Taj Mahal, hunt tigers in a Bengal jungle—try everything once." Read at a certain age, this stuff is irresistible. "I wanted to realize my youth while I still had it," Halliburton continued, "and yield to temptation before increasing years and responsibilities robbed me of the courage."

Oh, God—so did I! And so did thousands and thousands of American students like me who made the pilgrimage to Europe in the summer of 1968. Entire airlines were created to ferry us back and forth at discount rates. I was flying Air Bahama on its second day of service, and it, like its competitor for the student market, Icelandic Airlines, landed in Luxembourg because of the lower tariffs. The point was to get to Europe—anywhere in Europe—it was all the same to us. We were a generation that had turned away from things American, preferring instead European cars and movies and foods and philosophies, all of which we had been absorbing secondhand. Although America was without dispute the most advanced nation in the world, and the richest, and the freest, in 1968 my generation looked toward Europe with a feeling of extreme inadequacy.

For me that feeling was born in the novels of Ernest Hemingway. My immediate response to reading one of Hemingway's European novels, particularly *The Sun Also Rises,* was a longing to write myself into it. This was not so much a sense of identification with his world as simple envy. The ambience within his book seemed truer and more authentic than the world I lived in. I wanted to be a Hemingway man instead of a tortured adolescent. I wanted to live in his time instead of my own. I wanted to fish in his streams and drink in his bars and make love to his women and fight in his wars—not in my own. Hemingway had shown me that the proper relationship of an American artist to his country is exile. He made this choice appear noble and in many respects exquisite. I realize now that this was partly an illusion of his style, which has an infallibility about it that life itself does not.

The world abroad was filled with disconsolate Americans like me, who were on the run from the war, yes, but also from some premonitory nightmare of the people they were about to become. None of us could speak of our parents without irony, but the irony was a mirror of our future selves, the grasping and vapid selves we saw at the end of the process. We knew how it worked. You began with ideals (that was the privilege of youth), but age and compromise wore you down. You would need a job. You would marry. You would have children. Once you got the mortgage and the second car, all was lost. One day your child would stare at you ironically and you wouldn't understand.

And so we fled before it happened, and went to live in Katmandu or a commune in Ibiza. We were inoculating ourselves against smugness and materialism. We wanted to touch bottom. Until now we had lived indoors, protected against want and discomfort, but also against joy and the raw pleasures of real life. We had been born into a country that had half the income of the world. America had been generous with its wealth; we had given it away in stupefying quantities, but the money returned itself to us in the form of power. What had we done to deserve the curse of such good fortune? We embraced the globe with military bases and submarines and Peace Corps volunteers and multinational corporations, but we suffered the lovelessness of Midas. Was there any ally whose loyalty was not paid for? Was there anyone who didn't hate us for our wealth and and feel the impress of our power? We were the heirs of a newly created empire, but we were in flight from privilege. In Crete, old women in black dresses would go down to the beach to laugh at the Americans living in caves. All humanity wanted to live like Americans, and here were the Americans living like squirrels on nuts and seeds.

Of course the test of these swollen spiritual feelings was unfairly applied in Luxembourg; in relative terms one might as well be landing in Indianapolis. But it was Europe all right, with its well-advertised authentic Old World charm. I wanted it to be charming, and I wanted it to be authentic, but my experience in the new world was that each category excluded the other.

In the country I grew up in, charm—by which I mean a beguiling sense of place—was so rare it had to be captured and incarcerated like an animal in a zoo. Part of our American problem with charm is that it is usually an obstacle to progress, unless the charm itself can be merchandised. If there is a single charming house left unrazed in town, it necessarily becomes a restaurant or an antique store; no doubt it will have a historical marker in front of it as well, chronicling some negligible transaction but serving to point out that this house was once, after all, a charming home. Any city with a large enough claim on charm sets about turning itself into a resort or a convention center, with the result that whatever was charming about the city in the first place is either obliterated or else "preserved" in such a way that the charming becomes quaint—i.e., dead. I have watched this process happen in the New Orleans French Quarter. For years the city fathers wanted to build an expressway that would cut off the Quarter from the Mississippi River; there was even a proposal to line the expressway with Gay Nineties gaslights to help it blend in (gaslights = charm). In order to save the Quarter, the preservationists had it declared a historical district. That stopped the expressway, but the Quarter, as a living part of the city, was finished. It was now officially charming, with the result that oilmen and orthodontists from Houston and Dallas began buying it up, hotel chains surrounded the perimeter, the city renovated the funky areas near the waterfront, boutiques replaced the sailors' bars, and citizens were displaced by tourists. Now the French Quarter is no more authentic, in terms of being a real place to live, than is Williamsburg, Virginia.

It doesn't take long for an American to associate charm with doom. You stand, let us say, on some bright, untouched promontory on the edge of the sea and say to yourself: What a loss. What you are thinking is, Yes, it's lovely now, but wait until the Holiday Inn pops up, and the Burger King, and the Exxon station, and the usual retinue of billboards and trailer courts and strip joints and clapboard shacks that make up an American coastal community. Or else you are sitting in a little dive listening to jazz; there is an agreeable feeling of inconsequence; you almost—almost—dare to unwind and give yourself up to the genius of the place, but just let yourself do so and next week the bulldozer arrives, or the renovator appears. I think this is part of the appeal of amusement parks in America, such as Disneyland. They are artificially charming, authentically inauthentic; nothing more can happen here; one wanders through them with no feeling of loss.

The American approaches Europe mystified by the apparent permanence of charm. As I walked through Luxembourg on my first afternoon, absorbed in its beauty and relieved by the lowered tone of commerce, my thoughts were trailed by dread and suspicion. Could this last? Or was Europe itself actually a kind of amusement park for American tourists (and not to be trusted)? Perhaps the boulevards were lined with propped-up facades; perhaps the natives in their berets or their dirndls and lederhosen were paid by the management to affect a culture they no longer endorsed. It was charming, all right, but my American instinct was on the lookout for phoniness.

Still, I had to ask myself how charm could persist in Europe and exist hardly at all in my own country. The most immediate answer was age, which does bestow its dignity on even very ordinary man-made objects. One sees this in the older sections of the United States, New England and parts of the South, which have been civilized for a sufficient period of time that charm has built up an account. My own section of the country, the new world, is too recent for time to have had much effect, but in any case there is an indigenous loathing for old things. Most older buildings with any promise have long since been pushed down to make way for the new. Sunbelt cities that are themselves little more than a century old already have an archaeology comparable to that of Troy or Thebes; it's just that the civilizations that underlie the present have the lifespans of butterflies. In Texas the only old buildings that have been permitted to stand are the Spanish missions, which are so full of charm that they make a person woozy.

But it is not merely age that generates charm, or rather, allows charm to exist. Washington, D.C., and Dallas are both young cities, and yet Washington is charming in ways Dallas will never be. Washington is geologically prettier, but it is also built on a more human scale, owing to a height restriction that prevents commercial buildings from eclipsing the Capitol. Most of Europe was constructed before the advent of elevators—a growth hormone for American skylines, which are limited now only by their capacity to interfere with airline traffic. Dallas is just such a city of egotistical, heaven-aspiring skyscrapers, which are impressive from a distance, but when a person walks among them they make him feel puny and insignificant—he would have to be a hundred feet tall to feel at home on the sidewalks. In terms of proportion Washington is our only European city; it is also, like Paris and London and Berlin, a city of monuments and bureaucrats, benefiting from the carefree expenditure of public moneys.

I saw the European recipe for charm as being stone, Catholicism, stairways, bureaucracy, espresso, pigeons, and millennia.

It was too early for me to tell what effect all this charm had on the Europeans, but my own immediate response to it was relief, as if a tooth had suddenly stopped hurting. Leaving America, I had also left behind the ordinary garishness that crowds the American streets, the barrage of commercials filling the airwaves, the five o'clock rush, the frenzied pursuit by many million egos of wealth and stardom. These nuisances were present in Europe, but at a tolerable level, below what I now had to realize was the threshold of pain. Capitalism, at least in its ruthless new world incarnation, must be incompatible with charm.

Along with the environmental relief I was enjoying, there was the anonymity of travel. Until now I had been surrounded all my life by people who knew me and who expected me to behave in a particular way. For the first time I was traveling alone, and I discovered that luxurious, uncorseted feeling of being unknown. I might be anybody. It was a joy to leave behind the self I had always been, the person everyone knew, and become—what? I had come to Europe determined to drop off the boy and find the man, but I was caught in the middle of this exchange and was neither one nor the other. I was in the zone of Anything's Possible, the ideal romantic state, and yet one can exist in that atmosphere only briefly before the ego begins to dissolve.

In the Luxembourg twilight I passed a boy smoking a cigarette. I turned around and followed him. He was about my age. He was slender, and he walked with an abstracted, important air. A blue sweater hung around his shoulders. Something about the intensity of his smoking and thinking made me decide: that's my new self. I could smell his black tobacco and could nearly imagine the profundity of his thoughts. I followed my new self for several blocks, wondering where he might lead me, until some awareness of me broke his concentration, and he nervously speeded up and then boarded a bus. When he was gone I stopped at a kiosk and bought a package of Gauloise cigarettes and then retraced our steps, smoking and thinking, while the theatergoing me trailed behind, withholding judgment.

I spent my first night in Europe in the Bern railway station on a bench, my backpack at my feet, struggling for sleep along with a dozen other travelers, as a pair of German tourists talked loudly all through the night. I tried to hush them several times, but they stared at me furiously and only talked louder. Their rudeness was marvelous; they were simply inhuman. The other travelers were mostly Italians and Greeks, large families with shopping bags full of sausages and gifts, and they twisted about on the benches in various woefully resentful but acquiescent attitudes. I thought how all of us carry history about inside us, that centuries of conflict and struggle, prejudices, successes and failures, are hammered into us in the form of traits, which are as irrefutable as genes. I was suddenly very grateful to my father for winning the war.

How nice—I thought the next morning as the cog-rail train ascended beside the gorged Alpine streambeds—how nice to be Swiss. I was trying on nationalities. How enviable simply to withdraw from the quarrels of international strife. And yet, even as I thought that, I realized how foreign the idea of neutrality was to me; it rang of shirking, or cowardice; it brought to mind the schoolchild who shuns rough games and refuses to shout down injustice.

Richard Halliburton had given me my immediate destination: Zermatt, at the base of the Matterhorn, which Halliburton climbed in Chapter Two. I had never climbed anything greater than several flights of stairs; in fact, I had a fear of heights inherited from my father. My new self was an adventurer determined to cast aside all former neuroses. My old self, however, was grateful to discover that bad weather had closed the mountain to climbers.

I rolled out of Switzerland and into Spain, and then on to France, England, Scotland—I was determined to see it all—I was like a contest winner in a grocery store with five minutes of free shopping. As a consequence I spent most of my time on trains, or else standing on the side of a road with my thumb in the air. It didn't matter. Motion was the important thing, being free to bum along in my anonymous mode, Mr. Nobody on the road to Nowhere, in my blue jeans and an army jacket I acquired in Belfast, my backpack loaded with several changes of underwear and socks, a poncho, a handy clothesline my mother had given me, a washable Haspel suit I wore once, a copy of Arthur Frommer's *Europe on $5 a Day*, and four china plates I had purchased in Delft as a present for my mother (three survived).

I held on to my money jealously. My great temptation everywhere was food. Europe was filled with appetizing aromas I had never encountered. Even the most ordinary staples, bread and cheese, revealed unexpected nuances. I thought resentfully that I had never eaten real food until now, it had only been an American approximation; that my bread was not real bread, it was breadlike; and that the flavors of my life had been washed clean of subtlety.

On August 2, I celebrated my twenty-first birthday in the town of Montauban in southern France. I stopped at a small café on the roadside and examined the menu written on the blackboard outside. At the table I enjoyed a moment of self-pity as I thought about being alone on this significant anniversary, and I consoled myself with a glass of Beaujolais. The owner came by after my meal to serve the fruit. *"Americain?"* he asked. When I nodded he sat down.

"You pappa, he bang-bang in ze guerre?"

"Oui," I said, my one word of French.

The owner pointed to his eye. "I see him in Paris. Eisenhower—bravo!" Then he poured us each a brandy and offered a toast to America—a toast I myself would never have offered—and waived aside my check. That was a birthday present I have never forgotten.

I arrived at the Gare du Nord the following dawn, and rode the Métro to the Boulevard Saint-Michel. Never have I entered a city more wonderfully than on that morning, when I ascended from the subway tunnel into the heart of Paris before it had awakened. Only a few shopkeepers were out, sweeping the sidewalks and setting out their wares. What was beautiful about it was the absence of transition; I had slipped in through the night and under the suburbs, materializing in what I thought must be the center of life—Paris, at last.

There was a woman I wanted to see. Her name was Edith. She had been an exchange student at Sophie Newcomb College and a friend of Tamzon's. I remembered how pretty she was and how French, with her black eyes and black-black hair and her voluptuous European body. I wasn't certain what she thought of me, but she had given me her telephone number months ago, on the unlikely chance that I would ever get to Paris. I got a room in a cheap pension and waited until midmorning to call.

"Larry, you're here!"

She certainly was excited to hear from me. She insisted that I check out of the pension at once and come stay with her. "My parents are away for the month," she informed me.

Edith lived on Rue Gay-Lussac, a street named after the physicist who discovered that the density of a gas varies inversely with its temperature. I think there is a corollary in the realm of human behavior, in which heated expectations vaporize into—ah, lost hopes. I was walking on Edith's street, looking for her door, when I saw her coming in the other direction with a load of groceries and a large loaf of bread. She was beautiful. She was smiling. I thought about the wonderful meal she was going to prepare . . . and so on.

"Edith!" I cried. I had a tremendous grin on my face.

She looked up uncertainly. Recognition came slowly into her eyes. "Hello," she said. "What a coincidence this is! Do you know who else is in town?"

"No," I said, still grinning, but wondering.

"It's Larry Wright!" she said. "He's on his way over now!"

My hold on identity was shaky enough. Was there really another Larry Wright in town? Probably not. But clearly there was another Larry Wright—an ideal, non-me version—in her mind.

We enjoyed a polite dinner. Once reconciled to the me she had before her, Edith had been gracious enough to invite me in anyway. Of course I couldn't stay the night. All during the meal I could only think of my rival Larry Wright. I felt less than nothing. There was surely no possibility that someone would pretend to be me. But this someone, whoever he was, obviously possessed qualities I didn't have and hardly knew about. You can't fully appreciate the possibilities life offers to others until you've been confused with someone else and discovered how people might react to you if you weren't you. Now I knew with dismal clarity that there were men in the world who might call beautiful women in strange cities and send them scurrying to the grocery store for steak and candles, and in all innocence I could only pretend to be such a man.

After dinner Edith took me to see a Gary Cooper double feature that was playing in the basement of a coffeehouse. So this, I thought meanly, was the French underground now—a roomful of intellectuals sitting in folding chairs under the plumbing and electrical wiring watching *High Noon* and *The Hanging Tree* in 16 millimeter.

When I was in high school there was a single movie house in

Dallas that would occasionally show European films. My mother would take me, if they weren't too naughty (if they were, she would go alone). We were dying for sophistication. For two hours we could leave our repressed and moralistic hometown and watch life unfold in an alternative fashion—a more honest fashion, it seemed to me, and certainly more permissive and forgiving. If American movies were all action, French movies were all mood. Their comedies, which my mother loved, were concocted entirely out of nuance and whim. Once Mother took all three children to see *Monsieur Hulot's Holiday,* the Jacques Tati comedy, and she laughed so hard that the manager asked her to watch from the lobby. In college I discovered Truffaut, and then Renoir and Cocteau and Godard. In the early days of my love affair with Tamzon we went to see *A Man and a Woman,* and we were nearly incapacitated by passion. The final scene of that movie, when the lovers are embracing in the train station and the camera is revolving around them, made me dizzy with joy, and for days afterward I was humming the sound track and viewing life through the sentimental lens of Claude Lelouch. This was at a time when I was reading the French philosophers and novelists, and I had decided that the French mind floated above the ordinary world in some elevated atmosphere of its own.

But here was Gary Cooper, the new French idol. How many times had I seen these movies on late-night television! To see them again in France was to understand at last the power of the American Western, which is really the creation myth of America. I understood at once the appeal of America as an idea, as a possibility. America-as-Western was not sophisticated but elemental. I could see, as I glanced at the faces around me, that this was a European dream. It was individual man, called to his limits, facing evil and the prospect of death, but standing alone and in the cause of goodness, truth, justice.

However, making American Westerns requires a moral authority Hollywood had lost. The only good Westerns in the sixties were being made by the cynical Italians, and to see them as an American was to feel that a valuable legacy had been stolen and put to wrongful use. The whole point of the American Western was to show good triumphing over evil, to tell ourselves that fable again and again. It was no accident that the best Westerns tumbled out of the studios in the smug days of victory following World War II. The Western reaffirmed our vision of ourselves as a righteous people in an evil world, and it reminded us that by being courageous and true we would never fail to win.

And yet we had come to discover in Vietnam that the high-handed morality that was our most distinguishing characteristic as a nation had led us into an international comeuppance. What discouraged me as an American was the glee with which the world responded to our chastisement. We were to be made humble again. Now you could no longer show Gary Cooper movies to American students—we would hoot them off the screen. But in Paris I saw again in Gary Cooper the nobility of American innocence and its simple calling to goodness. I was touched, and felt singled out as an American.

All up and down the Boulevard Saint-Michel the cafés were crowded with American students and draft evaders—I even ran into several people I knew. English was the most common language on the street. There was a group of college boys from Auburn sitting next to me, drinking cappuccino and talking interestingly about the odor of European pussy. There were as well a number of American blacks on the street, who seemed to have captured a monopoly on the hashish trade. Most of them were ex-GIs, and they took me for a deserter because of my army jacket. One evening I bought a lid of hashish for ten francs and sat on the floor of my hotel room to smoke it. In a little while I began to hear distant sounds of thunder, then women's voices, and vacuum cleaners, and then the knock of the maid at my door. It was ten o'clock in the morning.

This was the day I went to the American embassy. I put on my Haspel suit for the occasion. At the desk I said I wanted to speak to someone about the consequences of exile. I was shown to the office of a young consular officer named Mr. Levine, who looked at the note the secretary handed him and said to me, "Don't do it."

"If you had to choose between Saigon and Paris," I said in an assured, perhaps derisive tone, "which would you prefer?"

Levine looked outside at the rain. It was a typically gloomy
Parisian summer day. "This city's filled with kids like you. They
don't do very well, most of them. They don't speak French, they
can't get jobs, they just feel lonely and out of place. After a while
they realize what they've given up—their home, their family, their
language—"

"But not their lives."

"Well, no." Levine went on to explain, however, that if I went
so far as to renounce my country and seek citizenship elsewhere,
I would lose certain liberties I had come to appreciate as an American. If I just decided to lay low in Paris until the end of the war,
I would be subject to prosecution.

Jail, exile, or war—those were my alternatives.

Levine shrugged. What was he supposed to say? He was speaking
for the United States of America. If he were speaking for Levine
he might have had an answer for me, but I doubt it. Nobody did,
those days. I left his office wondering why I had gone there. Perhaps I was just trying it on, the role of Exile, the part Hemingway
played so well (except that Hemingway could always go home).

I don't know why it is so much more pleasurable to read a book
on a train coach than in an armchair at home. There must be a
parallel between one's life and one's book, each of them pleasingly
held in suspense as they roll through possibilities. To be in that
parenthetical state between Point A and Point B, and Chapter One
and The End, is to be in a state of hammocky contentment, and
to arrive at both destinations simultaneously is, for me, a nearly
orgasmic form of melancholy.

In Dublin I went to the Martello Tower, where James Joyce
lived briefly, and where *Ulysses* begins. Near the castle on a spring-
board, pale naked men were diving into the chill Irish sea. In the
room where Buck Mulligan served a breakfast of toast and butter
and honey, I bought a copy of *A Portrait of the Artist as a Young
Man* and read again the passage in which Stephen Dedalus de-
clares his principles:

You have asked me what I would do and what I would not do. I will tell you what I will do and what I will not do. I will not serve that in which I no longer believe, whether it call itself my home, my fatherland, or my church: and I will try to express myself in some mode of life or art as freely as I can, using for my defence the only arms I allow myself to use— silence, exile, and cunning.

I repeated this credo again and again, and even wrote it down on the flyleaf. Silence, exile, and cunning: it was a slogan for me then, and perhaps a solution. On the other hand, I thought about living a small Joycean existence, avoiding the war and teaching languages in Trieste or Geneva. Was I really prepared to pay such a price to be in the service of Art? What opportunities for happiness was I willing to surrender for the chance to write? Silence, exile, and cunning: it suddenly seemed like a prescription for a life of bitter reclusion, a motto for a troll. I wanted to write, but I didn't care to disengage myself from the world.

I was measuring myself, as anyone who is twenty-one must do. Life until then had been all promise and possibility; now choices would have to be made. What did I want to be when I grew up? This was the river boundary I would have to cross into manhood. When I tried to summon the courage to declare myself a writer, I would remember the effrontery of that ambition, and I would well up with shame and resentment. I was nobody. I was empty inside. My life was no more than ordinary. I recalled the private conference I had had with my writing teacher at Tulane, after he had read a turbulent short story I had written about a doomed love affair, which was set beneath the equestrian statue in Jackson Square. My professor was not a successful writer himself. He published occasional poems in academic journals, and collected them in small vanity printings, but he was a handsome, gray-bearded man with the *gravitas* of Tolstoy. He told me sadly in his office that my writing reminded him of—what's that fellow's name? His eyes searched the ceiling. Who? Who? I was afraid he was going to say Flaubert, since I had been imitating him shamelessly. In any case,

I knew my whole life was waiting for my teacher's judgment.
"What's the name of that fellow who wrote *Exodus*?" he asked.
"Leon Uris?" I said in complete horror.
"Yeah. You write like Leon Uris."
He might as well have told me I had three days to live. It was
an unbearable prognosis. I was doomed with the talents of a popu-
lar writer. No one would ever take me seriously.

I began reading *The Tin Drum* in Dublin and read it as I traveled
past the graveyards of Holland and the battlefields of Belgium. I
was reading it in a pension in Amsterdam near Anne Frank's house.
I was putting off Germany. All over Europe there was testimony
of the evil that the Nazis had let loose on the world. Were the
Germans peculiarly capable of evil? Or were they merely victims
of a political culture they couldn't control? These were the questions Günter Grass was asking in *The Tin Drum*. I was asking
myself the same questions, because I was also a product of political
cultures widely regarded as evil—the Dallas of 1963, and the
United States of 1968.
    I recalled the puzzlement in my father's voice when he spoke of
the Germans. He had admired them as an enemy. They were
civilized in their approach to combat—not like the fanatical, suicidal Japanese, or the half-savage Chinese in Korea—and their skill
was unsurpassed. They would have won the war, my father believed, if it hadn't been for Hitler's frequent stupid meddling. One
of his most vivid memories of the war is the day he entered a village
near Cologne and came across the body of a dead German child,
a victim of artillery fire. German children are, of course, famously
beautiful, like porcelain dolls, and the sight of this dead boy
stopped my father in his tracks. Why? What caused the Germans
to begin this war, which would cost so many lives, including twenty
million civilians such as this boy in the street? Were the Germans
evil? A stupid question—but how else can it be framed? Was this
dead child evil? My father remembered seeing the slave girls in the
German homes, who had been torn away from their families in

Czechoslovakia and Poland. "How could a great religious, cultured people do this kind of thing?" my father asked himself. Was this the destiny of civilization, to destroy itself in some fantastic barbaric urge? There is a moral transfer that takes place between the victor and the vanquished, which George Bailey writes about in his splendid book, *Germans*. The loss of German dignity after the war was followed by "a collateral loss of shame" on the part of the victors. We can see this, as Bailey points out, in the expulsion of nearly three million Czechs of German ancestry from the Sudeten portion of Czechoslovakia immediately after the war, and the renewed persecution of Jews in the Soviet Union, for reasons that were substantially the same as the Nazi persecution. "For me the most disgusting and dismaying result of World War II and its aftermath is this: that the exposure and universal condemnation of the moral insanity of the Nazis ministered to the reinforcement of the moral insanity of the Communists," writes Bailey. But wasn't there also a similar if not identical loss of shame in our own country? Not immediately after the war—the rebuilding of Europe was all to our credit—but later, wasn't there a kind of delayed reaction, which turned us from the Good Samaritan into a dangerously prideful bully, convinced we could do no wrong? Had we somehow been transformed into the enemy we had once destroyed? Isn't that the danger of victory?

Now the children of the victors of that war were naming their own country "Amerika." You saw it spray-painted on the public walls and written into the headlines of underground newspapers, followed by swastikas. It was all over Europe as well. We were the successors of the Third Reich. My father was sputteringly furious at the comparison, but I was ambivalent. Were we so different from the Germans? Was there a real parallel between our engagement in Southeast Asia and the German occupation of Poland? What was the difference between our chosen role as the world's policeman and the German drive for international dominion?

I closed *The Tin Drum* in Bremen and sat in a café beside the square with the whimsical statue of the *Musicians of Bremen*—the donkey, the dog, the cat, and the rooster of the fairy tale. I was drinking good German beer. A pregnant mother was strolling an angelic child, who was laughing at a pigeon trying to mate. The pigeon was chasing his female quarry all over the square. It was comical; people stopped and pointed at the birds; the female was quick-walking and cutting sharp corners, and the male followed precisely behind her. He seemed to have a sense of irony about the occasion—he was looking about for sympathy—and he certainly had crowd appeal. He was the Chaplin of pigeons. We were all laughing now.

Later, as I stood on the autobahn waiting for a ride, I wondered how evil moves among us, like a virus. It was too simple to say that the Germans were evil and now they are not, or that we had been good once and now we were not. Our victory cheated us of a measure of self-knowledge. We had come away from that war thinking evil was far away, and we were immune, while the Europeans learned that it was always close at hand.

I went north to Denmark with a double purpose. I wanted to scout the Scandinavian countries, which were popular with draft resisters, and I had thoughts about going to Russia. All my life I had heard about Communism—my God, it was the subject of such hysteria in Dallas that . . . well, only incest and devil worship could be spoken of with the same degree of outrage. During the fifties our governor, Allan Shivers, had tried to make membership in the Communist party a capital crime (the legislature moderated the penalty to twenty years in prison). My image of Communism was formed by Herbert Philbrick, the double agent of Lee Harvey Oswald's favorite television show, "I Led Three Lives," who was always tracking down subversives in the suburbs, and by J. Edgar Hoover in *Masters of Deceit,* which was the text for virtually every high-school civics class in the state of Texas. Hoover made the lure of Communism seem irresistible, like heroin. Take the example of Jack, in what Hoover called "the Case of Lost Faith." Jack was an ordinary boy with nice manners and an inquiring mind—until "something started to happen to him, slowly but surely. His faith in God and religion seemed to be fading. As he later told FBI agents, he felt this loss already in high school." (Uh oh.) By the time he entered college, Jack was a "spiritual vacuum" into which rushed the philosophy of Marx and Engels. Jack's case was typical of the high-minded but misguided idealists who were drawn to Communism through a sincere—"though perverted"—desire to replace the faith of their childhood. "Many reasons cause individuals to join the Party," warned Hoover, "but undoubtedly most important is the Party's appeal to idealistic motivations, to a 'bright new world' where justice, peace, and freedom will replace strife, injustice and inhumanity."

Like Jack, I saw the appeal of the new world of Communism, even through the curtain of hysteria in Dallas. We talked about freedom all the time in Texas, and on my side of town we had plenty of it, but we seldom talked seriously about equality. As an American schoolchild I knew that all men were created equal, according to the Declaration of Independence, although if I looked at the child who was created in Highland Park versus the child born in South Dallas, it was hard to understand exactly what that proposition meant. What came clear to me was that freedom and equality were mutually exclusive; one came at the expense of the other. In the United States we were free but distressingly unequal; in the Soviet Union, as my father would say, all people were "equally unfree." In our arguments I found myself becoming a devil's advocate for Communism, especially in China or Vietnam, or any place where the downward pull of poverty and overpopulation was greater than the power of capitalism to save it. My father would point to Taiwan and South Korea and of course Japan, the capitalist response to Asian Communism. Name one successful Marxist economy, he would say. Well, Russia. Compared with the United States? East Germany. Compared with West Germany? And so it went, an argument I never won.

Could Communism tolerate freedom? This was the question posed to the whole world in 1968 by Czechoslovakia, which had suddenly decided to exercise freedom and see what happened.

Communism was still such a mystery to me that the big surprise of the Prague Spring was that the Czechs wanted to be just like us, especially the young Czechs, who began to grow their hair long and play guitars. On the news we saw people celebrating religious festivals that had been banned for twenty years, and speaking out against the Soviets, and performing forbidden plays. In their exuberance one could measure the cost of the spiritual oppression they had endured, until now. This was the great experiment of 1968: the attempt to be equal but free, to reconcile the two great doctrines of government, to "give Communism a human face," in the words of the new Czech leader, Alexander Dubček.

America was also bending toward a new balance, through Johnson's Great Society. He was the first president to talk with real passion about equality in our own country. "You do not wipe away the scars of centuries by saying: Now you are free to go where you want and do as you desire and choose the leaders you please," Johnson said in a memorable speech at Howard University in 1965. "You do not take a person who, for years, has been hobbled by chains and liberate him, bring him to the starting line of a race, and then say you are free to compete with all the others, and still just believe that you have been completely fair. . . . This is the next and more profound stage of civil rights. We seek not just . . . equality as a right and a theory but equality as a fact and equality as a result." Three years later it was obvious that the Great Society was sinking into the quicksand of Vietnam, along with everything else that was worthy about America, and yet it still seemed to me in 1968 that both sides, the Communist and the capitalist, were inclining toward the center, and that if Czechoslovakia succeeded the world would change.

That possibility ended on the night of August 20. I was in the state of newslessness that is usual with foreign travel. I had heard nothing, for instance, of the impending Democratic convention in Chicago, or of Mayor Richard Daley's plans to shut out the protesters. The morning after I arrived in Copenhagen I went to the Tourist Information Office and asked for directions to the Russian embassy. The girl at the desk looked at me queerly and told me how to get there by bus.

Several hundred people were standing in the street in front of the embassy, which had been cordoned off by Danish policemen. They were not a mob; they were well dressed and orderly, but they were standing there in tears, nearly all of them sobbing, and without having any idea of what had happened I approached the scene like an onlooker at a funeral. "You did not hear?" a policeman said incredulously. "The Russians invaded Czechoslovakia."

Surprisingly, I was admitted to the embassy to make my visa request. I waited in an anteroom with another man who was crying politely and holding a newspaper with the headline DUBČEK DØD. (Later in the afternoon we would learn that Dubček actually had been spared.) A consular officer came and spoke to the man briefly in Danish. I observed the proceedings as a mime of international relations: There was the Danish man's futile entreaty (perhaps he had relatives in Czechoslovakia), the Russian's imperious shrug, the Dane's rising anger and frustration, then a frozen look on the Russian's face that said "enough." The Dane threw the newspaper down on the table and left. Then the Russian turned to me.

"I'd like a visa."

The Russian laughed. He was, I realized, the first Russian I had ever seen. After hearing about them for so long, I was curious to see that he did not seem like a devil, just a beleaguered bureaucrat. "You can apply," he said, "but I can assure you it will be refused."

I was not the only American whose trip to Moscow was blocked by the invasion. In Washington, Lyndon Johnson was making plans for a secret summit meeting with Soviet Premier Aleksei Kosygin. Soon after Robert Kennedy's death Johnson developed misgivings about his declaration not to seek a second term. The polls showed Humphrey, the inevitable nominee, trailing Nixon by an apparently insuperable margin. Johnson imagined that if he could create a sudden, unexpected triumph, his party and his country might turn to him again. His first thought was a surprise escalation of the war, but at that point nothing short of victory could have brought him the renomination he desired. The other possibility was a significant change in our relations with the Soviets. Johnson made plans to fly to Moscow and return just in time to address the divided Democratic convention. It is still not known publicly what Johnson hoped to gain from the Soviets and what he was willing to concede, although scholars at the Johnson library say informally that what he had in mind was a freeze on development and deployment of nuclear weapons, an end to a nuclear arms race that has now cost America 750 billion dollars since 1945.

What if Johnson had gone to Moscow? Perhaps nothing; after all, the Soviets didn't think enough of the prospects for an agreement to cancel their invasion of Czechoslovakia on the evening before Johnson was scheduled to depart for the summit. Had he gone earlier, perhaps he would have gained the agreement he sought, perhaps the Soviets would not have sent their tanks rolling into Prague, perhaps Johnson would have been reelected, and so on. But this is a frustrating exercise. What happened is that freedom died in Czechoslovakia, and the goal of equality in America sank with the Great Society.

I read *Henderson the Rain King* on the Orient Express. A book read at exactly the right moment can change your life, and probably I needed to be outside of America to love Saul Bellow's American voice, the sound of the vivid democrat, overgrown and rude and too enthusiastic but full of humor and goodwill. As I read it I thought: I am that. I am that voice; that voice is America speaking in the person of Eugene Henderson, explaining himself, recognizing his huge flaws, and like me trying to find his real worth in the world. Outside the train windows the Austrian Alps lurched toward heaven in an absurdly beautiful tableau that set my American mind to thinking of beer commercials. And yet Bellow's voice, ironical, offhand, but also passionate and sincere, was riding with me, and as I listened I began to soften and forgive. I was going to the end of the continent, to Istanbul, but my mind was on America.

We leveled off in the long plains of Yugoslavia, which reminded me of Kansas, with its fields of grain and the sunflowers growing along the railroad track. Some Yugoslav workers got on the train, smelling of hard labor, and a student who rode in my coach for a hundred miles. He spoke a bit of English. He wanted my address.

People frequently did. There seemed to be something important about having someone's address in America, as if it were a refuge. We changed locomotives in Bulgaria. We were going backward through the age of technology. We had begun the trip with a swift German diesel that powered us over the Alps, but when we crossed through the Iron Curtain we picked up another engine, of Czechoslovakian manufacture. Now we hitched ourselves to a creeping Soviet castoff that made Bulgaria seem like the world's largest country. The passport control officer came aboard, wearing a hat with a big red star, like a cartoon Communist. In one little town, I think it was Popovica, we were held up for two hours. I tried to get off the train for a few moments to stretch my legs and smoke, but the train was surrounded by plainclothes security men, who shouted at me and pushed me back to my coach. We saw them taking a man off the train in handcuffs. Everyone was quiet for a while.

But we were finally out of Bulgaria and lumbering into Turkey, leaving behind the Communist world and entering the "free" one. Outside, on the blistered Turkish plains, emaciated cattle hid from the sun in the slender shadows of telephone poles. Inside, Henderson was talking to the noble African, King Dahfu, who asked him, "What kind of traveler are you?"

I wondered the same about myself. What was I after? Why was it so important to me, as it was to Henderson, to go *far, far*—as if I could leave myself behind?

"Oh . . . that depends," Henderson replied. "I don't know yet. It remains to be seen." And then he said, "I seem to be some kind of tourist."

"Or a wanderer," the King corrected.

I had no interest in seeing the sights in Istanbul, but somehow I saw them: the Blue Mosque, Haga Sophia, Topkapi Palace. There was something morose about visiting a collapsed empire, even if one was grateful for the collapse.

I had come far—not so far as Henderson, but far enough to feel that I was over the horizon. I could feel the stretch of time and space. But what was I here for? To find myself? Or just to go farther?

In part, of course, I was simply fleeing the pain of my ruined love affair. The conventional wisdom was oddly true: that the greater the distance between Tamzon and me, the less I felt the loss. At night, when I tried to shut her out of my mind, I imagined digging a hole the size of a grave and crawling inside it. In Istanbul I was finally able to sleep without this imaginary burial.

I met a Dutchman in a café near the Haga Sophia who asked me to join him for some hashish. We went to his room at the Hotel Gülhane around the corner. His roommate, a German artist, unwrapped a package of freshly pressed hash, which was still as pliable as modeling clay, and we smoked four joints in the little blue-and-white room with the chipped plaster and graffiti in many languages. Then the artist took a bottle of Dexedrine and emptied ten tablets into his hand, which he swallowed two by two.

We went onto the roof. It was half-covered by an awning. You could sleep here for two lira a day—about fifteen cents—and the roof was crowded with hippies propped against the walls in various states of stupor or lying in bedrolls. Nearly all of them were Americans.

All at once I knew—despite my melancholy and a certain will toward self-destruction, and despite the authentically romantic call of the mullahs from the minarets and the violent sunset over the Golden Horn, and despite the flight of hashish that was transporting my thoughts in and out of time and dimension—I suddenly knew that I had come far enough. There were no answers here, only a loss of questions in the fog of drugs and exile and loneliness. For years I had been running away from Dallas, and now from America, but I understood with something other than bitterness that I carried them inside me. I was Dallas. I was America. Here on the roof of the Hotel Gülhane I stopped running away from myself.

10 / CHOOSING

My father took me to lunch at the country club with a Marine Corps general. He was a squarish person with a muscular face and muscular opinions to match. He talked about gooks. He talked about sissies. He made his points with little karate chops on the tablecloth that sent tremors through the iced tea. At one point he described me as "red-blooded," which seemed to mean that I was okay and Marine Corps material. When he talked about duty and country and "our boys in *Veet*nam," I began to twitch, since the object of this luncheon was to get this banker's son into the general's reserve unit and keep me out of the war.

A week later our family doctor ran into me in the bank and asked what I planned to do about the draft. I said I hadn't decided yet. "I bet if we looked real hard at those kidneys of yours, we might find us a little problem," he said, winking. "Come by the office sometime and let's see what we can discover."

I was so astounded I didn't know how to respond. I knew my father would be furious if he discovered that one of his closest friends was helping me evade the draft. Even the general's offer of a six-month hitch in the reserves was highly distasteful to my father—and to me, for different reasons. My father had a low opinion of the reserves as a fighting force, and I wasn't sure that I could live with the naked exercise of privilege that had jumped me to the top of the waiting list.

And now I was being offered a way out of the draft entirely—on a trumped-up kidney complaint.

Until now I had not understood that there was a large conspiracy to keep white middle-class kids out of the war. I had thought we were doing it ourselves, through cleverness. Everybody had a secret prescription for failing the physical, such as eating twenty egg whites so that albumin would show up in the urinalysis, or drinking a pint of your own blood to simulate an ulcer (you threw it up—it had to be yours because they would test it). I had friends who declared themselves homosexuals, or who went on extreme diets to place themselves outside the minimum physical standards. About half of the eligible men in America failed their physicals during the Vietnam era, a rate of rejection that was two or three times what it was in other NATO countries. There were orthodontists who would fit you with a set of artificial braces (the Army wouldn't take you if your dental bills were too high), battalions of psychiatrists willing to diagnose cracks in the crockery, and a full division of lawyers spinning out tangled motions and applications that had no other purpose than to drag on and on through the court, until their clients reached the age of twenty-six, when they were safe from the draft. Despite several reforms in the Selective Service laws, approximately fifteen million men—6o percent of the eligible men in the Baby Boom generation—evaded the draft in one fashion or another.

But now it struck me that our evasions were a part of a design. We were expected to find a way out of the draft in the same way that laboratory mice are supposed to puzzle through a labyrinth. It was nothing more than a social experiment being conducted by General Lewis Hershey, director of the Selective Service System, to "channel" young men into becoming "more effective human beings in the national interest." Those who were smart enough to find the escape hatches would be protected. It was a system designed to be unfair, a system that suggested that some American boys were more expendable than others, but also that we were all just mice in the box.

Originally the draft was an appealingly democratic idea. It had worked well enough in World War II and Korea and beyond. I remembered the shock when Elvis Presley got drafted. They shaved his ducktail and sent him to Germany. There was an element of adult vengeance in this. Grown-ups hated Elvis the Pelvis; you had the feeling all along that they couldn't wait to get him in the Army and teach him manners. And yet the fact that Elvis was not above the draft impressed me. I really believed that every American man was obligated to serve. But during Vietnam it had become clear that people who mattered wouldn't have to go. The National Guard was stuffed with athletes who were too valuable as investments to risk in combat; at one time the Dallas Cowboys had ten players assigned to the same Guard division. A widespread call-up of the reserves would have eliminated professional sports for the duration of the war. The year I was facing graduation, 1969, there were 28,000 more college-trained men in the National Guard or the reserves than in all of the active branches of service combined. Only 1 percent of the guardsmen were black. Actor George Hamilton, who was dating Lyndon Johnson's daughter in the White House, got a hardship deferment because his mother, who lived in a Hollywood mansion, depended on his support. Joe Namath led the Jets to the Super Bowl on his IV-F knees. These contradictions made everyone cynical.

The only really conspicuous, important American to be hounded by the draft board during the sixties was Muhammad Ali. There was that same element of vindictiveness toward Ali as there had been with Elvis. Ali had to be disciplined because he was an egotistical black man, a sexual threat as well as a racial one. By the Army's own standards Ali was unfit to serve. He had scored 78 on the IQ test, below the minimum, and was classified I-Y, a limbo for undesirables who would be called only in the case of a national emergency. But after Ali became the heavyweight champion and converted to the Black Muslim religion, his hometown draft board in Louisville, Kentucky, reclassified him I-A, fit for service. Ali applied for conscientious objector status as a Muslim minister. He also hired the most prominent draft lawyer in the country, Hayden Covington, who was married to General Hershey's sister. Covington advised Ali to move to Houston, where he thought the fighter might get a fairer hearing. This was an unfathomable piece of strategy to anyone living in Texas, where the antiwar movement had only the most tentative hold. After he refused to step forward at his induction, Ali was convicted of draft evasion and sentenced to five years in prison. He was stripped of his title and forbidden to fight, but he stayed free on bond until the Supreme Court overruled the lower-court decision four years later, on technical grounds. About a hundred other Black Muslims went to jail for the same offense.

I had grown up with complicated feelings about Ali. We used to watch the "Cavalcade of Sports" every Friday night when I was a child, and I became a fan of Floyd Patterson. He was the first black man I consciously admired. Patterson was dignified and handsome, a favorite of John Kennedy's, and never the Uncle Tom he was sometimes depicted as during the Ali era. He belonged to that solemn train of black notables that included Ralph Bunche and Marian Anderson and Sidney Poitier, whose gravity and sense of personal fineness were so profound that the casual racism of the suburbs was completely refuted. But Patterson was demolished in two fights by a black ex-con named Sonny Liston. Liston was so devastating (Patterson hadn't lasted six minutes, total, in both fights) that we thought he'd never be beaten, that he'd be champion forever, with his scowling countenance and fourteen-inch knuckles. At the end of the first Patterson fight in 1962 a young fighter named Cassius Clay barged into the ring and began screaming at Liston, calling him an ugly bear, offering to fight him *right now*—it was an act, of course, but it was wild, chaotic, and with Patterson stretched out on the canvas it seemed that the era of the dignified black man was over, and some berserk force had arrived.

Like nearly every white person in America, I was put off by Clay's vanity. "I'm so pretty," he was always crying. By saying it he made us look at him. He *was* good-looking, even my mother admitted it. Maybe it was true he had stolen his act from Gorgeous George, the professional wrestler with the golden locks, but the notion of a black person being beautiful was entirely new to us. Already he was a revolution, this fantastically brash Negro—a revolution in sensibility. We tolerated him because we fully expected him to die in the ring.

Liston had the reputation of being a cat's-paw of the mob, and he liked to play with his image as the world's toughest man. He kept a pistol filled with blanks to shoot the occasional reporter, and once he played that trick on Clay when a member of the Liston entourage tipped off the challenger that the champion might be found in a particular casino shooting craps. Clay burst in and shouted, "I want you out of town by sunup! Las Vegas ain't big enough for both of us." Liston pulled his gun out of his pocket and began blazing away, although by the time the last shot was fired, Cassius Clay was back in his hotel room under the bed.

After loving Patterson so, I thought I would cheer for anyone who could knock Liston off the throne, but I could hardly bear to see him replaced by a twenty-two-year-old boy with the world's highest self-esteem, who had hurled his Olympic gold medal into the Ohio River. I couldn't cheer for either man. Symbolically and psychologically, it wasn't my fight.

In the seventh round Liston refused to answer the bell, and on February 25, 1964, the new champion became Cassius Clay—or Muhammad Ali, as he instructed us to call him the next day. He was determined to make us choke on him. It's a miracle he sailed through the sixties unmurdered. Maybe he saved himself because he expressed no interest in white women, although that disinterest was in itself the most extreme insult imaginable.

My hero, Patterson, came out of retirement to fight Ali. He said he was going to bring the title back to America. He refused to call the champion by his Muslim name. Patterson became a stand-in for the Great White Hope, and virtually every white sportswriter, politician, and editorialist was praying aloud that Patterson would regain the championship. Ali did not merely beat Patterson; he tortured him, keeping him on his feet for twelve rounds as he lectured him through his mouthpiece. I felt sick watching Patterson stagger around the ring, searching for the withheld right that would have finished him, but finding instead that beckoning, teasing, tormenting left jab. You could see the hate flooding out of Ali. Whatever he was saying to Patterson I felt he was saying to me as well. He was rebuking me for making a hero of such a man.

Patterson was never replaced in my pantheon; he was simply

crushed and pushed aside. Ali didn't ask us to make him a hero in the same quiet, dignified, demanding way that Patterson had. Ali didn't care about being liked, and that gave him extraordinary power. It was strange that a man with a measured intelligence just above that of a moron could hold the nation enthralled with quick flicks of his jabbing wit. He said what he thought without thinking. On the day Ali was reclassified I-A, in February 1966, a television reporter asked for his reaction, and Ali said, "I ain't got no quarrel with the Viet Cong."

At that time the antiwar movement was still small and tied mostly to the coasts, to Berkeley and Boston. Virtually every newspaper and magazine in the country supported the war, and so did the preponderance of politicians and the great majority of citizens. But underneath—that is to say, in my generation, among the students whose voices had not yet been heard—there was a smoldering apprehension that we were headed for disaster. It was the timing, in other words, that made Ali's statement so inflammatory. He was already an international potentate, almost a nation unto himself, and it was typical of his egotism that he would negotiate his own foreign policy. But as soon as he said it, I realized that I agreed with him; I had no quarrel with the Viet Cong either. Just having the heavyweight champion say that released a vast sense of permission inside me. I could allow myself to think about not going to war. It was not such a test of manhood after all.

As I faced the beginning of my senior year and the inevitability of graduation, all choices were available to me. I could enlist, as I had nearly done before. I could be drafted (and would be, if I did nothing). I could go to prison. I could choose exile. I could get out of it all on a doctor's lie. Since there was no clear ethical winner, in my opinion, the choice became aesthetic, a matter of style. Each role had its attraction—even prison, the most sincere alternative—but each was dreadful in its particulars. What kind of country, I wondered, would put all of its young men in a position where they had to do something morally wrong? On the other hand, what kind of young men were we, who would lie and cheat, and pull strings, and run away, to avoid duty to our country or danger to ourselves?

*   *   *

The fall of 1968 would be a season of significant encounters.
The first paragraph I read of the work of Søren Kierkegaard was
this famous, but to me hilarious, passage from *The Sickness Unto
Death:*

> Man is spirit. But what is spirit? Spirit is the self. But what
> is the self? The self is the relation which relates itself to its
> own self, or it is that in the relation which accounts for it that
> the relation relates itself to its own self; the self is not the
> relation but consists in the fact that the relation relates itself
> to its own self. Man is a synthesis of the infinite and the finite,
> of the temporal and the eternal, of freedom and necessity, in
> short it is a synthesis. A synthesis is a relation between two
> factors. So regarded man is not yet a self.

And of course I closed the book immediately. Who could digest
such nonsense? It was like trying to eat spaghetti politely; the
noodles were too long to get on the fork. And yet, forced to read
The Sickness Unto Death, I went on to *Fear and Trembling, Works
of Love, Concluding Unscientific Postscript*—in short, I had run
upon one of those writers whose authority I found compelling, who
seemed to be speaking about my condition in particular, and whose
work was filled with such humor, irony, and bell-ringing insights
that I sometimes had to read him standing up.
Either/Or, a pseudonymous work in two volumes, was the book
that most affected me. It was easy to see myself in the first part,
which consisted of the papers of a purely aesthetic man, whom
Kierkegaard refers to only as A, and my father in the second, which
is the work of B, an ethical man, a civil magistrate, who attempts
to correct the melancholy romanticism of his young friend. A is
open to the pleasures of the world, but he cannot enjoy them
because he cannot choose from among them; he cannot limit
himself; he must be arbitrary; he cherishes the accidental; he is lost
in the infinity of alternatives. His greatest enemy is boredom and

"everydayness," which he combats by constantly seeking new experiences, new women, new pleasures—all of which invariably disappoint him and keep him in despair. B has made his choices, he is settled down and content, but he is also in despair because he has not entered into the final stage of spiritual growth, in which one develops an absolute relation to God.

In the middle of my Kierkegaard sojourn my philosophy professor suggested that I might be interested in doing a paper on the influence of Kierkegaard on the work of a local writer, who was a former doctor, an amateur theologian and philosopher, and even something of a linguist. He had lately turned to writing fiction, and had won the National Book Award in 1962 for his first novel, *The Moviegoer*. His name was Walker Percy.

As soon as I encountered Binx Bolling, the hero of *The Moviegoer*, I experienced a nervous sense of recognition, for here was Kierkegaard's aesthetic man—detached and ironic, but curious and aware of mystery in the world, and he even, like me, drove a red MG (to "break the grip of everydayness"). Binx floats among the possibilities, unable to choose this or that. The specific character of his despair, or "malaise," is the feeling that "the world is lost to you, the world and the people in it, and there remains only you and the world and you no more able to be in the world than Banquo's ghost."

A month later I drove my MG over the Pontchartrain causeway to Covington, Louisiana, to interview Percy for the paper I was writing. For years I had idolized writers without ever having met one, and so as I approached Percy's handsome brick house, which was tucked under moss-draped live oaks above a sluggish bayou, I was giddy, nervous, and swollen with expectation. Also, I thought that Percy already knew everything about me, he knew my interior life. I felt like Binx Bolling going to meet his creator.

Indeed, Percy greeted me with a raised brow when he saw the MG wheel into his drive. He was out by the duck pond, introducing some new ducks he had just acquired to the older residents. We sat beside the pond in lawn chairs, with a bottle of whiskey between us, which steadily diminished as the afternoon wore on, and talked about writing and philosophy. He recalled for me the time he and his friend Shelby Foote drove to Oxford, Mississippi, to see Faulkner, but Percy had refused to get out of the car. "I just sat there reading *Gone With the Wind,*" he said.

The sun dropped behind the trees. Time was passing, the world was spinning, I was spinning, but I was full, I was overflowing. In the twilight—almost, I might say, under cover of darkness—I was moved to blurt out that I wanted to be a writer. It was the first time I had ever said it aloud. "Have you got any money?" Percy asked me solemnly.

"A couple of dollars," I said.

"I mean family money."

"We're just sorta middle class."

"It's a lot easier if you have money."

I stared into the black pond with a woozy smile. Here I am, talking to Walker Percy, and he's worried about my finances! I must be a serious person after all.

I met a woman in Archeology 301. She came wafting in ten minutes late on the first day of class, wearing a purple blouse with a scarf at her neck—a little too turned out, I thought, for the archeologists. She had an attractive vague way of not being embarrassed. "You must be Miss Murphy," the professor observed. She was. Roberta Murphy.

All semester we dug up Indian artifacts in a backwater slough in the sugarcane country called Lac des Allemands. A band of oystereaters had camped there a thousand years before. They had been a lazy and unimaginative tribe. The entire product of our dig was several baskets of broken shards and an unaccountable crumpled carton of Lucky Strikes that had somehow slipped into prehistory. Our professor was a bearded misanthrope who drank from a hip flask and spent the afternoons observing the legs of the Newcomb girls, which were fully revealed thanks to the current style of short shorts and miniskirts. At the end of the day busloads of convicts would pass by, on their way back to Angola Prison from the cane fields, and you could hear them moan when they passed the coeds. Fashion was having an effect.

Roberta had grown up in Mobile, Alabama, a doctor's daughter, the product of a "dilapidated aristocracy," as she called it, and she had a patina of learning and culture that brought up my old feelings of backwardness. She listened to opera. The only opera I had ever heard was on an experimental excursion to the Music Hall in Dallas when the Metropolitan came to town. My father and I had both fallen asleep. But when Roberta listened to opera she cried. "Can't you hear how beautiful it is?" she asked. I was dumbfounded and a little scared, but one day at twilight I lay on the floor of her apartment and listened to Leontyne Price sing *Tosca.* The windows were open, the curtains moved in the breeze, shadows of the oak trees swayed across the ceiling, and Puccini's wild sentiments crashed through me like a summer storm. Roberta was majoring in classical languages. In the evenings after she bathed, she would wrap her beautiful chestnut hair in a damp bun, put on a flannel robe and granny glasses, and translate Cicero, while Erik Satie's ethereal melodies played in the background. I was at a point in my life where I was acquiring new passions, new tastes that were individual and would last the rest of my life. The first time I heard Thelonious Monk was in Roberta's apartment, and it sounded like something that came from inside me. His quirky rendition of Irving Berlin's forgotten tune "(Just One Way to Say) I Love You" became, through a thousand playings, our song. It was not just Monk and Satie and Puccini I had a taste for, I realized now; it was Roberta—her company, the ambience she created, her laugh, the special way she used language. For her birthday I gave her an Irish setter which peed in every room of her apartment.

This was an entirely new kind of love affair, calmer but also friendlier, less turbulent but also more complex. Roberta was like ballast for me; when I was with her I felt that I was in the world, and not floating apart from it like a man in space. And yet even when I moved in with her, neither of us saw our relationship as a "romance." We were buddies.

* * *

On the night before graduation my parents came to town. Roberta and I were having a drink with a friend when they arrived, and before I finished the introductions my father and my friend began to argue about the war. I hadn't known how much anger my father still had; I thought after our many battles that there was no force left in his attack, that we were permanently stalemated. But now that my student deferment was ending and I was staring into the face of the war, something long deferred in my father was boiling to the surface.

We went to dinner at my favorite restaurant, Galatoire's, and when Mother asked what I recommended, I suggested the pompano.

What was it about my suggestion that set my father off? Perhaps it was the galling thought that I had been here before, educating my tastes with his money—pompano!—it was another measure of the waste of my life, at such an expense to him. Look at how I had turned out, full of half-baked opinions offered with a supercilious and patronizing air, just like the damn waiters in this place. . . .

We were sitting at a middle table, where my father's voice filled the room. I thought I might slit his throat with my steak knife. It was true I had more expensive tastes than my father, who had a begrudging attitude toward restaurants anyway—but then he was the son of a broken farmer and I was the son of a successful banker, and we were bound to have different values. In some way he couldn't prevent, he had made me into his opposite. He had wanted my life to be better than his, and easier, and it had been. But look at the consequences! Did he want a son who was at home with the wine list? Yes, in theory, to be at ease in society was a good thing—if it weren't for the truckload of attitudes that came with it. What kind of education had he bought for me after all? In my father's eyes I was a middle-class Fauntleroy, despite my posturing about radical politics. How dare I order pompano and attack capitalism?

The issue between us wasn't really the pompano, it was still and always the war. We both knew that a decision would have to be made within weeks, and my father was hating me in advance for making the wrong decision—whatever it was.

At this, their first meeting, my mother and Roberta seized the conversation with some aggressive small talk. My father and I looked at each other in fury, then turned away. At any moment we might have jumped up and exchanged blows, so we forced ourselves to stare at our nervous female companions. Vividly I understood why women despise the tyranny of men, those monsters of ego, who bring their wars into the family and fight them in public places.

"What are you doing after graduation?" Mother asked. Roberta didn't know. It was impossible to think about our relationship beyond the next several days. Within a month or two I would be in exile or in the Army or on my way to jail, so there certainly didn't seem to be much future in pursuing me. Roberta thought she might go to graduate school.

My own limited plans were to take a summer course in publishing at Radcliffe College and wait for the ax to fall. Graduation was a dismal prospect. I was going to have to leave behind two things I valued highly, love and safety.

After dinner, when I had driven my parents to their hotel, Mother made the mistake of asking me to come up to their room. The argument picked up again and finally spilled out into the parking lot, where it raged loud and clear, for everyone in the Fountainbleu to appreciate. "You have wasted your life and my money," my father charged. "You are fit for nothing. You understand nothing. I have spent a small fortune educating a snob and a traitor."

"I am not a snob."

"You're a disgrace!" my father shouted. "Look at you! You're not worthy to be an American. You don't care enough to defend your country!"

"My country is not under attack."

"The hell you say! The hell you say! You'll never get another cent out of me. I'm not going to support a subversive."

"I don't want your money," I said carelessly.

Mother was sobbing on the bed, begging us to stop, but we were alike in too many ways, and we had too many scores to settle, not only with each other but with the future and the past. It was my father's generation that had brought me to this point of having my life twisted by a war no one wanted to fight. How could he blame me if I hated him and his generation for being so goddamned wrongheaded and sure of themselves, for pushing the world around and picking fights they would send their sons to settle? Well, thanks very much! I don't want your fucking war! My father's face went purple. He said it was a damn shame the country was going to have to be handed over to the likes of me, a bunch of brain-washed sissies—!

When the management finally appeared we were screaming at each other about America. My father's last words to me were a slogan of the age, all the wisdom of his generation boiled down to a bumper sticker. "Love it or leave it," he said.

A few days later I drove across America from Dallas to Boston with the top down, hopped up on Dexedrine, my mind flying. I rode between the wheat fields and cow pastures, past the shotgunned road signs, across a country that was at war abroad and at war with itself, a country that was stewing in its own bitter juices. I despised America. I hated its meanness. It wasn't my country anymore. It had resurrected Richard Nixon from his own angry exile and made him President—Nixon, the hit man of the bourgeoisie—and as I drove across the vast belly of Nixon's America I felt defeated and afraid. Somehow, with graduation, the prospect of revolution had popped like a soap bubble; it had been an undergraduate fantasy after all, too embarrassing to even talk about now.

A revolution had come, all right, but it hadn't been mine. It was the victory of the new world. At the time it seemed that Nixon's election was a fluke, a detour in the march toward liberalism, brought about by the coincidence of Humphrey's unfortunate nomination and the vindictive response of the middle class toward the poor, the minorities, and the young. It was a choice that made no one very happy; the turnout was so low (61 percent) and the margin of victory so slim (43.4 percent to 42.7 percent), that in the end little more than a fourth of the electorate cast ballots for the man who became our president. It was a revolution nonetheless; the power had shifted inexorably to the new world, and Nixon was its first true expression.

My drive from Dallas to Boston was, in its way, a retreat from the victorious new world to the defeated old one. I came into the city after midnight, got lost, and finally came upon Harvard Square in the middle of the night—Harvard, the inner sanctum of the Eastern Establishment. It was like crossing the lines into the enemy camp. Spiritually, I felt that I must be home. (Of course, no one is less at home than the wandering Confederate.) I was too thrilled to sleep. When dawn came I was already walking across the campus in a state of worship, nodding at the few early risers, who avoided my dizzy smile as if it were an infection.

I was housed in a Radcliffe dorm with a boy from Kentucky, the only other southern male. We discovered that there was a certain exoticism attached to us, as if we were exchange students. One woman asked me, "Is that really the way you talk?" Most of the other students in the Publishing Procedures Course were from Ivy League schools, and some of them carried surnames I knew as brands of cake mix or automobiles. Here, firsthand, was Old Money. It was different from the New Money I had met in Texas. New Money had come out of the oil fields; it had come suddenly, in geysers, and was often just as suddenly gone, sucked away in a dry hole. New Money liked to display itself, in the form of heavy diamonds, even on men, but along with the plush cars and suburban mansions came a hostile attitude toward real elegance. There was a phrase in Texas that a man was "rich enough to wear white socks," which meant that he could walk into the Petroleum Club dressed like a field hand, cussin' and spittin' and scratchin' where it itches, and the men in the room would wink at each other and make knowing comments about his net worth.

Old Money didn't behave like that. Old Money invested itself cautiously, almost stingily; it did not reach for the check. Old Money was a lodge with secret ways of revealing itself, having to do with fashions and attitudes. By contrast with the windblown characters I had known in Texas, Old Money was like the pig who built his house of bricks; it spent itself on pedigrees and social connections designed to avoid failure. New Money was politically conservative but personally generous and openhanded. Old Money was oriented in the opposite direction; here people were politically liberal but sorry tippers.

Famous writers came to speak to us, or else we went to them. We took a bus trip to Cape Cod to meet Kurt Vonnegut, who addressed us while wearing a bright yellow nor'easter rain slicker on a warm, sunny day, and we were invited to Ipswich, where we bumped into John Updike in the movie theater. I was hungry for these encounters. If I had any doubt about my ambition it vanished when I returned to my dormitory room one evening to find the author of a recent best-selling potboiler sitting on my bed, surrounded by three fourths of the women in the course, several of whom were quite literally stroking him, rubbing his knees and hair—a vision of literary reward.

Roberta came to visit and brought our dog. We hid Stewart in the dorm, and when I finally took him out for a walk in the evening he was nearly delirious. He was in that state of frenzy when he bit a renowned liberal journalist who was our speaker for the day. For the rest of the course I was known as The Man Who Owns the Dog That Bit Jack Newfield.

In Harvard Square on a Sunday morning I first said the word "marriage" aloud to Roberta, not as a proposal, exactly, but as a possibility. Harvard Square was filled with dope addicts and spare-change panhandlers and student minstrels; everyone seemed to be drifting, unattached and unconcerned; there was a blissed-out tranquillity in the air that traveled on the mindless strains of a flute being badly played by an old man in hippie clothes and the rattle of tambourines from a conga line of Hare Krishnas who snaked around the trees. One felt a sense of insubstantialness, as if people might fly. A strong gust of wind would have cleared the park in a swirl of saffron robes and miniskirts. Marriage did not belong to life in this dimension; it was too nontranscendent, too troublesome, too square, too limiting. My voice cracked when I said it.

I was afraid I had offended her. The conceit of the times was that marriage was a sellout, a truckling under to the conventions of society. Roberta and I were in love, but to formalize that relationship through marriage would be a signal that we were caving in to the button-down mind-set of our parents' generation. Our generation was on the road to individual freedom, and marriage was a perverse detour, it was voluntary servitude, a cop-out in an age when all options should remain open.

"If you marry, you will regret it," warned Kierkegaard's aesthetic man; "if you do not marry, you will regret it; if you marry or do not marry, you will regret both; whether you marry or do not marry, you will regret both." I didn't want to lose Roberta. I wanted companionship, I wanted to feel grounded, to build up the lifelong intimacies that make up a profound relationship; on the other hand, I didn't want to remove myself from the possibility of other women, from the joys of superficial encounters. It was the age of the Pill and the Playboy Philosophy. Harvard Square was crowded with available but increasingly complicated women, who were in the middle of the sexual revolution. Bralessness had announced itself at the Miss America pageant the year before, when a TV actress stormed the stage trailing a string of burning brassieres. Women said they were turning against fashion; they no longer wanted to be treated as sex objects. And yet—my God! Nipples! On display! You could see them racing up and down inside T-shirts, like buoys in the surf. Moving breasts! My imagination was fully stoked all the time. Never before had there been so much to surrender. As a man I had the feeling of finally owning Boardwalk and Park Place; marriage did not seem to be a clever investment of my sexual capital.

And yet I could sense trouble brewing. On the edge of the square a woman with unshaven armpits cast a deprecating glance at me, then handed Roberta a flier entitled "The Myth of the Vaginal Orgasm." Until I read the flier I had never heard of the clitoris. Now it reared up like an angry and unsatisfied customer, demanding gratification. The flier was advising masturbation as a superior sexual experience. I felt ignorant, I felt threatened. Were men becoming optional? I had no doubt that women would give up men entirely once the reproduction problems were worked out; they would become self-propagating, like sponges.

Was marriage a form of oppression? I wasn't sure of Roberta's views on this, nor had I given much thought to the kind of wife I wanted to have. I wanted a partner, but did I want a full partner? "Equality" was a nervous word for me. Was it possible to have a marriage of equals? Was it desirable? What did it mean in 1969 for a man to mention marriage, even as a hypothesis, to a strong-willed woman? Roberta was noncommittal. "It's something to think about," she said, and I was relieved. At least she wasn't offended.

In the middle of the night I sat on a park bench, under the statue of the seated John Harvard, and I began to cry. My I-A draft notice had arrived in the mail.

Who was I? Suddenly everyone needed to know: the government, Roberta, my parents. I was going to have to declare myself, but I was invisible. There was no self to declare. I was just as much one thing as another, as much a soldier as a peacenik, as much a bachelor as a spouse, as much a patriot as a traitor. How could I say yes to one part of me and no to another?

Choose! Choose something!

But choosing was awful, it was like amputating limbs. There were so many consequences, involving life and death, love and sex, duty and honor. Every choice would define me, and limit me. I would become something, and not something else. I would have to have beliefs. And I would have to choose now.

Until this moment, birth and circumstance had defined me as the enemy. I had been a Dallasite during the Kennedy assassination, a white southerner during the civil rights movement, a man during the women's movement, and an American during the Vietnam War. As a consequence my life had been a series of disavowals. I had left Dallas, I had left the South. I was leaving the kind of man I had expected to become. Now the strongest urge I felt was to leave America.

But this was not an identity, this continual leaving. I must believe *something*.

When I was a child we had a toy called the Magic 8 Ball. You would ask it a question and shake the ball, and the answer would appear in a window. As I lay on the park bench the single answer that floated out of the obscure recesses of my mind was "Thou Shalt Not Kill." It was not very much of an answer, and certainly not an identity, but it was a beginning.

I decided to become a conscientious objector, or to try to, given that my draft board was in Dallas and could not be expected to hear my plea with much sympathy, and given as well my own ambivalence about my motives. That summer Henry Kissinger said in *Look* magazine, "Conscientious objection must be reserved for only the great moral issues, and Vietnam is not of this magnitude." What an infuriating piece of sophistry! In my opinion it was only in the great moral contests, for instance in the war against Nazi aggression, that a violent response could be justified. I would defend my country if it were attacked. I would have fought in World War II. I was not a pacifist. Moreover, I was not a member of any organized religion. There were 172,000 COs during the Vietnam era, and nearly all of them were members of nonviolent sects such as the Quakers or Mennonites or Jehovah's Witnesses. I was merely a lapsed Methodist. I doubted that I would be considered very seriously.

In my application to the Selective Service board, I described myself as a "Christian Existentialist," which meant—to me, at least—that I believed in the values of Christianity without really believing in God. I quoted Paul Tillich, who had written of "this affirmation of meaning within meaninglessness, of certitude within doubt," which is "not the God of traditional theism but the 'God above God,' the power of being, which works through those who have no name for it, not even God." I accepted the possibility that my conscience was tied to some larger power or urge, but even if it were not, my conscience had told me not to kill, and I would not. My conscience was all I had.

To my astonishment, my application was quickly approved. When I got the news I slept for two days. It was like the exhaustion that comes after a final lovers' quarrel. I was emotionally spent.

I had two weeks to find alternative service—typically, two years in a low-paying public service job, in a place that was not within commuting distance of your home. Many hospital orderlies were COs; however, since we were in the middle of a recession most of the bedpan jobs had been taken by people who really needed them. Also, I wanted desperately to get out of the country. I took a bus to New York, with the idea of getting a job at the United Nations. There were no positions available to me there, but I did get a list of American institutions abroad, many of which had offices nearby. At the top of the list was the American University in Cairo, whose office was across the street. I walked into the office and spoke to a man for ten minutes. He asked if I could leave for Egypt that night. I gathered he was short of teachers.

"No! I'd have to pack. My clothes are all in Boston."

"Tomorrow, then."

I hadn't expected it to be so easy. I hadn't even had a moment to think about what it might be like to spend the next two years in Egypt. I went back to Boston for a confused farewell to Roberta. The next day I was standing in John F. Kennedy Airport calling my parents to say that I was leaving America after all.

11 / EGYPT LAND

WELCOME AT CAIRO, said the sign on the airport—an unwelcome signal to an English teacher who had to teach his first class the following morning. It was midnight, Egyptian time, when I arrived in my new apartment and fell dead asleep, only to wake up two hours later, jet-lagged and bewildered. I wandered around the apartment and listened to the traffic and the pentatonic melodies of the doorman's transistor radio.

At seven a small, wiry man, with a distinguished face that reminded me of the actor Claude Rains, came into my apartment. He had his own key. He was carrying a shopping bag of groceries, and he introduced himself as Shaffei Mohammed Helal, my servant. "What you like for breakfast, mister?" he demanded.

Shaffei had learned to cook in the British army, a wretched school for chefs. In prerevolutionary days he had been a butler, which was a more suitable position for his aide-de-camp manner and military bearing. On that first morning he was in a grumpy mood, and he made breakfast into a noisy production. Later I learned that he was planning to have breakfast prepared before I awoke, as servants in Egypt were expected to do. The following morning he arrived half an hour earlier, but I was still on American time and wired on Arab coffee I had brewed myself. Every morning for the next two weeks he came in earlier and grumpier, trying to catch me asleep—but how could he? I was dropping from exhaustion right after dinner and often was asleep before the sun went down. One morning Shaffei arrived at four, haggard but determined, and found me making eggs. He slumped against the door and cried, "Mister, when you sleep?"

I did not relish the idea of having a servant. I still thought of myself as a radical; also, I was twenty-two and Shaffei was in his middle fifties, so our relationship was bound to be oddly balanced. As the months passed and our friendship grew, Shaffei became more and more the affectionate, if ever fussy, housewife. We would go shopping together, along the stalls of vegetable stands, past the butcher shops with the bleeding carcasses hung out for the flies, and Shaffei would take my hand, in the Arab fashion, and complain about prices.

As much as I loved him, I never grew to love his cooking. He did have a flair for presentation. A salad would be laid out with carrot spokes around a tomato hub, a banana pie would be garnished with concentric coins of fruit; it was all very pretty but emotionally uninvolving. Once I decided to upgrade his culinary skills by translating a recipe out of a Julia Child cookbook into the pidgin English we used to communicate. It was for a lamb roast. Shaffei sat in the kitchen with an intent look as I spoke about the marinade, "like wine soup" with thirty-five bay leaves—

"What is bay leave?"

"Add the onions, carrots, celery, never mind the juniper berries, two cups of vermouth, garlic, bouillon, cook in olive oil, season with—"

But now Shaffei was laughing. "Excuse me, mister, this is for one person?"

"Eight or ten."

"For the cost of this dinner I can feed two hundred."

And of course it did seem preposterous in revolutionary Egypt to dream of French cooking, so I laughed as well. Wasn't I a revolutionary too? And yet there was a grudging imperialist inside me who was dying for a first-class meal.

The street life of Cairo reminded me of a coral reef, a flamboyant but fragile ecology of vendors and beggars and entrepreneurs who raced about in shoals among the taxis and pedestrians. Every stoplight supported a jasmine seller and a windshield cleaner. On the sidewalks a family of three generations made a living selling baked yams and mint tea. Sometimes outside my apartment on Mahad Swissri fire-eaters and sword swallowers would appear, or a man with a dancing baboon, or a clown in a Charlie Chaplin suit, twirling his cane and tipping his derby. In the late afternoon the little daughter of a blind peanut vendor would lead her father by the hand. He wore a black *gallabiya* and a white turban, which was wrapped across his eyes. On his arm he carried a basket of unshelled peanuts, called *sudani* in Arabic. His daughter was no more than five years old, and she walked barefoot, and as they moved past my apartment her little voice shouted *"Sudani! Sudani!"* and he would echo *"Sudani!"* in a deep, echoing cry like a train whistle.

I lived on the island of Zamalek in the middle of the Nile, one island downriver from Roda, where Moses was found in the bullrushes. Each morning on my way to the university I passed a public school, where children in coffee-colored uniforms lined up to sing *"B'ladi, B'ladi"* ("My Country, My Country") at the top of their lungs while a xylophone and a drum inexpertly clanged and boomed after the tune, and the schoolmaster circulated among them with a short-handled whip. For a moment the entire street paused; the policeman in his wooden hut stood at attention, the doormen playing a game like checkers with bottle caps looked up and smiled, showing their gorgeous Nubian teeth, the harelipped beggar boy added the sound of his own sad voice, and then the song ended and the doormen resumed their game and the boy raced after taxis and the policeman took a nap.

Outside the school gates an old man in a white robe took piasters from the brown, groping hands poking through the rails and passed paper cones full of hot peanuts through the bars. His cart was an ancient baby carriage with a tin-can oven inside, and his paper cones were the homework papers given him by the schoolchildren. Every morning when he saw me coming he would call out, *"Sabah il kher!"* (May your morning be good.)

And I would respond, *"Sabah il nur!"* (May your morning be full of light.)

"Sabah il ishta!" he insisted, may your morning be as white as cream—or as fragrant as jasmine, as pure as honey; his formulations changed daily. It is a decorous and romantic language.

As soon as I passed the peanut vendor I was hailed by Samir the Artist, who stood outside his studio working on charcoal portraits of Omar Sharif, or Charlton Heston as Moses, or some iconic study of Gamal Abdel Nasser. "Good morning, my darling," he called out in English. "Did you see the Phantoms today?" The Phantoms were the American-made jets used by the Israeli air force. They would often buzz the city at dawn, streaking down the Nile just above the bridge tops, shattering every pane of glass along the Corniche with their explosive supersonic screech.

During the two years I was in Egypt, from 1969 to 1971, the ancient war between the Arabs and the Jews had gone stale, but it continued to be fought in a languid fashion, like two fighters grown arm-weary in the late rounds. Many of the windows in public buildings were blued and crisscrossed with masking tape. Soldiers with antique British rifles patrolled the city's bridges from sandbag turrets. At night you could see their shadows on the walls of the lantern-lit tents, reading, playing cards, sleeping in cots, their underwear drying on lines beside the busy bridge traffic.

The Nile itself was just another boulevard, crowded with water taxis speeding students to Cairo University, and feluccas that had to lower their masts to squeeze under the bridges, and houseboats constructed of reeds and cardboard, which drifted near the shoreline. Sheep on their way to slaughter took their final bath in the river, along with their naked shepherds. On holidays the Nile swarmed with rowboats, and sometimes a wedding party came along in several boats, followed by a band serenading the newlyweds. From every boat in the river came shouted congratulations, and young men would stand on the gunwales and dance as the band played some popular song everyone knew.

I liked to walk the length of the island, past the sidewalk café with its parti-colored chairs facing the water and the cats stalking about under the tables for scraps. Near the café is a mosque where Nasser and the Revolutionary Command Council plotted the coup against King Farouk in 1952, and beside that is the needle-shaped Cairo Tower, a silly-looking erection that was built with the three million dollars that the CIA gave Nasser as a bribe. The tower is spitefully placed directly across the Nile from the Hilton hotel.

Once I crossed the Kasr El Nil bridge, I stepped into Tahrir Square, the heart of Cairo, where traffic whirled about in a maelstrom and a million pedestrians flooded the sidewalks. It was always a relief to slip inside the gates of the American University and to leave the jostling, noisy crowd outside.

In 1969 there were no diplomatic relations between the United States and Egypt because of the Israeli war; the American embassy was closed down, and the business of citizens was conducted in a consular office tucked inside the grounds of the Spanish embassy. The only significant American presence in the country was the American University, and as a result the school had become a refuge for spies. The president of the university, Christopher Thoren, who has since died, was an elegant spook whose cover was blown by Philip Agee in *CIA Diary*, and there were other people in university administration who had important titles with no apparent duties. The young Americans like me who taught in the English Language Institute were always joking about being overheard in the privacy of our own apartments, but we were never certain who was listening, the Americans or the Egyptians or even the Russians, who lived across the street.

On my first morning in Cairo I entered a classroom filled with Egyptians, Palestinians, and Jordanians who constituted UG-14, the undergraduate class with the lowest level of achievement on the Michigan language exam. Many of them had already failed the test twice and had only one more opportunity to gain full admission to the university. Since I had no teaching experience at all, I had been given a class in which no one was expected to succeed. Most of them had learned English from teachers who didn't speak it. They had spent years conjugating verbs wrongly and learning to say "blease" and "sank you." When I came into the classroom I asked, "Does anyone here speak English?" and a voice in the back of the room said, "You do."

They reminded me of American high schoolers in the 1950s, with their innocent antics and dateless school dances and their apparent complacency. It was months later, after I had become a part of them, and they a part of me, that I realized they were not complacent, they were simply not alienated. They did not feel estranged from their countries or their religions, although few of them were especially patriotic or devout. They believed in progress; they had that same faith in the goodness of technology that my father's generation had had, but as a corollary they had absolutely no interest in the past. They were heirs to one of the oldest civilizations in the world, but they knew nothing about Ramses or Hatshepsut, and everything about the desalination of seawater or the construction of the Aswan Dam. They needed me because I was an instrument of progress; Egypt was building a technocratic society, and the language of technology was English. For most of them I was the last hope that they would be a part of that future.

Only one of my students was a troublemaker. His name was Medhet; he was a Jordanian from the West Bank. When he was a child an Israeli patrol had come through his village and shot a man to death in front of him. Some of the man's brains had splattered on him. Since then he had not been able to speak confidently. He stuttered terribly, and when the other students kidded him he would blow up in a tongue-tied tantrum. His great interest, he confided one day, was in Russian history. I gave him a book on Trotsky that was far too difficult for him, and yet he read it doggedly, week after week, all semester long. Just before he took the Michigan exam for his final time, he said he had dreamed last night in English. It was not my accomplishment; he was the one who read the book, he was the one who passed the test, but I was prouder of Medhet's success than of anything I had ever done.

It was strange that the Egyptians could be so cordial to Americans when Phantom jets were bombing their country. I think it was a relationship that only Americans can have with other peoples, in part because of our good qualities—we like children, we mix with the help—and in part because of our unfathomable democracy. Often my students would apologize to me for the actions of my own country. They did not hold me responsible for selling jets to Israel or refusing to assist the Arab cause. Their genuine feeling for the goodness of the American people was formed by Hollywood, which casts a spell over the entire world. The America of the movies is a land of such innocence and beauty that my students were predisposed toward forgiveness. They wanted to be on our side. Some of them had been born in villages in the Nile delta, or in Palestinian camps on the bloody West Bank, but they had grown up watching Doris Day driving carpool through the suburbs of the new world and Fred MacMurray smoking his pipe and telling bedtime stories. America had insinuated itself into their imaginations. They thought about it all the time, and they were bound to love it—but also hate it, because they knew that America did not love them; indeed, America scarcely thought about them at all.

In my students' minds, my country was in a state of cinematic timelessness. Chicago was still trapped in Prohibition and ruled by mobsters in double-breasted suits. When they learned I was from Texas, they imagined the Texas of a John Wayne Western—in other words, some Arizona parkland where the secrets of internal combustion had not yet been discovered. This proved a hazardous misconception for me when I went horseback riding with them in Giza, near the pyramids. My students insisted that I be given the very fastest Arabian stallion, and the owner produced a rearing, untamed beast that nearly rode me to Libya.

I often took my class to the movie theater, especially during Ramadan, the fasting period, when nothing is supposed to pass the lips between sunrise and sunset. We met each midnight for the special Ramadan features that helped keep people awake for the two A.M. meal. Once we watched *Barbarella*, Jane Fonda's science fiction sex epic, with the Russian national tennis team sitting in front of us, howling and pretending to cover their eyes. Another time we went to see *Midnight Cowboy*, which presented such a grimy picture of American urban life that my students came out of it feeling disoriented and glum. They couldn't believe America was like that. America was not just a place, it was an ideal, it was the promise of progress. America was what awaited their own countries if they worked hard and Allah smiled on them.

I wondered how my students could maintain their conceits about America given the Americans they had come to know. The teachers at the university fell into two camps, depending, I decided, on their attitude toward dirt. When the wind blows out of the desert nothing is clean, and for Americans the consequences can be demoralizing and even traumatic. Either they retreated to their shuttered apartments into mean little covens of snobbery and bigotry as the dust accumulated on their coffee tables like a Minnesota snowfall, or they forged ahead blithely behind a handshake and a smile, not minding the smell or the noise or the grit. I fell into this latter group; I was the American nincompoop in his most endearing incarnation, always popping up to help the servant get the dishes, and thanking thanking thanking and tipping tipping tipping—who could fail to love him and pity him and wonder at the waste of wealth and power that produced such a creature?

Directly across the street from me was the Novosti Press Agency, the Russian news service. I often watched a pair of blond children playing hide-and-seek behind a thick-waisted banyan tree and the tanklike Volga sedans parked in the drive. The Russians lived in partial quarantine. Unlike other foreigners, they had no servants; they moved in small groups through the food shops in Zamalek, inspecting things too closely, bargaining in gruff, rudimentary Arabic. It was said that their embassy forbade them to speak to Egyptians except to shop. You never saw them enjoying themselves in restaurants or nightclubs. Every other Friday night Novosti gave a party for their correspondents. I discovered that if I lay on the balcony outside my bedroom I could just see into their parlor, where the Russians were gathered around, sullenly drinking and playing old Teresa Brewer records on the phonograph. At two o'clock in the morning they would spill out into the street, smashed, and singing "Put another nickel in! In the nickelodeon!" I honestly could not decide if they were making fun of American culture or if they really admired Teresa Brewer.

One afternoon as I was walking to the Ghezira Sporting Club with my tennis racquet, a Russian offered me a lift in his Volga. His English was quite good. We played doubles together on several occasions thereafter. I thought this was quite humorous; I called us the "Big Powers" after we had teamed up to beat several European pairs. After a match Aleksei would buy us a couple of Stella beers and we would sit in the shade and talk about tennis, or he would quiz me about fine points of English grammar. Occasionally we would talk about Vietnam or American politics. He was not aggressively friendly, but he was often around. He spoke very little about Russia; he would shrug in a way that indicated I really shouldn't probe. "But life is very nice here, I think," he would say, indicating the bowlers rolling ninepins on the grass and the ponies coursing down the polo field and the weight lifters sunning their muscles in the garden.

After I met Aleksei I noticed that I became a subject of interest among people in the university administration. On several occasions I was invited to play tennis with an assistant to the president, who invited me to his apartment for tea and flattered me into talking about my views on the war, or the relative merits of Communism versus capitalism, or the responsible position of America in the world. I cleared my throat and said that capitalism was all right for America, but it couldn't solve the problems of the developing world. Socialism might. Or else Chinese Communism, but that didn't seem like much fun. And on and on in this vein, the reactionary leftist politics of the day, while the president's assistant nodded and said "Um-hm" and "I see what you mean." I think now how excruciating it must have been, both for the KGB and the CIA, to spend their time wrestling over this naive idealist. After a while they both lost interest and I found myself looking for new tennis partners.

One winter night in 1969, while I was camping in the desert, I was awakened by a series of explosions. I wrapped a blanket around me and stepped out of the tent into the chill desert air. On the horizon appeared great bulbing orange flashes. I counted the seconds between the burst and the rumbling sound of the explosion and figured them to be coming from Helwan, the industrial district. The light from the bombs silhouetted the city skyline and glinted

off the pyramids. I could just see the black images of the Israeli jets
like angry bees diving into the glow of the fires. It was splendid.

In the morning I returned my camel to its owner, and asked if
the man had seen the bombing. He turned away and kicked at the
sand. "The bombs!" I said. "Didn't you see the bombs in Helwan
last night?"

He continued to study the sand as if he hadn't heard me. Finally
he said, "No bombs in Helwan last night."

The war was always just offstage. Sometimes the Israelis would
race over the city in the middle of the day, for the hell of it, and
fifteen minutes later the empty sky would be filled with antiaircraft
shells as the defenders reached their posts. All across the city
Cairenes would flock to the rooftops to view the fireworks. An
American girl I knew was hospitalized with hepatitis near a district
that was frequently bombed at night. In the morning the nuns
would gather the shrapnel and use it to mulch the roses.

The newspapers seldom reported the raids at all. They concentrated their attention on the successes, real or imagined, at the Suez
Canal. Few days passed without the announcement of another
Israeli jet downed, sometimes with a photo but usually "seen crashing across the Canal." Most of my students listened to the BBC
for news about the war. The Israelis seemed invulnerable to them,
like wizards, and they felt diffident; they thought the whole world
was laughing at the Egyptians, who were too backward to operate
the machines of modern warfare, who had picked a war with Israel
and lost it in six days.

The identity they most longed for, then, was that of their enemy.
Their admiration for the Israelis was heartbreaking; every time a
Phantom flew overhead, unmolested, it was a refutation to their
right to inhabit the modern world. When they struck a match, one
of those perfidious Egyptian matches with a head that flies off, they
would laugh self-consciously and call it an "Israeli match," as if the
clever Israelis had contrived a scheme to set Egyptians on fire. The
Egyptians had lived in the desert for three thousand years, but they
had not made it "bloom," as they heard the Israelis had in a single
generation. Civilization may have been born here, but it never

grew; it stayed perpetually primitive. Indeed, the fellahin, the rural proletariat, were still plowing their fields with water buffalo and drawing water with the Archimedes screw; as soon as you left Cairo you shed two thousand years of progress. The city was a small bit of almost modern life set in a country that had not changed since the Ptolemys. Until Nasser dammed the Nile, Cairo was an electric island, and even now when you flew into Egypt at night what you saw was black, black, black, then Cairo like a bonfire. My students were mortified by their past, which surrounded them, which they could easily see from the vantage of any structure taller than five stories—the pyramids, that single great eruption of monument building, thinking, and art, then century after century of colonial occupation, which had kept them frozen in time at the beginning of history.

The Six-Day War of 1967 might have toppled the Nasser regime—that had been the object of the Israeli invasion—and yet the grossness of that defeat had had the opposite effect. When Nasser announced his resignation after losing the Sinai along with his entire air force, the country had rallied behind him and demanded that he stay in office—it was not an orchestrated display by a Third World strongman, it was a spontaneous national response. Nasser was the father of the revolution, the architect of modernizing Egypt. He had absurd dreams of uniting the entire Arab world into a single socialist empire; but it was not until the moment of his abject humiliation that he became a true symbol of proud, broken, resolute Egypt.

It was strange for me to have fled one war, only to find myself in another. Many of the American teachers, including me, were still waging an antiwar campaign against America in Vietnam on the campus of the American University. When Nixon ordered the invasion of Cambodia, we wore black armbands in protest. We held teach-ins. These actions were regarded with disbelief by the Egyptians and with alarm by the university administration. But we never lurched into the arena of the Middle East war; for most of us it was an abstraction, even though we speculated frequently about new hostilities. In the fall of 1970 there was a brief, mismatched war between Jordan and the Palestine Liberation Organization, and there was a great deal of talk about the evacuation of the American community from Egypt, should the war spread. And there was always the threat of another Israeli invasion. Everyone knew the Israelis could enter Cairo at will.

I knew that their war wasn't my affair. On the other hand, I couldn't stand the idea of seeing my students killed. I thought about how much love and effort are required to draw a single human being through the complexities of childhood and adolescence, and what a vessel of knowledge and experience each of us is, how valuable and filled with potential. My students might die in the service of History, but their own histories would be cut short in some miserable inconclusive exchange along the canal, or some heroic charge in the service of a misbegotten war. I had no investment in their wounded national pride, but I cared about my students and I fretted about their futures, and in that way their war became my enemy, along with my own.

I began to pester Shaffei about artichokes. I was dying for one. Roberta used to boil them and serve them whole with a vinaigrette dip. I couldn't find the word in my English-Arabic dictionary, and when I tried to describe them to Shaffei his face became suspicious—he thought I was talking about pine cones. Finally I went on a patrol of vegetable stands and discovered a lovely bunch of artichokes hidden away with the turnips in the back of the store. I bought two of them and took them home to Shaffei. "Ah, mister, you buy *karshuf.*" It is actually the word from which "artichoke" is derived.

That night I had artichokes. And the next. And the next. Shaffei was demonstrating his remorse. After a week on this diet I realized it was not artichokes I was longing for, but Roberta. Compared with loneliness, marriage no longer seemed like such a dismal alternative.

And besides, I was entertaining the notion that we might get married under Moslem law, which would permit me three addi-

tional wives. This was ideal. Even in my greediest moments I knew
I could be content with four wives at a time; moreover, the divorce
laws were fantastically simple ("I divorce thee, I divorce thee, I
divorce thee"). There were obstacles to overcome—such as per-
suading Roberta to convert—but first she had to be willing to
marry me and move to Egypt.

Our proposals crossed in the mail. I wrote begging her to come;
she wrote that she was coming anyway. Negotiations began. The
Moslem gambit did not even merit a response. Roberta demanded
to be married in Athens. She was a classics major, after all.

The only man in Greece who could marry us was an ecumenical
preacher who happened to be a former Nazi. He had been booted
out of Egypt because he was suspected of spying for the Israelis.
One can imagine how he responded to me, the conscientious
objector. We spoke briefly about Egypt, and he recalled how much
he loathed the Egyptians, who were always lounging about in their
pajamas, spending their life in chatter, whereas the Israelis were
such hard workers, so efficient, such great warriors. I admired the
Israelis too, for many reasons, but hearing them so described by a
former storm trooper made me sentimental about the gentleness
and sociability of the Egyptians. I said I hoped the Egyptians would
not come away from their long war with the Israelis more like
them, in the way that the Jews had fled Europe with the stamp of
Germany on their souls.

Roberta and I were married on January 22, 1970, in a depressing
ceremony. It seemed to me a bad omen to be married by a Nazi.
But afterward my best man, Larry Gray, brought out a bottle of
Veuve Cliquot, and we climbed to the top of the Acropolis. It was
the first full moon of the decade. The Parthenon was before us,
forbiddingly holy. We went inside its roofless sanctuary and knelt
on the floor of broken limestone, and were baptized in champagne
to the memory of old gods.

On September 28, 1970, at night, a ululating wail spread across
Cairo. It was a terrifying sound, loud, ubiquitous, pulsing—you

would expect to hear such a noise at Armageddon. Nasser was dead. The wailing continued all night. We heard stories the next week about mass suicides, people leaping out of windows from grief. Muezzins chanted from the mosques to comfort the people. The next morning it was as if Cairo itself had died. There were no cars in the streets. The city was hushed and afraid. Shaffei arrived, ashen and red-eyed. "The people are like sand in the streets," he said.

After noon, bands of young men in flatbed trucks ranged through the city crying, "Gamal Abdel Nasser lives! We are all Gamal Abdel Nasser!" In Alexandria in 1952 an assassin had fired three shots at Nasser while he was making a speech. "Let them kill me!" he had said then. "Now you are all Gamal Abdel Nasser."

Between the death and the funeral nothing transpired in the city. Without the fumes of automobiles and factories, the Cairo smog lifted; the air became pure and the stars vivid. There was no city smell, no traffic roar.

While Cairo remained breathless, the trains were bringing the fellahin from the countryside. They crammed into boxcars and rode on tops of buses. Millions simply walked. We knew they were coming, and yet the streets of the city remained vacant.

But on the morning of the funeral they suddenly appeared. I stood on my balcony and saw five million—ten million?—Egyptians standing on the bank of the ancient river, facing Zamalek. For as far as I could see there was not a single space of unoccupied pavement. I couldn't even see the trees on the Corniche; they had become people-trees.

Finally the dignitaries were in place and the procession began its slow advance into the city. I had joined the other Americans on the roof. Of course I was remembering Kennedy's funeral, and the assembly of the high and mighty half-stepping toward Arlington. When the cortege reached the Kasr El Nil bridge, the crowd on the mainland suddenly burst through the police line and rushed for the body. We could see the soldiers trying to beat their way through the mob with nightsticks and rifle butts. The bridge itself began to tremble. The vibration was visible to us a mile away. Many of the diplomats broke ranks and retreated; one could imagine their panic in the middle of such a convulsion. The horse drawing the caisson skittered as the flag was torn from the coffin and immediately shredded. Somehow the cortege crossed the bridge. It moved with awful force as the policemen beat a path through the mass.

I thought again about the mischief that great men cause. Who could know how many people died to make the new world Nasser foresaw for his country and the Arab nations? He had stirred up war and revolution across half of Africa and the Levant. He had freed his people from the corruption of royalty and colonialism. But he had oppressed them as well and squandered their meager resources on foreign adventures. The power of his will had been like the procession that now shoved his corpse through the grieving millions. How many were yet to die in his path? And yet this was a man his own people celebrated as their national savior.

Why do people struggle? I recognized how naive my question was, but as I watched the calamity below, and sensed the tragedies that must follow, I felt bewildered by the object of so much passion and death. What Nasser represented to the Egyptian people was a sense of their own worth in the world, a feeling of equality with the colonial powers that had oppressed them for so many centuries. I understood their resentments. I felt in smaller ways the same urgent desire for redress. I thought how much of my life existed in this tension of being between stops, between the person I was and the person I was struggling to be, although the distance I would have to travel was incomparably less than that of my students. I had grown up in the new world and looked toward the East with a sense of inadequacy and resentment and shame. Now I saw in the torment before me the measure of those same feelings in the Egyptian people. They were creating their own new world. The ultimate object of their resentments was the colossus of wealth and power that was my country. As I stood among the tanning, detached Americans on the roof, I felt a quick stab of despair. I imagined how we must look to the Egyptians below. How far they must feel from closing the distance between themselves and us. Equality, justice, freedom, pride—what a bloody struggle lay ahead.

12 / WHITE MAN

In 1971 I was twenty-four years old, married, back in America, and looking for work. At that time in Texas there was only one publication where a liberal young writer could make a name for himself: the *Texas Observer,* a little muckraking biweekly tabloid in Austin published by Ronnie Dugger and edited then by Kaye Northcott and Molly Ivins. In the past it had been home to Willie Morris, Billy Lee Brammer, Robert Sherrill, and occasionally to J. Frank Dobie and Robert Coles. With the thought that it could be home to me as well, I had driven down to Austin one scorching August afternoon and been politely turned away. On the way home I was gasping for breath. What had I expected? How were they to know I could write, when all I had to offer was my own presumption? Suddenly my vision suffered a break—the road split apart and the landscape tilted. I hit the brakes and skidded wildly onto the shoulder. It was fear breaking through. For forty minutes I sat on the side of the highway with the hundred-degree breeze stirring idly through my windows as the traffic boomed past. What kind of life awaited me? My prospects looked as bleak as that vast and featureless Texas prairie, an empty table under a hard sky filled with circling buzzards. If I couldn't be a writer, what then?

I didn't know anybody my age with the least interest in business. When recruiters came to campus they sat at empty tables thumbing through their own brochures. Everyone I knew regarded business as evil. Our brief against business began with Exhibit One, the

206 / IN THE NEW WORLD

Vietnam War, which like all our wars had the economy soaring. Corporations were growing fat off defense contracts, which were so profitable and such boondoggles you wondered how capitalism survived peacetime. Business had an interest in keeping the war going, and the young, who would have to fight, had an interest in bringing the war to a stop. We were natural antagonists.

We were just catching on to the price we had to pay personally and as a nation for other people's profits. Lakes and streams had turned into sewers; the city air was horribly visible; cancer rates were rising and so were birth defects; wildlife was in real jeopardy; the seashore was coated with tar from oil spills; roadsides were littered with nonrefundable bottles and empty sacks of franchise food; tomatoes tasted like cardboard and pizzas were covered with plastic cheese; freeways burst through neighborhoods like flash floods; nattering jingles lodged in our minds—*Brush-a brush-a brush-a! With the new Ipana! See the USA, in your Chevrolet*—so that we were constantly advertising products to ourselves. We lived in a world of greedy commerce that was killing us, deforming us, ruining nature, and making us vain, insecure, and slightly insane.

And was it surprising that the results of the American business culture, the products themselves, were shoddy and often dangerous? When Ralph Nader published his exposé of the Chevrolet Corvair in 1965, *Unsafe at Any Speed: The Designed-in Dangers of the American Automobile,* he became a campus hero and the bane of the business world. General Motors hired private detectives to discredit Nader, and prostitutes to lure him into compromise, but he proved almost pathologically viceless, the first saint of the consumer movement. After Nader the reputation of American products plummeted. If you wanted a good car you bought a Volvo or a Volkswagen. Stereos? Televisions? Buy Japanese. Shoes? Leather goods? Go Italian. The only reliable American products were armaments and blue jeans.

All of these movements—the peace movement, environmentalism, consumerism—were separate fronts of an antibusiness crusade, which was itself a part of the larger generational war. On the one side stood our parents, with money in their pockets, advertising the blessings of capitalism in the forms of split-level houses in the suburbs and two-car garages and a place in the country; and on the other side were their children, the sophisticated consumers. Who were nonetheless bemoaning the consequences of affluence, which were war, materialism, and the corruption not only of the human spirit but of the planet as well.

We had seized the high ground, all right, but where did that leave us now that we were ready to be somebody? Mere money wouldn't do. We had to service our ideals. We had to find personal fulfillment. Of course, by setting such high standards for ourselves we were rebuking our parents. We were saying that we would not allow ourselves to turn out like them—crass and thwarted. Being rich wasn't the same as being fulfilled. The secret we didn't allow ourselves to admit was that we expected to have everything— idealism, fulfillment, and money too. The money was stipulated. We assumed that the prodigious productive energy of our parents had already projected the economy toward ever greater wealth and that therefore we could turn away from the task of stoking the engine of that economy, which was business, and go on to more important and creative lives.

That summer Roberta and I set out for North Carolina in a three-hundred-dollar six-cylinder Ford van. Hemingway had authorized the use of newspapers as the first step in a writing career, and North Carolina supported a surprising number of fine liberal papers, such as the *Greensboro Daily News, Raleigh News & Observer, Charlotte Observer,* and W. J. Cash's old paper, the *Charlotte News.* We stopped in New Orleans, where I left applications at the *Times-Picayune* (Faulkner started there) and the *Vieux Carré Courier,* then we went to Mobile to visit Roberta's family, and I saw the editor of the *Press-Register.* The disinterest that marked my passage through the newsrooms of the South was giving me a first-class case of midnight chills.

Certainly I was coming into the world at a difficult time. Never in history had so many college graduates hit the streets. The Baby Boom's enemy was itself; we were all arriving at the same conclusions, getting the same degrees, competing for the same jobs. And for the first time we—that is, we white men—were competing against women and minorities. It turned out that everyone wanted to be somebody, not just me. The problem was we all wanted to be the same person.

The highway from the Alabama Gulf Coast to the North Carolina Blue Ridge went through some of the least-developed farmland in the Western world. It was a separate, defeated country buried inside America. As we drove through Georgia and South Carolina we could still see traces of cotton terraces etched on the hillsides, and abandoned stone chimneys standing like totems of a lost civilization. I often thought, during the waning days of Vietnam, about the frequently heard statement that America had never lost a war. No one ever said that in the South. The Civil War was more than a century old, but the defeat endured. When Sherman's troops marched through Georgia—one of them was my father's maternal grandfather—they described the state as the breadbasket of the Confederacy; they wrote home about the fat meat in the smoke-houses and the bounty of grain and vegetables, which reminded them of Ohio. When they left, Georgia no longer reminded anyone of Ohio. The small plantation in my mother's family had been directly in Sherman's path, and the discovery that my father's kin had been a second lieutenant in the Illinois Cavalry very nearly disqualified him from being my mother's husband, in the view of her father. Her father's father had been with Lee, all the way to Appomattox.

Now, in my own time, the war still left its mark on the land. There was no longer an agrarian economy in the South; it had been replaced after the war by the sharecropping of cotton, a plant that seems to be designed by nature to destroy the soil and break the human spirit. When the cotton economy went bust, a giant migration evacuated the rural South. Seventy-five percent of Georgia reverted to forest, a condition that approximated colonial times, except now the trees were post oaks or unvariegated pine barrens controlled by giant paper corporations. The people who remained on the land, woodcutters and marginal farmers, lived an existence as mean and deprived as the lives of trolls.

The legacy of that war could be seen in the poverty, the ignorance, the despair of the South as it still was. But something else was happening as well. I thought about it as we crossed the Savannah River and noticed black people fishing out of motorboats and using rods and reels. It was the first time I'd ever seen Negroes in boats. Somehow during the two years I had been out of the country, the civil rights movement had taken another evolutionary step, off the bank and into the boat. I also saw my first black motorcyclist and, on a municipal course in Charlotte, my first black golfer. Each of these sightings was a revelation, not only about the increasing affluence and social mobility of black people but also about my own presumptions. I remember thinking, It's okay to play golf now.

I saw the changes and felt relieved—relieved of the guilt of privilege. I wanted America to become a land of freedom and equality, as it had been advertised for so long, but there was another side to these changes that I was just beginning to understand. The reason I couldn't find a job, I was told as I went from one newspaper to the next, was that I was white and male, and every major paper in the country was staffed by people who were exactly like me in those respects. The editors just shrugged when I came in. I was a year too late. Now they only wanted women or blacks or Hispanics.

It felt queer to be the victim of discrimination, while at the same time approving of it. Minorities deserved good jobs. Women should be allowed to compete fairly with men. It was right that they should be given preference, I told myself with increasing desperation as one door after another was closed to me. After I had spoken to the editor of the *Charlotte Observer* I was finally offered a tryout with an affiliated paper in South Carolina, the *Rock Hill Herald.* That afternoon I drove to Rock Hill and failed the typing test.

A friend of Roberta's, Frye Gaillard, who had grown up with her in Mobile and was now working at the *Observer,* told me about a defunct civil rights magazine in Nashville called the *Race Rela-*

tions Reporter, which had recently been brought back to life by a grant from the Edna McConnell Clark Foundation. Frye arranged an interview for me with the editor, Jim Leeson.

I expected to meet the stereotypical southern liberal, that hunched and wincing figure in a dirty seersucker suit. Leeson turned out to be a tall, slender bachelor with a facial resemblance to Montgomery Clift. His interview with me consisted mainly of a game of tennis, which he played in street shoes. I won. We went out to dinner the same evening with Steve Nickeson, the associate editor, a rawboned cowboy from Wyoming who seemed uncertain about why I was in town. It crossed my mind that I might be the victim of one of Frye's practical jokes. The next day, as I was getting ready to drive back to North Carolina, in a state of frustration and dread that is difficult to describe, Leeson told me to report to work in thirty days. He never did say what my salary would be.

One could, and I did, spend many hours puzzling out the complicated impulses that fit together in the person of Jim Leeson. Although he might correctly be described as a professional liberal, he was in other respects a tireless reactionary. For years he waged a one-man campaign against the use of seat belts; in his opinion, millions would die who might otherwise be thrown free of the wreckage. He opposed gun control on the premise that few people got killed who didn't need killing, but he opposed birth control for rather opposite reasons. He lived the life of a solitary gentleman farmer outside Franklin, Tennessee, employing convict labor, and he spent his free time listening to organ music and writing letters to the editor. He once ran for office—he aspired to be a squire, which is a county magistrate in Tennessee—but I always had the feeling that if he was elected he would empty the jails and declare a state of anarchy in the Big East Fork district of Williamson County. Apparently the voters felt the same way.

Leeson came to the office every day in a cheap black suit and a skinny tie—he always dressed like a Mormon missionary—and he expected his employees to maintain his standards of decorum. My first sin was being caught with my bare feet airing in the window on a sultry summer day, when a foundation man chanced to visit.

After that, I was never entirely in Leeson's favor. He was a solitary man who seemed to prefer grudges to friends. At the same time, his cynicism served him well in a time of radical change. Once a Puerto Rican militant came into the office demanding reparations for past injustice. Leeson heard him out politely, and then said, "Look, sport, we don't have money for handouts." That became a story everyone loved to tell about Leeson; no one had ever imagined calling a Puerto Rican militant "sport."

The office of the Race Relations Information Center, which Leeson oversaw, was a two-story Victorian house across the street from the campus of Vanderbilt University. For nearly two decades the center, which was first known as the Southern Education Reporting Service, had been recording and investigating the civil rights movement in America. Often it had provided the only reliable, dispassionate reporting available on the knotted problems of school desegregation, and later on such equally complicated matters as Indian water rights and bilingual education.

In many respects Leeson's contrariness was exactly the corrective a white liberal needed when foraying into the complicated and schismatic world of American race relations during the early seventies. The movement had spawned many movements. One no longer knew whether to speak of Negroes or blacks or Afro-Americans, or Chicanos or Hispanics, or Indians or Native Americans. There were always new constituencies. Now the problem of desegregation was not an absolute moral choice between right and wrong, it was a million agonizing compromises between what was practicable, or constitutional, or politically feasible. Federal courts were overwhelmed with class-action suits for greater desegregation in the schools, increased representation of minorities in jobs and political offices, protection of migrant farmworkers in the Sunbelt and immigrant factory workers in the sweatshops of the big northern cities. The political solutions involved busing and quotas and huge new bureaucracies and discrimination in a new form—that is, official, government-enforced discrimination against the white male majority. The old alliances, such as blacks and Jews, were breaking apart, and unexpected new ones, such as blacks and Wallacites, were being formed. American society was in metamorphosis; it would no longer be only the land of the permanent black underclass or the immobilized Hispanic peon; it would be—something else. Now the creature itself, whatever it was, was beginning to emerge.

Reporting on this process was an ideal education for a provincial young man whose politics and sympathies had been formed largely secondhand. It was an education in struggle and resistance, accommodation and change. Naturally I was full of prejudice, especially toward the white southern man—myself, in other words.

Nashville was the first place I'd ever lived that was obviously pretty, but like many pretty things it was also vain and remote and a bit shallow. The Nashville I am speaking of is Old Nashville, a city of fine old families, as stiff a bunch of honkies as a person would ever hope to encounter. This Nashville lived in the mansions of Belle Meade and went to the polo matches and the steeplechases and carried on endless conversations about china patterns and sports cars. They were polished, attractive people in most respects, and quite literate, although there was something dismal even about that. "Oh, Ginsberg," you might hear at a party, or "Oh, Styron." The sophistication, the lassitude, the world-weariness, gave them European airs. "What do you do?" I asked a socially prominent couple at a small dinner party. "We take a lot of walks," said the wife, and her husband added, "We're trying to cut down on the meat we eat."

There was another Nashville, the Nashville of country music and "The Grand Ole Opry." It had been in the background all of my life, especially on those long road trips of my childhood, when my father was pushing on to the next motel and Mother would fool with the radio, trying to find a clear-channel station in the staticky night, and then WSM in Nashville would come yodeling through. It was primitive and tacky, but Mother left it on. Perhaps she was remembering her own father, who sold musical instruments for the Gibson company in the Southeast, picking out the same songs on his ukulele. My father's father played the fiddle at the square dances in Kansas. For them the country tunes of Grandpa Jones and Tennessee Ernie Ford, the how*dee*s of Minnie Pearl, the white gospel songs and the brokenhearted-lover blues of Ernest Tubbs and Kitty Wells, were sounds of their childhoods, sounds they had gladly left behind in the big-band era of their adolescence. At home they listened to the comfortable, inoffensive sounds of their middle age, to Perry Como and Liberace and the light classics of Arthur Fiedler—the music my generation would laugh at. But there was power in those country songs, and when the headlights were poking through the night, and Mother and Daddy sat in the front seat with their pensive faces glowing from the instrument lights, I would lie in the back with my sleeping sisters and listen to those loOoOoOonesome blues.

In Nashville the stars of the Opry lived off in mansions of their own. Minnie Pearl played tennis with the governor. They contributed abundantly to the presidential campaigns of George Wallace and Richard Nixon; in fact, Nixon's favorite song, he claimed, was Merle Haggard's "Okie From Muskogee" ("We don't smoke marijuana in Muskogee / We don't take our trips on LSD / We don't burn our draft cards down on Main Street / We like livin' right and bein' free"). Country music had always been mixed up with the right-wing preachers and the golden-voiced fascists who jumped out of the radio in the dark, the voices that told us America was going to hell, but we could bring it back if only we would send the hippies to the barbershop and bomb the commies and stop the advance of the nigra. Now it had become the voice of Nixon's Silent Majority, and I recognized it—it was the same reactionary urge I had grown up with in Dallas. It was the politics of the new world, set to music.

When I finally went to see the Opry, a full year after moving to Nashville, I did so in the spirit of an anthropologist visiting some exotic white tribe. The Opry was still housed in Ryman Auditorium, an old gospel tabernacle built by a reformed riverboat operator named Tom Ryman, which is how it came to be called "the Mother Church of Country Music." Down on the stage dozens of people who seemed to have nothing to do with the show were milling about. Overhead were billboards for chewing tobacco and shaving cream. There was a feeling when you first entered the small, steeply banked auditorium that was like the feeling of coming into a minor-league ballpark and beholding the manicured grass and crisp chalk lines, and the advertisements along the outfield fence. It was a feeling that everything was just about right, that something real could happen here. A woman was singing about going home to Kentucky, and when she finished, a man on the other side of the stage signaled for us to applaud. Then Hank Snow came on the stage, a little man in a spangled suit, and the place exploded in the flashes of Instamatics; it was like heat lightning over the deep rumble of Hank Snow's voice.

I did not suddenly fall in love with country music, but I could sense that something was happening in America that country music was expressing. It was a phenomenon, a white awakening. It was not just the music of the truck stops and the oil fields; it was coming out of the suburbs and the office towers of the new world. If you listened to the lyrics you could hear the anxiety of an uprooted people in the midst of an extraordinary social upheaval. They were the songs of a people who lived in the cities now but who longed for the old certainties of country life, whose families were shaken by the loss of values and the changing sex roles— people who were liberated by the automobile and the Pill and a steady paycheck, but who felt alone and confused. After I began to listen to the words, I often came down to the Opry, sometimes just to stand outside the windows in the alley, absorbing the sentiments and feeling a racial urge to be a part of my own kind.

But in 1974 the Ryman was closed down as a fire hazard, and the Opry moved into an amusement park. On opening night Richard Nixon came to play "God Bless America" on the piano, and whatever bridge it was that had been opened between me and country music closed again.

On my second day at work a Baptist preacher with a broad-brimmed Amish hat, black clothes, and work boots came into my office and introduced himself. "My name is Will Campbell," he said, "and I wonder if you would take a moment to cut my hair." When he took off his hat I realized that wouldn't be much of a task. He had a sort of friar's fringe that ran behind his ears, and I obliged him with a pair of stationery scissors.

Will was a legend in the civil rights movement, although not a hero—he was too original for that. He had come out of the Mississippi Delta, the son of a poor cotton farmer, and had gone to war in the Pacific, then to Yale Divinity School, then home to the South to preach. He was the only white man to join Martin Luther King in forming the Southern Christian Leadership Conference. He had walked through the mobs in Little Rock in 1957 to escort black children to Central High. And yet he was known now mainly as the preacher who ministered to the Ku Klux Klan.

Will's motto was "We are all bastards but God loves us anyway." It was an infuriating formula because he proposed that blacks and whites were truly equal, which meant that they were equally capable of evil. Liberals tried to idolize Will, but they wound up choking on him. He described himself as a racist and refused to condemn the Klan; instead he went to their homes and meeting rooms and spoke to them about love. In 1966 he was one of several southern churchmen to visit James Meredith after he had been shot during his March on Mississippi, but afterward, Will was the only preacher who went to see the man who shot him. In Will's equation, Meredith and his assailant were equally deserving; they were both bastards but God loved them anyway.

He had been kicked out of the Student Non-Violent Coordinating Committee, along with all the other whites, by Stokeley Carmichael and Rap Brown, when the movement turned to Black Power. "There came a time when they said, 'Look, Will, we think we have our own people pretty well under control now, and maybe you should go home and work with your own people.' " Will thought about who those people were. "My people are Kluxers and crackers and rednecks. They'd kill me," he protested, but he knew that Carmichael and Brown were right. Someone needed to minister to Will's people; the movement would never advance until white people had been made ready to accept the changes.

I romanticized Will without really hearing him. His message was that I would have to accept myself as a white Southern man, but I was never more ashamed of myself in that respect. Everywhere I went I saw the damage caused to minorities by white culture. Also, Will was addressing me as a person, and I wasn't one yet. Who I was now was the Witness. This is the persona of the reporter—objective, disinterested, colorless, a neutral observer—a role I was eager to play, this ready-made character who was no one, but who had rights to go anywhere, ask anything. For a young man on the run from himself, it is a beguiling sanctuary.

I learned that in personal respects, the Witness is invisible. He may have opinions, but he does not express them, or else he disguises them so that they blend with the color of the times. People accept him as a classless, raceless, genderless convention, which gives him the authority to walk through the burning slums or to ascend the whispering marbled towers of the people in charge. He is a receptacle for other people's stories, a kind of mailbox where others deposit their thoughts. He is welcomed by Indian chiefs in the Painted Desert and movie stars in Beverly Hills and the condemned on Death Row. It requires an adjustment in the Witness's self-esteem when he realizes that people are not speaking to him but past him, to the public he is presumed to represent. He can rightfully be seen as a godsend or an avenging angel or a prurient snoop, but in any case he is understood as a force and not as a personality. In time the Witness may demand his own identity, in which case he becomes like any other citizen with prejudices and allegiances. He may even join a political party or campaign for a cause, but then he has become visible and unsuitable for his job. He will suffer a dizzying loss of access and importance. But if he stays in the profession, the Witness comes to value his neutrality above any competing quality. He scours his identity until he is free of reaction, with the exception of a cellular response to excitement and change. At this stage of refinement he is nearly divine, he is a saint, but he is invisible even to himself. His only approaches to his lost humanity are alcohol and sarcasm.

Had I understood these dangers as clearly then as I do now, I would still have chosen journalism as a profession, if only for the sensation of seeing life as others live it and the privilege of witnessing America and carrying to the public that quickly forgotten commodity, the news.

The civil rights revolution of the sixties was over by the time I began my report on it. The major marches had been marched, the great speeches spoken, the martyrs killed, the legislation enacted. Now there was another period, more subtle than before, a time of lawyers and bureaucrats. The movement had left the streets and gone indoors, into the white man's world, the boardrooms and courthouses and chambers of power, and it was here, of course, where I felt more at home. I knew who these people were in a way that, blinded by sympathy and remorse, I could never really know the cynical black kids in Bedford-Stuyvesant or the hungry Navajo child in a desert hogan. I had seen enough of America to discover the consequences of the white man's culture. I thought then that whiteness was evil, almost helplessly so; at least that's how I imagined it.

And yet in these same boardrooms and courthouses and chambers of power I was seeing an accommodation that was unique in a world where races and tribes and sects were everywhere struggling for power and everywhere being crushed by the pitiless majorities. What was constant in the world was revolt and repression, a bloody inertia. Only America was changing. There was resistance, but there was not slaughter, as well there might have been, given how complete was the control of this country by white men. The civil rights revolution was to a large extent a battle for the conscience of these men—for *my* conscience—and it was successful because the white majority had the will to change.

I saw this in Mississippi, in a redneck pulpwood cutter who set aside his native prejudices to form a labor union of woodcutters, both black and white. I saw it in a North Carolina Klansman who ran for the school board with black support. These were men who were struggling against everything they had been brought up to believe, struggling, really, against themselves. I saw it also in the more remote but consequential actions of white politicians and judges and businessmen, whom I gave little enough credit at the time, but who were working out the same moral questions as I was. Our minds were the stage upon which this drama had to be played, because in order for minorities to acquire power, white men had to release it.

Usually these victories of conscience were small and unspoken. Perhaps they were only expressed in the voting booth, where minorities were beginning to be elected with widespread white support; or when the governor of Florida started his own program of affirmative action; or when my father decided at last to hire a black teller in the bank; or even in the moment when a man in Waycross, Georgia, or Boston's Southie determined not to say "nigger" anymore. This was all, as I say, accommodation: incremental decisions made slowly, reluctantly, with much backsliding and more than a little hypocrisy.

In total, however, it was no less than a revolution. I didn't see it as such then; I believed America was such a repressive society that the changes I was seeing were not just inadequate, they were counterrevolutionary. We spoke then about the civil rights movement being "co-opted," just as the antiwar movement had been, and women's liberation, and the consumer movement, and the environmental movement, and gay rights, and so on. When changes were institutionalized and made a part of the formal machinery of government, they were taken out of the hands of the people in the streets. Every victory seemed to be, in some obscure fashion, a setback. There was a scrambling for new issues; the movement would not be defeated by success.

All the world was criticizing America for its repression, and yet nowhere else was there even a beginning of a plan for racial justice. Scarcely anyone recognized what was really happening in America, which was a profound, exhaustive, remarkably peaceful revolution—an extension of our first revolution two hundred years before.

I was also learning about black people, not only as a reporter but as a coworker and a friend. The first black reporter Leeson hired with his new grant money was a slight and dapper young man from the *Chicago Daily Defender* named Anthony Griggs. We had nothing in common. I liked Ray Charles and Tony liked Bach. I was reading Richard Wright and Tony was a fanatic about Vladimir Nabokov, to the point that he had adopted Nabokov's hobby, butterfly collecting.

There was between us, and between our cultures, a yearning for each other. It was partly curiosity and partly the romance of ancient enemies. I wanted to be blacker and Tony wanted to be whiter. We each had discovered in the other's culture some completion of ourself, an answer to a need that our own culture hadn't supplied.

The second black reporter Leeson hired was a dauntingly smart and, I thought, unfriendly woman who worked in her office with her door closed and her desk surrounded with mirrors. In an editorial meeting she proposed to write a story about herself, a black woman coming back to the South. I thought the idea was patronizing and phony; after all, she'd come back to the South because she had gotten a job, not because of some emotional gravitation. Also, Leeson's primary rule of writing was to eliminate the first person. If we had an opinion, we learned to quote a "seasoned observer" or an "interested bystander." To my astonishment, Leeson said he thought her story was a fine idea.

"Well, I don't," I said blithely, and said why. I quoted Leeson's own rules to him. What about objectivity? detachment? The reader is not supposed to know who we are; we should be race-neutral. It seemed to me that if we started bending the rules, our readers would distrust us. We would become partisans. Hadn't he said those very things? Was he bending the rules because the other reporter was black? Leeson looked at me with narrowed eyes. He did not like to be challenged.

I look back at myself then with a mixture of admiration and impatience. I can see how doctrinaire I was being, how punctilious and inflexible. I had already gotten a reputation as a Young Turk in the office, and I compounded that impression by writing a long memo to everyone on the editorial staff proposing a number of sensible changes in the format of the magazine. Leeson called me into his office. The memo was on his desk. "I want you to start looking for another job," he told me.

I felt like an egg that had just been cracked open. Everything inside was falling.

"But why?"

"I just don't think you can get along with black people."

That was an accusation I would never forgive, but also never stop wondering about, and worrying that it was true.

I was unemployed again. Fired. At first it seemed that everything had been taken away from me, and I would never recover. I would live in a permanent state of semidisgrace. And yet the truth was that I was immeasurably better off than I had been when I set off on the road to be somebody. Now, at least, I knew what I was; that couldn't be taken away from me. I was a writer, goddammit.

13 / THE NIXON AGE

Of course, the greatest mystery of our era was Richard Nixon. He was the most enduring political figure of my lifetime and, except for John Kennedy, the most precocious. Nixon had none of the qualities we associate with modern leaders. He was square, not cool; he was empty of charisma; he was intensely shy—"an introvert in an extrovert's profession," as he said of himself—and so stiff that when Sammy Davis, Jr., hugged him at the Republican convention in 1972 it was one of the most surprising gestures I have ever seen. No one had ever touched Nixon before; he posted an electric fence between himself and everyone else, including his wife. From his earliest entry into politics, Nixon was hated intensely, and even his supporters had to forgive his awkward manner. Despite defeats that would have ended most political careers he went on to become president and to receive the greatest mandate of his time. Few people loved Nixon, as they had loved Eisenhower and Kennedy, and yet Nixon was popular in a way these men had never been. He was a force that was not appealing but irresistible nonetheless. He was a democratic urge, and more than any of his many opponents he represented the fears and hopes and aspirations of his age.

When Nixon arrived in Congress in 1946, on a wave of savage redbaiting that would set the tone of domestic and international politics for the next quarter century, he was already a controversial figure. A psychiatrist who moved to Southern California the same year Nixon was elected observed then the mixed reactions that

Nixon evoked. "I was struck," wrote Leo Rangell, "with a feeling of something awesome and uncanny, even, if you will believe it now, ominous and frightening, in the public's willing acceptance of the style and tone of his words; the uncritical and compliant acceptance of the artificiality, the obvious opportunism, the insincerity, and the questionable credibility which came across in his every utterance. Nixon at once polarized people into those who felt this way about him and those who did not." The emotional rift that Nixon opened in California's Twelfth District in the first postwar election would eventually become the fault line of American politics. Four years later it split the state of California, with Nixon's election to the Senate over Helen Gahagan Douglas. Two years after that, Nixon was on the winning ticket with Eisenhower, and the entire country began to arrange itself on one side or the other, either pro-Nixon or con.

My parents didn't love Nixon, but he came to represent them in ways they couldn't control. They feared and hated Communism, and here was Congressman Nixon, the foremost anti-Communist in the country. They loved Eisenhower, their hero, and here was Vice President Nixon, the Eisenhower loyalist and chief defender, although Ike himself treated Nixon like an unwanted pet. They were proud of their country, and here was Nixon the goodwill ambassador being stoned in Caracas or standing up to Khrushchev in the kitchen debate. Nixon made claims on their emotions without their consent. He began to personify certain attitudes they endorsed. Their vision of America had become, in subtle ways, Nixon's America.

Nixon appealed to another constituency of emotions that were not so easy to admire or understand. He never cared to play the role of the rustic, he was always yearning for dignity and status, and yet when he had first come to Washington the *Post* had him spotted as "the greenest Congressman in town." His friend and congressional classmate John Kennedy summed him up abruptly: "No class." That was an insult that implicitly included the millions of Americans who were, like my parents, earnest strivers, self-made people, who like Nixon had seen their own parents fail and who knew more of hardship than of ease. Kennedy had meant no class in the sense of stylelessness and gracelessness, but it was true that Nixon, and people like Nixon, were classless in the economic sense as well. They were "upwardly mobile." They had not grown up in a world of crystal and careful manners; many of them were just now learning which fork to use at dinner. And yet people who had lived near the bottom of society, whose childhood world had been a squalid city block or a godforsaken stretch of farmland, were now buying fancy homes and sending their children to private schools. Even in Dallas there were many fortunes larger than that of the Kennedys, but Dallas had the curse of new money—that is, the awkwardness of learning how to spend it. The owners of those fortunes had more money than power, more ambition than position, more enthusiasm than taste. Hard work and money were their only resources. In the battle of merit versus privilege they had seen the advantages of old wealth, with its connections and credentials and privilege. From these millions of no-class Americans, Nixon drew upon deep reservoirs of resentment. Nixon was their angry representative, their score settler, "a kind of dragon slayer," as he later declared himself.

He began by whipping Alger Hiss. Although Hiss had had his own tortured beginnings in Baltimore (his father committed suicide when Alger was three), by the time he appeared before the House Un-American Activities Committee in 1948 he was an advertisement for the Eastern Establishment. Unlike Congressman Nixon, Hiss was witty, handsome, beautifully dressed. He was a product of excellent schools, Johns Hopkins and Harvard Law. He had been a secretary for Oliver Wendell Holmes, Jr., and had gone on to practice in prestigious firms in Boston and New York, before drifting into government—and the Communist party. He had risen through the State Department like a bubble toward the surface. He had stood at Roosevelt's shoulder at the Yalta Conference and had helped to found the United Nations. He was a protégé of Dean Acheson and John Foster Dulles, the rulers of the Establishment. He was also a Soviet spy, according to his former friend and party comrade Whittaker Chambers, who would be-

come Richard Nixon's chief witness in the case against Alger Hiss.
Nixon might have gone to Harvard like Hiss did. Harvard had
awarded Nixon an academic prize in high school, but he couldn't
afford to go there. He went to his hometown college in Whittier
instead, and after that, to law school at Duke University on a $250
tuition scholarship, earning extra money by working in the library.
The big firms in New York gave him the cold shoulder; Nixon, the
star student, couldn't even get a job at the FBI. He went back to
Whittier and became a divorce lawyer. Then he went to war, where
Alger Hiss was too important to go.

Until this point my father's life parallels Nixon's almost exactly—the local college, the meager law school scholarship, the
years of deprivation and struggle and rejection, and at last the war.
It's no wonder that men like my father, who had started with so
little, would look at Hiss with the same cool loathing that Nixon
did. Hiss seemed to have everything they wanted, and what he had
was, in some unsaid way, *really theirs.* Hiss, they thought, had not
earned his easy access to money and power by hard work, nor had
he fought to defend the system that gave it to him. No. He had
been handed everything on the silver platter of class. That's what
Nixon hated about Alger Hiss. As Robert Stripling, HUAC's chief
investigator, later said, "Nixon had set his hat for Hiss. It was a
personal thing. He was no more concerned whether Hiss was [a
Communist] than a billy goat!"

Nixon nailed Hiss, but even after Hiss was convicted of perjury
many members of the Eastern Establishment continued to defend
him and deny his guilt. Thus the Establishment protected itself.
It was Nixon who would not leave well enough alone—Nixon and
the resentful, avenging no-class Americans that he represented.
They believed instinctively that Hiss was in league with the Communists, and the ringing denials of Hiss's guilt from the polished
chambers of power gave shape to the conspiracy. "No feature of
the Hiss case is more obvious or more troubling as history," Whittaker Chambers wrote later, "than the jagged fissure, which it did
not so much open as reveal, between the plain men and women of
the nation, and those who affected to act, think and speak for

them. It was not invariably, but in general, the 'best people' who were for Alger Hiss and who were prepared to go to almost any length to protect and defend him."

The Hiss case brought Nixon attention—it even got him on the ticket with Eisenhower—but it also made him the permanent enemy of the liberal Eastern Establishment. The hatred directed at Nixon after that would always have an element of classism—the wealthy, the privileged, the intellectuals on one side, and Nixon on the other, with the Forgotten Americans, the Silent Majority.

Nixon knew where the lines were drawn. When his personal political fund was uncovered in the 1952 campaign (SECRET RICH MEN'S TRUST FUND KEEPS NIXON IN STYLE FAR BEYOND HIS SALARY, said the *New York Post*) and Eisenhower was preparing to dump him from the ticket, Nixon defended himself before what was then the largest television audience ever. "What I am going to do—and incidentally this is unprecedented in the history of American politics—I am going at this time to give this television and radio audience a complete financial history, everything I have earned, everything I have spent, everything I owe," said Nixon, and out it came, the failed family grocery store, the inconsequential war record ("I guess I'm entitled to a couple of battle stars"), his wife's job as a stenographer, their 1950 Oldsmobile, their modest inheritances, their mortgages, a loan of $4,500 from the Riggs Bank in Washington, another of $3,500 from his parents, no stocks, no bonds, no interest in any business. "I should say this, that Pat doesn't have a mink coat, but she does have a respectable Republican cloth coat." And of course, the dog, perhaps the most famous campaign donation in history, "black and white, spotted, and our little girl, Tricia, the six-year-old, named it Checkers."

In describing himself, Nixon might have been describing my parents, and millions of other Americans who had worked hard but were still on the outside, who did not—"like Governor Stevenson"—inherit fortunes, who had ambitions but no advantages. The speech made Nixon into a national figure, almost on a par with Eisenhower himself. The unofficial count of letters and telegrams sent to Nixon, Eisenhower, local television stations, and party offices was more than two million, containing three million signatures. Republican headquarters in Washington alone received three hundred thousand letters and telegrams, and petitions signed by a million people. Nixon had discovered an electorate no one had known was there.

In some subconscious way the attacks on Nixon after that—for instance, the editorial derision directed at the speech, Stevenson's erudite loathing, Eisenhower's obvious snubs, the Herblock cartoons—would always reflect upon those same people who had spontaneously identified themselves with Nixon. They had not chosen Nixon to lead them, but they had seen themselves in Nixon's place, and they believed that what happened to Nixon would have happened to them, because of who they were. In their opinion Nixon was under attack not because he was unscrupulous but because he was an outsider, a usurper, the avenger of the new world.

Until the Checkers speech my father had no real idea who Nixon was. Of course he had heard of Eisenhower's puzzling selection of the thirty-nine-year-old freshman senator from California, and he had read Nixon's name in the newspapers during the Hiss trial, but he had never *seen* Nixon until this moment, when Nixon was fighting for his reputation and his career. It was an arresting moment in my father's life. Before the Checkers speech, Nixon was no one in my father's mind; after the speech, Daddy was a Nixon man.

The presidential election of 1960 divided America for the rest of the generation between Kennedy haters and Nixon haters. It was a contest of class more than of issues. For people like my parents, the Kennedys were the kind of people they dreamed of being, but the Nixons were the kind of people they were. They didn't hold it against Kennedy personally—at least my mother didn't; she voted for him—but just by being unapologetically himself Kennedy had made them feel less real. He was aboveground and they were somewhere below.

It was precisely those qualities in my parents that were like Nixon that caused me to gravitate to Kennedy. Perhaps a similar allure of wealth and glamour had drawn my father to Roosevelt in his own teenaged years. Money seemed to give Kennedy and Roosevelt extra vitality, despite their chronic poor health. Nixon, on the other hand, was fit but worn; the drudgery of life told on him. He longed for native charm. He wished to be a man of wealth and influence. He would have liked to be handsome. Instead, he was Nixon, with the ski-jump nose and the bulldog jowls, the mortgages that were both personally burdensome and yet embarrassingly modest, a man who could never get off a funny line, a Vice President whom even the President refused to take seriously. The gap between Kennedy's natural gifts and those of Nixon was like the distance between a god and a mortal. Kennedy was the existential goal, the American dream personified, a completely secure personality.

Whereas, Nixon! My own earliest feelings about Nixon were sensations of sympathy and discomfort, what one might experience when watching a performer flub his lines—or if not actually flub them, carry them off so poorly that one is too aware of the effort, the *acting*, the awkward reaching of the man for the role. There was always that feeling about Nixon, the amateur actor, of the leadenness, the pretense, the hopeless mortality of community theater.

"This is a man of many masks," said Adlai Stevenson in 1956. "Who can say they have seen his real face?" Stevenson was one of the first to speculate on the phenomenon of multiple Nixons. Even when I was a child, and Nixon was Vice President, I was hearing of the New Nixon. He was always undergoing renovation, always reforming himself. He was a sinner yearning for salvation, but not very earnestly. Herb Klein, one of Nixon's press secretaries, wrote that every campaign began with a New Nixon, who disappeared midway as the candidate began to feel mistreated by the press and gradually withdrew into himself. "We would start out with daily press conferences and end with none." The problem with the New Nixon was that he was invariably accused of being the Old Nixon in disguise. Herblock caricatured the New Nixon in 1960 as a smiling, well-shaven mask covering the familiar stubbled monster underneath.

And yet it was wrong to say, as Stevenson did, that we had never

seen the real Nixon. The reality of the man was dismayingly evident. What we saw in Nixon was a duality we didn't see in the more
polished performers on the public stage. In Eisenhower we saw the
contented hero playing out his presidency on the golf course. In
Kennedy we saw the American prince assuming his throne. In
Nixon we saw ourselves, neither hero nor prince, but a man of
extraordinary ordinariness who was straining to become something
more. His vices were as common as his talents. One would never
say about Nixon, as Lyndon Johnson's bitterest critics admitted of
him, that he was larger than life. He was exactly life-size. One saw
Nixon in a way one never saw Kennedy. Kennedy showed us what
he wanted us to see. Nixon showed us himself showing us what he
wanted us to see.

In the space between the man and the mask, Old Nixon and
New, lay the anxiety of the age. Most Americans, at least the silent
majority of them, were a part of the vast and expectant middle
class. They were not, or did not feel themselves to be, as stable or
as static an institution as the European bourgeoisie. They were
emergent. They were fluid. They were moving off the land and into
the suburbs, out of the old metropolises of the North and East and
into the booming cities of the new world. Ambition and uncertainty were their distinguishing features. Nixon, more than any
other politician, represented the aspiration of this grasping, highly
charged middle class to better itself. Old Nixon was the aggressive,
no-class newcomer on the make. He was fearful of falling off the
track, of sliding back to his origins. He was resentful of those ahead
of him in line, those who already had it made. Old Nixon dreamed
of the day when he would finally arrive, and then he could become
the gracious and secure New Nixon, able to relax, let down, cultivate friends, be generous to his enemies. But the lesson everyone
drew from Old Nixon is that he would never catch up to New
Nixon, and this knowledge was alienation itself, for if Nixon
couldn't close the distance, how could we?

The New Nixon mask might have had another face: John F.
Kennedy. It hit Nixon during the first debate, when Kennedy
opened with a surprise attack on Communism and the do-nothing

Eisenhower administration. Nixon was watching another Nixon, the ruthless campaigner, hitting the same notes as Nixon himself. "The things that Senator Kennedy has said, many of us can agree with. . . . I subscribe completely to the spirit that Senator Kennedy has expressed tonight . . . ." Mumble, mumble, what could he say? Kennedy was using all of Nixon's old themes, bashing Khrushchev, Castro, the Chinese; he was even lying in the clever way Nixon would lie: Kennedy accused the administration of coddling Castro (when he had already been briefed on the plans for the Cuban invasion); he spoke of a missile gap (when none existed). Nixon was nearly speechless. He cast an occasional lovesick glance at the tan and handsome and wealthy and secure and sexy and charming politician who was destroying him. *That* was the Nixon that Nixon longed to be.

Richard Nixon had come into office as a peace candidate. Of course, in 1968, all the candidates were peace candidates in varying degrees, but only Nixon claimed to have a "secret plan" to end the war, which he wouldn't divulge until he was sitting in the White House. In his campaign speeches, Nixon would even pat his breast pocket when he alluded to the plan, as if it were right there. All through the campaign, Nixon's secret plan tantalized the country, and no doubt on that basis many people voted for him instead of Humphrey, who was never able to escape his image as the happy warrior. I didn't vote for either man. The first ballot I ever cast for president was one of thirty thousand given that year to the candidate of the Peace and Freedom party, Eldridge Cleaver, who fled into exile soon after the election.

My father saw Nixon as a great president; more than that, Nixon was *his* president. Nixon inspired in him a belligerent sense of well-being. My father rarely cursed, but after Nixon's election the expletive "by God!" appeared in his lexicon. We were going to *by God!* take care of the mess in Vietnam, and the *by God!* hippies who don't appreciate this country, and the *by God!* Eastern liberals who would sell us out to the first passing Communist. He agreed with Vice President Spiro Agnew's attacks on the "effete corps of impudent snobs" who controlled the television networks and the "nattering nabobs of negativism" who put America down. When Nixon called the campus protesters "bums," my father picked up the term and used it as his own, because in his opinion all the *by God!* bums should be shipped off to the nearest army post for a uniform and a haircut.

My father was not a vindictive man. But Nixon touched a nerve no other politician had reached in him, and his response was a prideful, defensive reflex. He resonated to the angry vibrations of the Nixon administration, which shook the media, the high-class liberals, and the Ivy League academics of the Eastern Establishment—"the men," Henry Kissinger said, whom Nixon "revered and despised, whose approbation he both cherished and scorned." Kissinger might have described my father's feelings similarly. Like Nixon, my father saw the country divided between "us" and "them." *We* were the hard workers, the hard-liners, the patriots, the deserving middle class, the good white people of Middle America; *they* were the people of privilege, who had grown soft and passive, the eggheads who preached surrender, the upstart Negroes, the craven, pampered young, the noisy minority. Us-versus-Them, Nixon's line of fracture, divided generations, regions, races, classes, and families. My father was one of us and I was one of them.

I am trying to account for my own hatred of Nixon, which was as intense as I have ever felt for a public man. I had thought I hated him because of his politics. And yet Nixon's politics were as liberal as mine. Despite his rhetoric, his record is that of the most liberal president of the postwar era. Instead of dismantling the Great Society, he expanded it; indeed, the only Johnson program he killed was a Job Corps summer camp. When he came into office 45 percent of the federal budget was being spent on defense and 32 percent for "human resources." By fiscal 1973 those figures were reversed. Nixon increased Social Security benefits by 51 percent. He raised spending for the arts by 500 percent. He eliminated taxes for low-income families and raised the minimum wage. He quintupled the enrollment in the jobs program. He created the Environmental Protection Agency. He brought civil rights to the North. He created the "Philadelphia Plan," which required minority business participation in federal construction contracts. He initiated a parks program and a mass transit funding authority. He expanded school lunch programs, and health and safety regulations; he extended unemployment benefits and vastly increased the food stamp program. Nixon may have been prodded by a Democratic Congress, but it was the liberals who killed his Family Assistance Plan, which would have provided grants for the indigent and the working poor, as well as money for job training and day care. Nixon's own platform in 1972 included a "full employment" budget, a national health plan, and federal revenue sharing.

Revenue sharing was the most radical of Nixon's social reforms, not only because it brought aid to the cities but also because it broke the power of local establishments. Suddenly federal grants were in the hands of minorities, and it was revenue sharing, almost as much as the vote, that put blacks and Hispanics and Indians on local panels and commissions and in the community agencies where leadership begins. The slogan of the Left—my own slogan at the time—was "Power to the people," and more than any other measure revenue sharing brought real power to people who were disenfranchised by race or circumstance. Always one to take more credit than he deserved, Nixon called his plan "no less than the New American Revolution."

In every respect these were programs that conservatives historically opposed and liberals historically supported. Nixon considered himself a moderate conservative, and yet he overthrew the first principle of conservatism, a limited government, by offering the nation's first $200 billion budget. As for the principle of free trade, Nixon responded with wage-price controls and a 10 percent tariff on imports. Much of what conservatives hate most about the liberal record is on the Nixon side of the ledger: income transfer payments to the poor, for instance, minority hiring quotas, indexing of Social Security benefits to inflation, closing the gold window. It was

Nixon, the legendary anti-Communist, who opened China, who brought detente with the Russians and negotiated the first disarmament treaty. Once again there seemed to be two Nixons, a conservative Old one and a liberal New one, thrashing out between themselves the ideology of the age.

In each of the big triumphs of Nixon's presidency, such as his trip to China, there was an automatic denial of its meaning. This denial took two forms. One was "he didn't want to do it, but he had to." In the many instances of social reform, it was easy to think that Nixon was pandering to a liberal majority, although in fact no such majority existed. The other form of denial was "only Nixon could have gotten away with it." This was a way of saying that only a man with Nixon's reputation as a conservative could, for instance, deal with the Soviets in a responsible manner; it was at the same time a way of excusing Johnson and Kennedy for not doing what Nixon did. Only Nixon could go to China. Only Nixon could negotiate arms control. Only Nixon could end the war.

It was the war, finally, that made me hate Nixon. Like everyone in the country, I was waiting to hear what his secret plan was. After he got into the White House we expected some dramatic announcement. Months dragged on, the war continued, and Nixon did nothing. We drew the obvious conclusion: Nixon had lied.

But Nixon did have a secret plan, and it's interesting to discover how much Nixon himself subscribed to the "only Nixon" myth. H. R. Haldeman, Nixon's chief of staff, relates how Nixon revealed his scheme to him as they were walking on a foggy beach during the 1968 campaign. "I'm the only man in the country who can do it," Nixon said. "I call it the Madman Theory, Bob. I want the North Vietnamese to believe I've reached the point where I might do *anything* to stop the war. We'll just slip the word to them that, 'for God's sake, you know Nixon is obsessed about Communism. We can't restrain him when he's angry—and he has his hand on the nuclear button'—and Ho Chi Minh himself will be in Paris in two days begging for peace."

Nixon's secret plan was inspired by Eisenhower, who also came into office facing a stalemated war. Ike got word to the Chinese that he would use nuclear weapons unless a truce was signed immediately. Within weeks the Korean War was over. The North Vietnamese, however, lived in a world with a more complicated nuclear balance of power, and they recognized the Madman Theory as a bluff. Nixon, like Johnson and Kennedy before him, was caught in the quagmire.

Vietnam became Mr. Nixon's War on November 3, 1969, when he finally went on television to outline his plans to end the war. I assumed, and prayed, that the President was going to propose a series of troop reductions as a prelude to total withdrawal. Instead he asked "the great silent majority" of Americans to support the war until the North Vietnamese could be made to negotiate or the South Vietnamese could learn to defend themselves. "I pledged in my campaign for the presidency to end the war in a way that we could win the peace," Nixon said.

"The more support I can have from the American people, the sooner that pledge can be redeemed; for the more divided we are at home, the less likely the enemy is to negotiate at Paris.

"Let us be united for peace. Let us also be united against defeat. Because let us understand: North Vietnam cannot defeat or humiliate the United States. Only Americans can do that."

Nixon would boast that the Silent Majority speech changed the course of history. Once again he had found his vast constituency. He had done so by turning the war into an anti-Establishment issue, placing Us ("the great silent majority") on one side and Them ("a vocal minority") on the other. A Gallup poll showed three quarters of the population in agreement with the President. Nixon stacked his desk with thousands of congratulatory telegrams and letters. And then he began to wage four more years of war.

I heard the speech in New Orleans, in my final year at college, and I realized then that the war would never go away. It was waiting for me, it had some incomprehensible power of its own to endure despite morality and the stated goals of our national policy. Nixon had promised to get us out of the war, and now he was telling us the same thing that Johnson and Kennedy had concluded: the way out was further in.

My father adopted Nixon's slogan, "Peace with Honor." Mine was "Peace Now." Either alternative was surrounded by tragedy. In my father's view, abandoning our ally was cowardly and would lead to the loss of Cambodia, Laos, Burma, Thailand; he believed in the domino theory. Like Nixon, he thought America must keep up appearances, even in a bad situation like Vietnam. Honor meant keeping our commitments, even if our ally was not altogether honorable himself. The consequences of Peace Now were the humiliation of the United States, the advance of Communism, the probable slaughter of millions who depended on us for defense, and also, most profoundly, a repudiation of the values our country represented and for which my father had fought.

He had felt these sentiments before the Silent Majority speech. However, before the speech, Vietnam had been *their* war. He blamed Kennedy's poor judgment for getting us into Vietnam; he blamed Johnson's bad management for extending the war; he thought that the striped-pants set in the State Department and the Ivy League heroes of the New Frontier had made foolish calculations and unnecessary commitments. But after the speech his attitudes changed. By making Vietnam Mr. Nixon's War, Nixon also made it my father's war. It came to represent him, and his way of life, his values—*his* as opposed to *theirs*. Thus my opposition to the war became, in subtle but unbearable ways, more personal than it had been previously. There was another domino theory at work, which affected the dynamics of my own family. I could not push against the war without striking Nixon, and when Nixon fell, he fell against the Silent Majority, that endless line of no-class Americans that included my parents.

Watergate was such joy. For nearly two years no one spoke of anything else. It was a national obsession, a slow-moving coup d'état. Because it was such a spectacle and lasted so long, Watergate became as much a part of my life as a war or an economic depression or some other ongoing national calamity, and yet I experienced it not as disaster but as theater. One read the papers or watched television with a thrilling sense of *what next?* Everyone's life had the same focus. The self felt diminished against the imposing backdrop of historic goings-on. At parties it did not matter so much who you were but what you knew, or what original construction you might place on the latest developments. There was a mood in the air that was both apprehensive and excited, and in my case included a thankful feeling of confirmation, for my own bubble of paranoia had burst. Everything I suspected was true, and more.

The economy went to hell, and it was easy to believe, especially during the Watergate Summer of 1973, that no one was working anymore. It was like having the World Series on all the time; everyone was home watching TV. During the Senate hearings the days were filled with performance and the nights with between-the-acts rehashings. Because it was theater, because it was tragedy, one always had the sense of momentum, of gathering pressure, of inevitable climax. Nixon would fall. We wondered seriously if he would somehow take us all with him, start another war or blow up the world.

I was jobless and trying to make a living as a free-lance writer, and for me Watergate was a psychic plaster sopping up my excess despair. Or else, let's say, it was a drug, always available in the form of commentary or speculation; I did not have to think about myself, I could think about Nixon instead, of his fantastic public tragedy, and not of my own private sense of failure. I could sink into Watergate like an opium dream.

Watergate did not really begin, as a public concern, until well after the break-in of the Democratic National Headquarters on June 17, 1972. "Five men," said the story in the Sunday *Washington Post*, "one of whom said he is a former employe of the Central Intelligence Agency, were arrested at 2:30 a.m. yesterday in what authorities described as an elaborate plot to bug the offices of the Democratic National Committee here.

"Three of the men were native-born Cubans, and another was

said to have trained Cuban exiles for guerrilla activity after the 1961 Bay of Pigs invasion.

"There was no immediate explanation as to why the five suspects would want to bug the Democratic National Committee, or whether or not they were working for any other individuals or organizations . . ."

On Monday we learned that the former CIA man, James McCord, was the director of security for the Committee to Reelect the President (CREEP). This was interesting news, but it did not appear to have much of a future life. Many newspapers didn't bother to report it; *The New York Times* buried the original Watergate story on page 50. John Mitchell, the former attorney general who was directing the President's reelection campaign, fired McCord, saying the break-in was "wholly inconsistent with the principles upon which we are conducting our campaign." Ron Ziegler, the White House press officer, refused to comment on the "third-rate burglary attempt." Who could doubt that the Watergate affair would end with that statement?

And yet there were subterranean forces that had been urged into action. The Democratic National Committee filed suit for a million dollars against CREEP; the FBI began an investigation; the two police reporters for the *Washington Post*, Bob Woodward and Carl Bernstein, continued to follow up their initial story of the break-in; a grand jury subpoenaed witnesses; and Texas congressman Wright Patman announced that he was going to begin his own inquiry, in the House Banking and Currency Committee, to track down the source of the several thousand dollars found on the burglars after their arrest. By August that money had been traced to CREEP.

There were other signals coming to the surface. Mitchell's voluble wife, Martha, a brassy, defiant, unstable woman whose late-night telephone calls to reporters had made her a celebrity and whose attacks on students and liberal judges had made her the most popular fund-raiser in the Republican party, began to issue public demands that her husband get out of politics. She called the reelection campaign "a cops and robbers game." In the middle of one of her notorious phone calls, this one to reporter Helen Thomas, she revealed that she had given her husband an ultimatum to get out of politics. "I'm sick and tired of the whole operation," she said. Then, according to Thomas, Martha cried out, "You just get away!" and the phone went dead. When Thomas called back, an operator told her that "Mrs. Mitchell is indisposed and cannot talk." Martha later claimed that a CREEP security man had jerked the phone out of the wall, then had thrown her against the window, smashing the glass and cutting her hand (it required eleven stitches). She described herself as a "political prisoner."

Even though the election was approaching and Nixon was certain to win, Watergate and the "dirty tricks" of the administration were becoming a part of the background of everyday life. We began to expect more disclosures. Nixon himself did not seem to be worried, however. He wrote in his diary that the latest attacks by the *Post* were the "last burp of the Eastern Establishment." He intended to bury that Establishment in the coming election.

I was a McGovern supporter in 1972; I even ran as a McGovern delegate in our Dallas precinct convention (the Wallacites swamped us); but I was never a McGovern enthusiast. Someone pointed out to me that McGovern had the same astrological sign as Calvin Coolidge—they were Cancers—and there did seem to be a psychic resemblance between them; they both had that sanctimonious air. What I remember most about McGovern's personal qualities was his preternatural ability to nap. Photographs of the campaign would show the candidate splayed out on a hotel bed with his shoes on, or reclining in his airplane seat, sound asleep. His platform was to pull out of Vietnam in ninety days (Kissinger had already announced that peace was "at hand"), cut back on the military budget (Nixon had reduced it substantially), increase busing to achieve a racial balance in the schools, forgive draft dodgers and deserters, civilize overly harsh penalties for possession of certain drugs, and give a thousand dollars to every man, woman, and child in America, whether they needed it or not. As William Safire,

Nixon's former speechwriter, pointed out, in the Us-versus-Them America that Nixon had created, McGovern's central message was "I'm 'them.' "

McGovern dumped his first choice for running mate, Senator Thomas Eagleton of Missouri, because of a prior history of mental problems that Eagleton had failed to disclose; after that, McGovern offered second place to senators Hubert Humphrey, Edward Kennedy, Abraham Ribicoff, Gaylord Nelson, Edmund Muskie, and Florida's governor, Reubin Askew, all of whom turned him down. His seventh choice, Sargent Shriver, the former director of the Peace Corps and a Kennedy in-law, accepted. My father declared McGovern to be the most foolish man in the history of American politics, and although I defended him, as I watched his campaign fumble it was hard to find reasons to support him, other than that he wasn't Nixon.

McGovern wanted to make Watergate the central issue of the campaign. He called the Nixon administration a "cutthroat crew . . . a corrupt regime," and warned that the nation faced a "moral and constitutional crisis of unprecedented dimensions" due to Nixon's "widespread abuse of power." It was not clear to me if voters ignored McGovern's prophecy because they believed it wasn't true or because they were more afraid of having McGovern in the White House than Nixon. After the election, when the country was paralyzed and Nixon was in disgrace, polls showed that Nixon would still be chosen if the election were held again and McGovern was the opponent. More people seemed to distrust McGovern, who was widely described as the most decent man in politics, than distrusted Nixon even at the brink of impeachment.

"Here is a situation where the Eastern Establishment media finally has a candidate who almost totally shares their views," Nixon told his staff. McGovern counted on the newly enfranchised youth vote, the 11.5 million people between the ages of eighteen and twenty-one. Much of his campaign strategy was to register these voters, but in the end, few of them voted. He hoped to capture the Catholics (both Eagleton and Shriver are Catholic), but Nixon overwhelmed him; Catholic voters in New York, for instance, went for Nixon two-to-one over McGovern. He had expected the women's vote, but received only 38 percent of it. In the end he carried the black vote, the campus vote, and the vote of 85 percent of the foreign car owners—that is, the snob vote. The raw core of the Eastern Establishment was defined by seventeen electoral votes: Massachusetts and the District of Columbia. McGovern considered moving to England.

On December 7, 1972, a White House secretary confirmed the existence of a secret "plumbers unit," which was created after a former Defense Department aide named Daniel Ellsberg leaked the Pentagon history of the Vietnam War to *The New York Times*. Ellsberg was on trial in Los Angeles, and the judge declared a mistrial the following day. In Chicago, on December 8, a United Airlines jet crashed into a row of houses near Midway Airport, killing forty-five people. It was not until the day after the crash that one of the bodies was identified as Mrs. E. Howard Hunt. A Chicago policeman found her purse, containing $10,000 in hundred-dollar bills.

In January, Senator Sam Ervin, a white-haired North Carolina Democrat and an ancient foe of civil rights, agreed to preside over a select committee to investigate the Watergate caper (it was not yet called a scandal). The first Watergate trial opened in John Sirica's court on January 8, 1973, and twelve days later the sequestered jury in that case watched the inaugural parade for Richard Nixon's second term.

"To one who was in the White House and became somewhat familiar with its interworkings," said John Dean, the former counsel to the President, reading his 245-page opening statement to the Senate Watergate Committee in a dry monotone, "the Watergate matter was an inevitable outgrowth of a climate of excessive concern over the political impact of demonstrators, excessive concern over leaks, an insatiable appetite for political intelligence, all coupled with a do-it-yourself White House staff, regardless of the law."

The Watergate hearings are black-and-white memories to me

now. Since I didn't own a color television set, I remember the Watergate committee as a collection of gray men in gray suits, sitting on an elevated dais and observing the witnesses across a blinding wash of klieg lights. Sam Ervin was seventy-six years old and in the final term of his obscure senatorial career. At times cranky, sputtering, rambling, and speaking in a gravelly drawl that had an Andy Devine squeak in the back of it, he might easily have been a model of the blowhard southern segregationist politician, and yet he became a national idol, an instant folk hero, based on his firm grasp of the verities of Shakespeare, the Scriptures, and the Constitution. The gush of affection I felt for Sam Ervin during those hearings was largely nostalgia for the lost values of faith and honor and even very elemental literacy. It was as if he had been exhumed from another century and had thundered into Nixon's new world, an age in which morality was determined by the J. Walter Thompson ad executives who ran the Nixon White House. The other Democratic members of the committee were Herman Talmadge of Georgia, a cigar smoker who asked the most piercing questions; Daniel Inouye of Hawaii, whose valiant military career ended when an arm was blown off in the Po Valley in World War II (John Ehrlichman's lawyer called him "a little Jap"); Joseph Montoya of New Mexico, an inane man who wanted to know if the witnesses had achieved "peace of mind" now that they had confessed. Howard Baker of Tennessee led the Republican minority. He wore glen-plaid suits, and he slumped in his chair, resting his chin on his fist. Baker drummed one question over and over: "What did the President know and when did he know it?" making clear the true object of the hearings, which was to determine whether there was a case for impeachment. Lowell Weicker, Jr., of Connecticut, one of the few remaining self-described liberals in the Republican party, was a passionate but ineffective questioner. Edward Gurney of Florida was quickly identified as the White House's man on the committee, whose assignment was to break down the credibility of Nixon's accusers.

Dean sat in the witness chair for an entire week in June. Behind him, amid the celebrities who had used their influence to get into the gallery, posed Dean's cameolike wife, Maureen, with her un-wavering, devoted stare. "Mo" Dean became an inadvertent sexual object during the hearings; the camera was always including her; and despite her prim outfits and severe hairstyle, there was a female lushness about her that caused my mind to wander from her husband's testimony. She reminded me of a blonde, grown-up Annette Funicello, facing life outside the Mickey Mouse Club. And in fact, perversely, there was some buried kinship between the Mouseketeers and these lost figures whose careers and aspirations were exploding before our delighted eyes—Porter, Magruder, Chapin, Sloan—young men who could easily have passed for adult versions of Bobby, Tommy, Cubby, and Jay Jay.

In that hearing room, filled with the clearings of throats and the impulsive mortal sound of motor-driven cameras (a sound like the death of insects in a bug light), Dean spoke of White House wiretaps of newsmen; tentative plans to blow up the Brookings Institution, a Democratic think tank; secret intelligence operations to discredit or embarrass opponents, to blackmail Democratic delegates through the use of prostitutes, and even to kidnap demonstrators and shanghai them (monterrey them?) to Mexico. At the direction of the White House a pair of ex-cops, Anthony Ulasewicz and John Caulfield, conducted political espionage on such persons as Edward Kennedy, the Smothers Brothers, and Dick Dixon, a comedian who imitated the President. A young man named Donald Segretti dogged the Democratic candidates and played tricks on them, such as writing the famous "Canuck" letter accusing Ed Muskie of making a slur on Americans of French-Canadian descent. This was all a prelude to the actual break-in at the Democratic National Committee and the subsequent White House cover-up, which John Dean directed and Richard Nixon knew about.

It was not just the vicarious thrill of watching powerful men disgrace themselves that held me in thrall to the television set all summer. It was mental tonic; it was discovering that my apprehensions and even my delusions were true, that I hadn't guessed the half of it. Also, I felt a peculiar sense of identity with the witnesses—not with their actions but with their paranoia, which mirrored my own. I intuitively understood the frightened, bitter, irrational feelings that had caused otherwise good men to go wrong. They were Nixon's victims too, victims of his galvanizing paranoia. In a way Nixon had driven us all crazy. There was no telling what anyone would do anymore. Everyone was berserk.

There was another depressing identity I felt within the witnesses, many of whom were also defendants in the various Watergate trials: they were preponderantly from the new world, which could now be defined as that stretch of the country from Key Biscayne to San Clemente—Nixon's America. Kleindienst, Strachan, Kalmbach, Haldeman; one watched them succeed each other in the witness chair, different men, but with similar accents and a particular sameness of background and outlook. By the end of 1974, twenty-eight of the thirty-eight men who were indicted for Watergate involvement and related offenses were from California, Arizona, Florida, and elsewhere in the South and West. This had the effect of condemning not only Nixon and his men but the entire class of new world Americans. The subtext of the Watergate hearings was an Establishment desire to roll back the power of such men.

Weicker was asking questions about the administration's use of the FBI and the IRS to gather information about political opponents, when Dean mentioned that the White House "maintained an 'enemies list,' which was rather extensive and continually being updated." Dean produced a memo he had written to Haldeman and Ehrlichman in August 1971, which addressed "the matter of how we can maximize the fact of our incumbency in dealing with persons known to be active in their opposition to our Administration. Stated a bit more bluntly—how can we use the available Federal machinery to screw our political enemies." The enemies list included 216 people, many of them predictable members of the Eastern Establishment, such as senators Kennedy, Mondale, McGovern; virtually all of the Congressional Black Caucus; fourteen labor leaders; the presidents of Harvard, Yale, and M.I.T., *The New York Times*, the *Washington Post*, the *St. Louis Post-*

Dispatch, along with nearly sixty reporters and political columnists; more than fifty businessmen, such as the chairmen of IBM and United Artists; sixteen academics, including linguist Noam Chomsky, economist John Kenneth Galbraith, and Edwin Land, the inventor of the Polaroid camera. Several of the enemies had actually voted for Nixon. Houston heart surgeon Michael DeBakey had worked in the Nixon reelection campaign. The celebrities on the list included, as one might expect, Jane Fonda and Dick Gregory, but also actors Carol Channing, Gregory Peck, Bill Cosby, Steve McQueen, Paul Newman, Barbra Streisand, and Tony Randall, and the otherwise nonpolitical quarterback of the Jets, Joe Namath.

One understood how Naziism could come to America. It would come in the form of Mouseketeers wearing Brooks Brothers suits and tortoiseshell eyeglasses.

The business of spying on political opponents was as ancient as politics; the age of electronics only made the espionage easier. Adlai Stevenson had tapped the Kennedy phone lines at the 1960 convention; Kennedy secretly taped more than six hundred conversations in the White House, a practice Johnson made routine. Johnson had bugged Goldwater in 1964 and had ordered the FBI to bug Nixon's campaign plane in 1968. The press, which was moralizing over Watergate, had always been willing to publish material that it knew to be stolen, such as the Pentagon Papers (and after Watergate, portions of the Kissinger and Haldeman memoirs). In the 1968 campaign, NBC had managed to bug both the Republican party headquarters and the Democratic platform committee. "I had been in politics too long," Nixon writes in his memoirs, "and seen everything from dirty tricks to vote fraud. I could not muster much moral outrage over a political bugging."

Still, he brooded about Kennedy's use of wiretaps on newsmen and Martin Luther King. When he came into office he found an elaborate bugging system already in place, and ordered it removed. (That was a mistake, Haldeman admitted later; Johnson had operated his taping system with a switch under his desk, but Nixon's was voice-activated.) Nixon had even discovered a bug Johnson left under his bed at Camp David. "Most of my advisors argued that if I revealed the activities of previous administrations, it would look as if I were trying to divert attention from myself by smearing others," Nixon recalls. "In the end . . . we did nothing."

Once the White House tapes were revealed, a frenzy took hold. One expected Nixon would destroy them, but the need to have them public was aching; it was like adolescent sexual longing— anything you wanted so much you couldn't expect to get. Everyone was tantalized by the knowledge that Nixon was closeted with the absolute truth. Did he know about the cover-up? Did he direct it? If he was innocent, why didn't he let us hear the tapes? Facing the prospect of impeachment and a contempt-of-court citation if he didn't give up the tapes, Nixon agreed to surrender seven tapes to Judge Sirica. One of them had an eighteen-and-a-half-minute gap in the middle of it, which according to experts contained "at least five, perhaps as many as nine" separate erasures. Nixon's national security adviser, Alexander Haig, testified in Judge Sirica's court that "sinister forces" may have caused the tape to erase itself.

Hundreds more tapes were subpoenaed. In April 1974, Nixon came on TV with a stack of blue loose-leaf binders behind him. "These are the transcripts of . . . forty-two tapes which I have made. There are thirteen hundred pages of them. I am turning them over to the Special Prosecutor and to the House Judiciary Committee. More than that, I have also decided that these should be made available to the American public." He would not surrender the tapes themselves. Material not related to Watergate had been omitted, as had the profanity. "Everything that is relevant is included," Nixon lied.

The transcripts hit the papers the next day. Even though they had been doctored to improve the President's case (he left out, for instance, the March 17, 1973, meeting with Mitchell, in which he told the former attorney general to "stonewall it, contain it, take the Fifth"), the transcripts persuaded a near majority of Americans that Nixon should be impeached. One read them with bewilderment, because Nixon said they would demonstrate his innocence. What they showed instead was the moral confusion, the flight from truth, the cowering paranoia, the threadbare rationalizations that characterized the Nixon White House. "This is just the last gasp of our hardest opponents," we read Nixon saying, and he continued, almost incoherently: "They got the hell kicked out of them in the election. There is not a Watergate around in this town, not so much our opponents, even the media, but the basic thing is the Establishment. The Establishment is dying, and so they've got to show that despite the success we have had in foreign policy and in the election, they've got to show that it is just wrong because of this [Watergate]. They are trying to use this as the whole thing."

From the beginning of the Watergate investigation, one sensed that events were being overtaken by theater. Men began to act in accord with certain theatrical conventions: Ervin was playing the hero, the press was the chorus, the White House spear-carriers trundled forth to their separate disgraces, and over all of them Nixon loomed, the immense protagonist, too mighty to be destroyed by anyone but himself. Of course, life is not art; it is not coherent and satisfying; at any moment one could expect the drama to end in a frustrating compromise. But as one read the transcripts, one gradually realized that Nixon was trapped in his own character; he was designed for tragedy and could no more escape his destiny than Lear or Macbeth.

Several times during the various meetings Nixon recorded with his aides, Nixon discussed Alger Hiss, his old antagonist. "I always hark back to the Hiss case," he said when Dean suggested meeting with Ervin in executive session. "We did that in the Hiss case." Nixon reminds Haldeman: "Hiss was destroyed because he lied— perjury. Chambers was destroyed because he was an informer, but Chambers knew he was going to be destroyed." "His constant analogies with the Hiss case and Watergate baffled me," Dean later wrote in his memoirs. "I thought the President had everything backward. I identified with *Hiss*, not the investigators, and I winced whenever the President talked about how he had 'nailed' him." But perhaps Nixon understood in the murky, symbolic re-

gion of his brain, below the level of conscious thought, that the
forces he had brought into play in the Hiss case, which had brought
him fame, would also bring him ruin. It was Nixon against the
Establishment once again, the new world against the old. As theater, the Hiss case was Nixon's Oedipal crime. He had nailed Hiss,
but now he had become Hiss, and John Dean would be his Whittaker Chambers.

Alger Hiss himself turned into a campus hero; he paraded around
the country as Nixon's first victim. One saw Nixon masks everywhere, especially on Halloween, when children went from house to
house doing passable imitations of the grotesque Nixon victory
posture, with his hands over his head and his fingers making Vs.
Instead of "trick or treat," they would quote Nixon's statement at
a Disney World press conference: "I am not a crook."

Although one still spoke in general terms about Watergate, one
no longer spoke of it as a caper, or an affair, or even a scandal, but
as a probe. Watergate had become the name of the incision into
the body of the American government. The corruption was not
confined to a single break-in, it was endemic. Under scrutiny, the
administration dissolved. In the Justice Department, for instance,
two attorney generals were convicted of criminal offenses; John
Mitchell was jailed for conspiracy, perjury, and obstruction of justice; his successor, Richard Kleindienst, pleaded guilty to the misdemeanor of failing to answer "accurately and fully" a question
that had been asked him during his confirmation hearings. The
question had to do with whether or not ITT had bribed Nixon with
a $400,000 campaign donation, in order to keep the government
from appealing three antitrust suits. Kleindienst told Senator
Kennedy: "I was not importuned; I was not pressured; I was not
directed . . ." Later Kleindienst admitted that Ehrlichman had
phoned him to say the President wanted him to drop the appeal,
and when Kleindienst balked, Nixon called him personally. "Listen, you son of a bitch, don't you understand the English language?" Nixon barked. "Don't appeal that goddamn case, and

that's all there is to it!" The turmoil in the Justice Department was noisier than that in other departments of government, but all over Washington agency heads and top aides were quietly resigning. Impeachment still seemed a remote eventuality, largely because of the man who would succeed Nixon, the intemperate reactionary, Spiro Agnew, one man more hated and feared by the Eastern Establishment than Richard Nixon. Agnew called himself Nixon's "insurance policy," and indeed the prospect of an Agnew presidency worried even moderate Republicans like my father, but astonishingly, Agnew was caught in an old crime and resigned, after pleading guilty to a single count of tax evasion. He had been taking bribes his entire political career.

Then came the indictment of Nixon's heir apparent, his former secretary of the treasury, John Connally, for accepting a bribe from the dairy industry to increase milk-price supports. Connally was Nixon's choice to succeed him in 1976; in Nixon's opinion, Connally was the only member of his cabinet with the proper "fire in his belly" to make a great president. He would have chosen Connally over Gerald Ford to succeed Spiro Agnew, but he concluded that the Democratic Senate would never approve a man who had recently deserted their party.

Connally was my father's favorite politician. He had been a strong governor of Texas, and many Texans liked to see themselves in his image, which was powerful and bluff but not buffoonish, as Lyndon Johnson had often seemed. Connally was acquitted in the milk-fund case, but his political career was ruined. Was it a coincidence that Nixon and his most likely successors, Agnew and Connally, would be swept out of power and contention? Was it a conspiracy on the part of the Eastern Establishment? Or was there a cultural failing in the new world that brought such men to disgrace? Coincidentally, Texas politics was involved in a scandal of its own, which had just seen the speaker of the Texas House and another legislator convicted of receiving bribes, and had led to the defeat of the governor and the lieutenant governor in the last election. The lieutenant governor of California was on trial for perjury. And then three members of the Senate Watergate Committee from the South and West were charged with various political offenses. Joseph Montoya said he was shocked to discover that his own campaign financial report contained forgeries and that $100,000 of illegal contributions had been laundered through phony committees. Edward Gurney, who was the first Republican senator from Florida since Reconstruction, became the first senator indicted in fifty years, for bribery, perjury, and conspiracy. Herman Talmadge found himself under investigation by the Senate Ethics Committee for his longtime habit of letting friends literally stuff his pockets with cash—a practice that differed very little from the crimes that had brought down Spiro Agnew.

It was a sour feeling to recall the piousness of these men as they sat on the dais of the Watergate tribunal. I wondered whether corruption and politics were so much of a piece that trying to separate them was like trying to rub the grain out of wood. Certainly the Europeans were sneering at our naïveté; in fact, the rest of the world was dumbfounded. Americans were deposing their strongest president since Eisenhower, perhaps since Roosevelt—and for what? For trying to minimize the damage of a routine campaign offense.

In the middle of the Watergate investigation and the Agnew resignation, Nixon suddenly put the armed forces on full alert, DEFCON 3, ostensibly because of the Yom Kippur War between Israel and Egypt and Syria, but there was an awful feeling that he was threatening us as well, his awakened constituents.

During this period the news changed—that is, not the information that is the news but the sensation of hearing the news. The expectations a person felt when he turned on television or picked up a newspaper were intense; one had become habituated to surprises. People spoke of being Watergate junkies, and it was appropriate, because there was that same tension of addiction, that same anxiety when one has gotten too far away from the supplier (television), and for many of us, that same unhealthy pallor that came from sitting inside all day. In the middle of Watergate summer Roberta and I went to a Tennessee state park with friends and spent the entire vacation in the lodge, with the other guests, watching the only TV. We were, as Nixon and my mother agreed, wallowing in Watergate. In Mother's opinion the whole affair had gone on too long; it was turning people into well-informed bores. First Vietnam, now Watergate. No one read anything except newspapers, nothing was funny unless it was also cynical. Life was losing its grace.

The House Judiciary Committee was already considering impeachment proceedings in June 1974, when a Washington grand jury named Nixon an unindicted coconspirator in the Watergate cover-up. Nixon left the country. First he went to Egypt, where President Sadat awarded him the Order of the Nile. The television coverage showed millions of Egyptians lining the streets as they had done during Nasser's funeral, only now they were cheering Nixon as if he were their only friend in the world. Then he flew to Saudia Arabia, Syria, Israel. Even in extremist Syria he insisted on riding in open limousines. In Cairo he had plunged impulsively into the crowd, and the Secret Service had to wrest him loose. One had the feeling that he was looking for martyrdom, if one can speak of such an ideal political death as that, being crushed by an adoring mob.

Even before Nixon left for the Middle East, reporters had noticed that he was limping and occasionally wincing. The White House physician confirmed that Nixon was suffering from phlebitis; a blood clot was lodged in a vein in his left leg. If the clot should break loose and travel to the lungs or heart, Nixon might die. He should stay home in bed, his doctor advised; instead he went tramping down to the pyramids and strolling around the palace in Jidda, daring death, making a show of it. When he came back to Washington he was obviously in pain, but he left again two weeks later for a NATO conference in Brussels, and then on to Russia for a summit meeting with Brezhnev. He was already making plans to go to Japan in August.

I believed that the Nixon presidency would end soon, either through impeachment or resignation or even the death he so obviously longed for. I wanted it for him, but I didn't want it on my conscience. I was afraid he would commit suicide, leaving a note to future historians who would not interpret this action as the final act of a mawkish, self-pitying man. They would not understand him as we understood him; they would see him as a victim of class rivalry, regional prejudice, partisan political attacks, and something else that was hard to define but that had to do with the hatred schoolchildren direct at the marginal personalities, the shy people in the back of the room, the overachievers, the ungainly, the boys who cry too easily—that kind of reactionary hatred felt toward the less-than-perfect people who threaten us with their flaws and their frailties. As one grows up, one tries to put aside such intolerance, but Nixon had called it up again and again, that image of the child whom nobody wanted to play with, who wouldn't go home. And since I had sometimes been that child, I felt a loathing for myself, and remembered dreams of my own death when my parents and would-be friends came to my funeral, begging for forgiveness and understanding. I understood Nixon's craving for the peace and joy and vindication of the grave.

In July the Supreme Court ruled that Nixon would have to surrender additional tapes subpoenaed in various Watergate trials. Four days later the House Judiciary Committee began to vote on the Articles of Impeachment. This was an arcane procedure, this solemn televised event conducted by a bland New Jersey Democrat named Peter Rodino; the ceremony and language had a medieval flair—the execution of kings must have been carried out in similar seriousness and formality. After seven months of deliberation the committee recommended impeachment on three counts: first, obstruction of justice in the cover-up, including making false statements, counseling witnesses to lie under oath, paying hush money, and interfering with the FBI investigation; second, misusing the powers of his office by manipulating the IRS, the FBI, and the Secret Service, with the object of harassing his enemies; and third, failing to comply with the subpoenas issued by the Judiciary Committee. The committee declined to endorse impeachment on the grounds of tax evasion, or violating the Constitution in the secret bombing of Cambodia.

Now what? The tension was unbearable. Would Nixon defy the Supreme Court? Would he destroy the remaining tapes? Would he tough it out and face an impeachment trial in the Senate? Already tickets were being printed for the trial, and television networks were making secret arrangements to cover it. The newspapers made occasional reference to Andrew Johnson, the only president who ever suffered impeachment, but Johnson was an uncomfortable precedent. From a southerner's point of view, Johnson's impeachment was a historic disgrace; he had tried to soften the punishment of Reconstruction, against the wishes of a vindictive Congress, and when he fired his scheming and disloyal secretary of war, Edwin Stanton, Congress sought revenge. Johnson was acquitted by a single vote. Reflecting upon that impeachment, 106 years before, I worried that we too were caught up in the winds of the moment and that Nixon might triumph in the history books.

Until now, the tapes had only proved that Nixon was evil, not that he was guilty. Nearly two weeks after the Supreme Court decision, Nixon appeared on television once again to release three transcripts of conversations he had had with Haldeman on June 23, 1972, six days after the break-in. He was also turning over the sixty-four tapes Sirica had subpoenaed. Nixon admitted that "portions of the tapes of these June 23 conversations are at variance with certain of my previous statements." I realized as soon as he said it that Nixon must be caught in a lie so obvious that he had lost all hope. "A House vote of impeachment is, as a practical matter, virtually a foregone conclusion," he admitted, and "the issue will therefore go to trial in the Senate."

Nixon would lose—even he knew that—and yet the extraordinary buoyancy that had kept him afloat in public life for twenty-eight years, that had brought him back to the surface after suffering defeats and scandals and the loathing of millions, would not let him sink away gracefully. "I insisted on a full investigation and prosecution of those guilty," he claimed once again, knowing that the very tapes he was releasing demonstrated the falsity of that statement. Nixon was asking us not to forgive him but to be blind to the obvious, to see things from his perspective—in other words, to lie to ourselves as he had lied to us. I felt very weary. I finally had had enough of Watergate. Curiosity had been satisfied, in my case. There was no longer any question about the outcome. The prospect of watching Nixon on trial exhausted me. Watergate had been like a Roman banquet at which I had gorged myself—my appetite had been a part of the depravity—but now that I was glutted and nauseated, Nixon was calling for the main course.

In the new transcripts, Haldeman comes to Nixon to report on the FBI investigation, which was going "in some directions we don't want it to go." Dean and Mitchell have agreed, says Haldeman, that the way to stop the investigation is to have CIA assistant director Vernon Walters call acting FBI director L. Patrick Gray and "Just say 'Stay the hell out of this, ah, business here, we don't want you to go any further on it.' " Nixon gets the picture. Haldeman can simply tell the CIA that " 'The President just feels that'— ah, without going into details—don't lie to them to the extent to say no involvement, but just say 'This is a comedy of errors,' without getting into it," says Nixon, and "that they should call the FBI and say we wish for the country, 'Don't go any further into this case, period!' "

Now everyone in the country could read the very words Nixon had used to order the cover-up. But even with his guilt clearly established, his conviction in the Senate a certainty, Nixon held out—for what? A pardon? A deal with the prosecutors? Or perhaps some darker solution. His doctor had cleared his room of any possibly lethal drugs. His secretary of defense had countermanded in advance any military action the President might initiate. Nixon was in a condition that was hard to define. He was President, but he no longer had any powers.

Nixon finally did resign, on August 9, 1974, and a month later President Ford pardoned him. It was difficult to believe that there had not been some tacit deal between the two old friends, who had known each other since Ford came to Congress in 1948. I wasn't shocked. By now I was utterly cynical. But I didn't want to see Nixon on trial forever and ever; nor did I want to see him sent to prison, and have to worry about the justice of that. I was tired of hating Nixon. The pardon at least had taken him off the stage, and I was grateful for it.

For most of my life I had been thinking about Nixon and Kennedy. They were the dominant figures of my time. One was martyred and the other disgraced, but until the moment Nixon stood in the door of the White House helicopter and waved farewell—in one long stroke, as if he could erase the memories like a chalkboard—the politics of my country was played out in the forces these two men represented. One could not let go of Kennedy, finally, until his old antagonist had fallen.

I had never known an America in which Nixon was not in power, or hauntingly outside it. My political thoughts were organized with him in mind, and to have him gone, not dead but silenced, was to remove a central pillar from my philosophy, that Nixon Must Be Opposed. The Nixonless world felt weirdly vacant to me.

In his farewell address, Nixon told members of his staff and Cabinet, "Never be petty. Always remember: others may hate you. Those who hate you don't win unless you hate them. And then you destroy yourself." That, indeed, was the moral of Watergate. It was a lesson I had not yet learned. I couldn't shake off my own hatred of Nixon, even though I knew he must be the most wretched man in the universe. I followed the progress of his phlebitis with morbid interest. When it flared up in the fall, Nixon refused to go to the hospital, saying he would never come out alive. His doctor said he had lost the will to survive. One didn't know if Nixon was really so ill or if he was dodging the subpoenas to testify in the many Watergate trials. Judge Sirica sent a panel of doctors to examine him, and they agreed he was too sick to testify. A piece of the clot had broken loose and lodged in his lungs. Finally Nixon underwent surgery, and went into shock because of intestinal bleeding. Pneumonia followed. He was in critical condition most of October and November.

I went back to Dallas for Thanksgiving dinner. For seven years my father and I had been enemies, first because of the war and then because of Nixon, but now we looked at each other without anger once again. I saw what all this had done to him. The man he identified as "*my* president"—in the way people do who only expect to have one president in their lifetime who stands for what they stand for—had shown himself to be a liar and a scoundrel. My father's judgment was shaken. He had defended Nixon for two decades, he had believed in him completely, but he realized now that he had been dreadfully wrong.

In some unexpected, unlikely fashion, Watergate had made it possible for me to love my father again. I saw in him now an appealing humility, which replaced the old bullying sense of certainty. That part had been the Nixon part and it was gone. However, the Nixon part of me was still present, still rueful and petty and paranoid, and as my father carved the turkey and my mother poured the wine, I offered a toast. "To phlebitis," I said.

Mother drew a breath and set down her glass. My father stopped carving and looked at me. He no longer had the energy for argument. He lifted his glass and said, "To us—just us, the family."

14 / TURNINGS

Approaching thirty, Roberta and I began to think of children. No one we knew had them. No one we knew really wanted them. In the age of the Pill, "accidents" didn't happen the way they used to, and if they did, the Supreme Court had ruled that abortions were a constitutional privilege. In the past, the age of cumbersome and imperfect contraception, children had been almost inevitable, a penalty of spontaneous carnality. Now they were optional; we could be childless without being chaste or even very careful. The brief moment between courtship and parenthood had become elastic, and in our case it had already stretched across five years of married life, but we began to feel the pressure of middle age and mortality. If we were going to have children, now was the time.

These deliberations felt entirely new. My parents had dived into childbearing with characteristic postwar fervor. For them, marriage was a license to get on with what they really wanted in life, which was several children as soon as possible. My father married my mother six weeks after he met her, and by the time he was shipped off to Europe he had accomplished his biological task. That first baby was born dead, but by the time my father came home from Korea in 1952, his three children were waiting for him. "It seems rather strange now," my mother had said to me, "but nearly everyone wanted to have a baby. Somehow the fact that the father might never return made the wives even more eager to have a child. It must be some sort of biological instinct to preserve the race."

My generation felt a different urge. The planet was already too crowded, too polluted; we lived with the prospect of nuclear apocalypse. Bringing babies into such a world seemed irresponsible and cruel. When I saw people my age with two or three children, I quietly condemned them. They must be greedy, naive, obtuse. I certainly didn't envy or admire them. They were the wrong people to have children; the right people were people like me, who knew better.

These were all rationalizations of a culture that had turned against children. I wasn't really planning my own family on the basis of world population growth or the likelihood of nuclear war. Children made me nervous. I was uncertain how to behave around them. As an adult I thought that the introduction of children into restaurants or movie theaters was a savage breach of etiquette. Their mere presence was a rebuke. In a purely animal sense, Roberta and I understood that we were designed to procreate, nurture, and die, leaving our progeny behind, but as a twentieth-century man and woman we felt a different imperative, which was to get ahead. Children were dead weight, a renunciation of our modern-adult lives.

This was a contemporary moment: deciding to go off the Pill. It was a decision to be chewed over at length during late-night dinners we would never enjoy again, or idly speculated upon some lazy Sunday morning when we were cuddled up in bed with the newspapers—how could we choose to surrender such quiet pleasures for the chaos of children? We were not afraid of the big responsibilities of parenthood; it was the day-to-dayness, the dreary moments of standing in line at the grocery store with a bawling infant, the countless diaper changings, and the middle-of-the-night feedings that wore down our imagination. At the same time, we had a primitive longing for consequences. We wanted our marriage to have an object other than companionship. We were ready to get on with the serious moments of life. We wanted—what? To create our own people, to become a family and not just a married couple. And so we went off the Pill. It was like taking off the final vestment, becoming naked in a thrilling way known only to the ancients; one felt exposed to the sky and the whims of the gods.

Now that I was a prospective parent, I looked at the world through a different lens. To have children, or even to imagine having them, required certain political adjustments. One need not become more conservative, although it seemed every parent did, but one must become less blithe. One must focus on schools and property taxes and interest rates, and upon the background wash of pornography and violence and drug use. Tolerance ebbed. I wanted to clear a safe space for my children, but safety was expensive and hard to find. I began to dream about money. For the first time in my life I looked at the Dow Jones industrial averages and saw a connection between the capitalist economy and the rest of my life. I did not really approve of these changes in myself, because conservatism, even in my hesitant turning toward it, was a movement backward, to the Dallas of my childhood. It was tied in my mind to square values, religious extremism, racism, and rabid anti-Communism. Nonetheless, I was beginning to see myself not as a liberal bohemian writer but as an uninvested, uninsured, marginal American.

This was a time when my values were being shaken for other reasons as well. Charles Manson had taken the radical chatter of revolution, the fantasy literature of Heinlein and Hesse, the interior mysteries of the Beatles' music—all of them secret signposts of my generation—plus a kind of idle, collective feeling that we were all more like each other than we were like our parents, and he had breathed it all horribly to life. He had forged a hippie commune into a gang of murderers. They killed between thirty-five and forty people, most of them not wealthy or well known or even much missed, but because they had killed actress Sharon Tate (who was eight months pregnant), and coffee heiress Abigail Folger, and hairstylist Jay Sebring, and a wealthy grocer named Leno LaBianca, and his wife (they stuck a fork in her abdomen), and because they had scribbled on the walls in their victims' blood the radical slogan of the day, "Death to Pigs," Manson became a hero in the radical community. "Offing those rich pigs with their own knives and forks, and then eating a meal in the same room—far out!" cheered Bernardine Dohrn at a Students for a Democratic Society (S.D.S.) convention. During a recess in the Chicago Seven trial, Yippie leader Jerry Rubin went to Los Angeles to speak to Charles Manson in jail. "I fell in love with Charlie Manson the first time I saw his cherub face and sparkling eyes on TV," Rubin wrote. Manson became an underground hero. He had his own column in the *Los Angeles Free Press*. *Rolling Stone* described him as "this smiling, dancing music man [who] offered a refreshing short cut, a genuine and revolutionary new morality that redefines or rather eliminates the historic boundaries between life and death."

Until then, when I spoke of revolution it was nothing more than an emphatic way of speaking of economic and political changes. I did not mean murder. After the Manson killings, I began to speak more carefully. I pulled back from the easy loathing of the middle class, which had become habitual in the writings of the underground press. Being a liberal had always involved having certain sentimental ties to the radical Left. After Manson, those ties snapped.

It's strange that my generation would find so much significance in assassinations and sensational murders. But we lived in an age of symbolic action. Manson was important to us because we saw in him the degeneration of our own lives and thinking. He had fostered the idea that he was Jesus, which his disciples truly seemed to believe. One underground paper published a sketch of Manson nailed to the cross, with a plaque above his head that said HIPPIE. There had always been, in the hippie movement, a spiritual yearning, a search for the countercultural Jesus, who was not clutched by the capitalists and the hypocritical, warmongering middle class. One could reject Jesus, but to accept and worship Manson suggested the insanity that yawned ahead when old values were thrown aside without new ones to replace them. It showed the bankruptcy of the revolutionary agenda, which was calling not for a new order but for chaos. When one of Manson's followers, Lynette ("Squeaky") Fromme, dressed up in a Little Red Riding Hood outfit and tried to shoot Gerald Ford in the genitals, it seemed to me that symbolic action had raced into new territory, the age itself had broken loose from anything like familiar reality, and the weird gesture had become paramount.

The airports were filled with religious extremists, but they were strangely different from the hot-eyed fanatics I had known in Dallas. They were selling not salvation but bliss. There was a monastic allure about the cults, which beckoned even to reasonable people who felt bewildered by their lives and wanted to retreat from complexity. One could shave one's head and put on saffron robes and sell Tootsie Rolls on the street corner. I felt a similar urge at times, but it was like the small compulsion one feels to jump out of windows when one is high, high off the ground. It was a call to the withered spirit to take flight from the towers of material desire to the self-effacement that awaits like a concrete slab. And of course one knew friends who made the leap.

The cults reconstructed the idea of the family so that it ran horizontally across the generations, and not vertically from one generation to the next. People wanted to be together without the burdens of children and aging parents. It seemed to me a way of staying in school, a dormitory life that might last—well, if not forever, at least for longer.

There was a gravitation from radical politics to radical religion. Loss of faith in the one led to a search for faith in the other (perhaps this is a cycle). Rennie Davis, for instance, cofounder of S.D.S., a man whose politics I had followed with interest, went to India in 1973 and became an acolyte of the sixteen-year-old guru, Maharaj Ji; Davis said he would "crawl across the face of the earth to kiss the feet of the Perfect Master." The line between matters that were properly spiritual and those that were necessarily political had become smeared. How were we supposed to deal with Third World insurgencies, now that our confidence had been shaken in Vietnam? During the Nicaraguan revolution, when the Sandinistas were fighting in the suburbs of Managua, the dictator Anastasio Somoza was hiding in his bunker, and an American delegation was desperately trying to negotiate peace, another American group of fifty transcendental meditationists booked a room in the Intercontinental Hotel and tried to levitate for peace. Newsmen found them hopping around the ballroom "like frogs." They said they had been sent by the Maharishi Mahesh Yogi to persuade Somoza to surrender his weapons and follow TM. Was this the future of the resistance?

I could criticize these religions because they seemed to me so transparently bogus, so rash and dramatic—and in the cases of Manson and, later, of Jim Jones, cults of personality, not of the spirit, which could become so crushingly evil. And yet I too felt spiritually empty. The prospect of parenthood made me feel it all the more keenly. I disagreed with what my parents had told me about God, but as a child I had been reassured by their belief. Now my belief in the supernatural was limited to an embarrassed half-acceptance of certain truths of astrology.

This was not a religion one could pass on to children. It did not answer questions about how and why we are here. It did not make one feel a part of a larger effort. I could face being an adult without answers to these questions, but as a parent I wanted to give my children the same religious comforts I had experienced as a child, even if they rejected them. Agnosticism was a chilly prospect for children, no matter what their sign.

And yet having children, the deliberate act of creation, was such an act of faith that it mocked my doubt. I thought about the resolution I made as an undergraduate, as I was wading through the existential philosophers, never to have children until I understood the purpose of life (undergraduates are allowed to think categorically). The point of life can't be just to go on and on, aimlessly, one generation producing the next, with no goal in mind. That is what I told myself, fiercely, at the age of twenty. At thirty, I was ready to accept that life must be perpetuated, regardless of its object, and that the act of making more life was both grave and joyful, a godlike power, the most severe responsibility and the closest approach to divinity I was likely to have.

John Gordon Wright was born April 10, 1976. His sister, Caroline Murphy Wright, came five years later, on October 20, 1981.

In the realm of politics I remained a believer, which is to say I was still a liberal. But ten years after the birth of the Great Society I was no longer devout. By now it was evident even to me that the primary consequences of liberalism were bureaucracy and taxes. Some of the good things that were supposed to happen did happen. The proportion of Americans living in poverty in 1959 was 22 percent; ten years later it was 12 percent; by 1979 it was down to 6 percent. Schools were integrated. Women entered careers that previously had been closed to them. The quality of our air and water was improving. In these respects the Great Society was a triumph.

But in other respects I was outdone with liberal thinking. Serious crimes had risen by 232 percent between 1960 and 1975. Liberal thinking replied this really wasn't so, it was an apparition, a function of better record keeping, although the truth was obvious to everyone. Murder, rape, robbery—these were regular features of every daily paper, but no longer front-page material. Enormous tragedy had become an ordinary event. During the New York City blackout of 1965, police reported fewer than one hundred arrests; when the same thing happened in 1977, more than three thousand looters were arrested. One didn't have to be robbed or beaten to feel intimidated by the advance of crime. I recall how, when I was growing up, my father would leave the car unlocked and running at the curbside while he ran into a store. People seldom thought about locking their houses at night. Now my parents' house was protected by an expensive security system, every door was bolted and chained, and despite these precautions they had been burglarized several times. Roberta was a modern working woman, and yet she was afraid to go out after dark. We assumed that bad things would happen, and when they did we blamed ourselves for not being properly prepared.

I agreed that poverty and racial oppression engendered crime. I supported programs, such as legal aid, designed to protect the rights of the accused. I approved of the Supreme Court rulings in *Miranda*, which required that every suspect be notified of his right to counsel, and in *Furman* v. *Georgia*, which briefly outlawed the death penalty. But I was disturbed by the apparently guilty people who were allowed to go free because of technicalities in the law.

For some reason these people had become a part of the liberal constituency. There was a general sense of approval in the liberal community for defense lawyers, and a corresponding loathing for prosecutors. Punishment was seen as repression. It was the same mentality that encouraged shoplifting, looting, and telephone fraud as a means of striking back at the Establishment, of "ripping off the system." However, as an investigative reporter I spent many hours in various prisons talking to convicts, and my liberal reflexes began to change. Most of the men I met had been damaged in childhood. It was easy to see how their miserable lives would direct them into lawlessness. But there was as well a contempt for their victims. The rapist who was stimulated by the way a woman dressed, the hitchhiker who murdered the man who gave him a ride—they believed that their victims had deserved what had been done to them, as if beauty and kindness were provocative acts. I had no way of knowing if this was a modern attitude, encouraged by a permissive society that excused the criminal and blamed the victim; perhaps criminals have always pardoned themselves in this manner. Being a liberal, I believed in rehabilitation; however, I was certain that nothing could be done to repair these men until they acknowledged the pain they had caused other people. The missing emotion was remorse.

There was a class of criminals, especially black criminals in the South, who were designated "political prisoners." My first published article was about the trial of three such men in North Carolina, who were convicted of burning down a stable and killing fifteen horses. They became known as the Charlotte 3, or the Lazy B 3. I had written of the trial as an injustice, because like most liberal whites I was impressed by the defendants, who were attractive, well-educated black men. One was a published poet, another had a doctorate in chemistry, another was a college student majoring in business administration. They had been organizing in the black community, using money from white churches. After their convictions they became an international cause célèbre. Angela Davis came to Charlotte to raise money for their defense fund. "Another year, another Christmas, has passed," wrote Tom

Wicker in *The New York Times,* "and T. J. Reddy, James Grant and Charles Parker are still in prison." Amnesty International listed them as "prisoners of conscience," in the same category as political prisoners in the gulags of Siberia or the dungeons of Chile. Two years after reporting on their trial, I went back to North Carolina to write a story for *New Times* magazine and uncovered two previously unknown witnesses to the crime. In effect, I proved that the convicted men were guilty, certainly one of the most indifferent triumphs in a reporter's career. What surprised me was the response from white liberals, who felt betrayed—not by the Charlotte 3, but by me. For many of them, the guilt of the men was not as important as the cause the men represented, which was the black political revolution in its terrorist phase. At bottom, liberals approved of the crime.

Liberals believe in the perfectibility of man. By the middle seventies this hypothesis had swollen to include the corollary notion that we are all perfect in our own way and no one can stand in judgment of another. Liberal judges became the enemy of the patrolman, who watched criminals go back on the street before the cops had finished their paperwork. Teachers lost their philosophical warrant for issuing grades; students who would otherwise be failed were passed along and ignored. The falling standards of education were reflected in the plummeting Scholastic Achievement Test scores (Is it significant that the fall in SAT scores began with the Kennedy assassination?) and also in lawsuits brought against schools by high school graduates who were unable to read. When I reported on education, I was dismayed by the willingness of administrators to simplify textbooks in order to give the appearance of success. In all of this there was a retreat from the rigor society requires in order to distinguish success from failure and to reward good and punish evil.

I had a small political epiphany in a grocery store in 1974 while I was standing in line behind a young man with modishly long hair, a mustache, a pipe in his mouth, and a copy of the *The New York Review of Books* under his arm. He might have been me in every particular. We could easily have exchanged grocery carts—

yoghurt, Orowheat bread, organic fruits and vegetables, Perrier water, et cetera—we were just beginning the health phase; jogging and quitting smoking loomed ahead. He was hip, he was intellectual, he was discriminating—like me. When he paid for his groceries he used food stamps.

I was shocked because my liberalism was directed at people who were not like me. My first reaction to the young man ahead of me in line was outrage. It seemed an especially low form of stealing, like taking money from the collection plate at church. At home, when I considered the episode more coolly, I wondered about the condescension that was at the heart of my liberalism. Government subsidies such as food stamps and welfare and even unemployment compensation were for people hindered by race or circumstance, not for people like me. And yet I too could qualify for some forms of relief. I realized I had different standards for minorities and the underprivileged, standards I would never accept for myself. My politics were compensatory, patronizing.

And I had gradually begun to hate the degradation that accompanied the liberal attitude toward freedom of expression. I had grown up in a city where cleanliness and order were prized above all other virtues, where sexual expression was highly controlled, and conformity was enforced through churches, schools, parents, and the abundant presence of policemen. Dallas was stricter than most cities, but in sixties' America it was not out of place. It may have been a repressive society, but one felt safe then, and the decorum that still existed between the sexes allowed for the play of romance. Oh, I had hated living in that breathless confinement. Now I wanted to retrieve something from that time—the discipline, I suppose, and some of the innocence. Once in Brooklyn I was pushing Gordon in his stroller through a park at twilight. There was broken glass everywhere. The walls were spray-painted with profanity. A park bench had been burned. I had a strong sense of apocalypse. I could understand the wild-eyed certainty of the street-corner preacher when he said the end was near. And when I turned the corner I came upon two people fucking on the sidewalk. I was frozen. It was as much as I could stand.

* * *

Another blow to my liberalism was the fall of Saigon. I had been
expecting it, without really caring very deeply. I suppose this is the
sin the world resents most about America, that it can create such
mischief in the lives of other people without giving much thought
to the consequences. It was April 29, 1975. On the news, I watched
the helicopters taking off from the roof of the American embassy,
leaving behind thousands who had come to depend on us, who
stood outside the gates with their possessions in their hands. Their
state of mind may be understood by the fact that while they stood
there a rain of singed but intact hundred-dollar bills fell unnoticed
among them, as the marines on the roof tried ineffectually to
dispose of seven million dollars with a flamethrower.

We were abandoning them, and abandoning their country,
which had by now become partly American, so powerfully had we
affected it. For months we had seen the end coming, as the South
Vietnamese troops retreated from the highland provinces and millions of refugees fled toward Saigon and the coastal cities. The
North Vietnamese watched them flee, seldom harassing them; in
one case, when South Vietnamese troops were evacuating Hue, the
North Vietnamese rolled a column of tanks to the edge of the city
and lit the evacuation route with their powerful headlights. And
yet the panic that ensued was spectacular. Three hundred South
Vietnamese soldiers stormed a World Airways jumbo jet in Da
Nang and pushed the civilians off the plane; many people died
trying to board the flight, some had already been killed on the
runway when the jet had landed, and when it took off, people were
clinging to its wings and undercarriage. They all fell into the sea.
The remaining soldiers stripped off their uniforms and went on a
rampage, killing, in one instance, twenty-five refugees crammed
onto the fantail of an American ship, apparently for no other reason
than their anger that others would escape, but not them. In this
chaos, Americans had seized the idea of getting as many orphans
out of Vietnam as possible. There were massive, confused airlifts
of children, only some of whom were offspring of American service-

men and not all of whom were orphans. It was a bewildering exodus. One of the C-5A transports crashed, killing over a hundred children. The North Vietnamese charged us with kidnapping.

In the middle of this fantastic downfall in the last days of South Vietnam, two Hollywood producers at the Academy Awards ceremony accepted their Oscar for the film documentary *Hearts and Minds* by reading "greetings of friendship" from the leader of the North Vietnamese Communist party. There was an outcry, but what struck me is that the catastrophe of the fall of Saigon would be played out in much the same fashion in America as the war had been: that is, as a controversy on TV.

I felt ambivalent. I wanted to believe the North Vietnamese were better than we, and ready for friendship. In the meantime, in the other war, the real one, people were selling their children and burning their money, mothers were wading into the sea with their babies, and chaos, frenzy, and fear had broken down anything like ordered behavior.

As I watched the fall of Saigon from my living room, I was heaving with relief and guilt. It was like a final release from a long and ugly illness, a death one had come to wish for. The Vietnam War was over. Fifty thousand people gathered in Central Park to celebrate peace and sing the old songs of the antiwar movement and hear the speeches one more time.

Two weeks before Saigon fell, the Khmer Rouge completed its conquest of Cambodia; the Pathet Lao consolidated its victory in Laos a few months later. Since Eisenhower, I had been hearing about the domino theory, and although I had ridiculed it, I had to admit that some of the dominoes had fallen as predicted. Who knew what consequences lay ahead? Vietnam was now the third-largest Communist country in the world, with the third-largest army in the world, larger even than our own. What would I propose to do if Vietnam marched on Thailand? I had no answer.

The news from Southeast Asia suddenly stopped. The reporters were expelled. We were living on rumors, and the rumors were awful. We heard that the capital of Cambodia had been evacuated, hundreds of thousands of people were being sent into the countryside; it was a bizarre, almost prehistorical attack on urbanity. In Vietnam much of the population was being sent to reeducation camps, for indoctrination or execution. We heard these things through diplomatic sources, but there was not the usual film footage that had documented the history of the war. Then the boat people began to appear, often hundreds of them on a single fragile raft, drifting in the South China Sea in hopes of reaching the international shipping lanes. At first it was not so dramatic. One expected the end of the war to cause panic and dislocation before the new order took hold. But the boat people kept coming. Passing freighters would pick them up, but there were so many of them, and more and more every month, so that the freighters would steam two hundred miles off course just to avoid the burden of taking on these passengers, who would cause them to be refused docking rights in most Asian countries. It had become one of the world's major emigrations, increasing each year, and the stories of the refugees were appalling. Vietnam was purging its entire ethnic Chinese population, more than a million people, and the government was charging them as much as $3,000 apiece for the privilege of being driven into the sea in open boats toward freedom or death. By 1979 this heinous extortion had replaced the export of coal as Vietnam's primary source of hard currency. The migration continued more than a decade after the fall of Saigon. According to the United Nations, more than half a million Vietnamese have fled their country by boat; the American ambassador to the United Nations places the total number of boat people at four times that figure. The estimates are complicated by the likelihood that as many die on their journey as those who survive to be counted.

At the same time hundreds of thousands of refugees were walking out of Laos and Cambodia, many of them settling into camps on the Thai border. They spoke of the bloodbath that had often been predicted, but that I had never believed. A quarter of the population of Cambodia, starved to death or murdered? Two million people dead? Had my father proposed such a figure to me, I would have said, "What kind of monsters do you think they are?" The monsters were on our side, I believed. I could quote the terrible figures. We had dropped seven million tons of bombs in Vietnam, twice as many as we dropped in World War II; that was five hundred pounds of explosive for every human being in Vietnam. It was genocide, I said; we were waging a war against the people and the land itself. But the truth was that the rate of population growth during the war in both South Vietnam and North Vietnam was approximately twice what it was in the United States during the same period. One could scarcely call this genocide; it was merely war. In fact, the percentage of civilians killed was far lower than in Korea, and no higher than World War II. Now that the war was over I was learning what genocide really meant.

"Certainly today the record is clear for all to see," Nixon summed up from his bitter exile: "a Communist peace kills more than an anti-Communist war." I wasn't ready to swallow this axiom entirely, but I realized that for most of my life I had accepted a certain willful blindness toward any negative consequences of Communism.

I was shaken by my willingness to disbelieve the truth, which was evident all during the war, that our enemy was not perfect after all. Did this mean that the war in Indochina had been morally defensible? Had I been wrong all along? Or was Vietnam simply a tragedy we could not prevent, and had made worse by trying? I now began to reconsider America's role in a world that was, to me, newly complex.

15 / MY PRESIDENT

We were living in Atlanta, Georgia, in 1974 when the outgoing governor announced he was a candidate for president. The headline in the *Atlanta Constitution* read JIMMY CARTER'S RUNNING FOR WHAT? A few months before, he had made an appearance as a mystery guest on "What's My Line?" One of the panelists guessed he was a mystic and asked if he recruited nuns.

It was exciting to have a Georgian in the presidential race, but at the time I was more interested in who was going to replace Carter in the governor's office. His immediate predecessor, and likely successor, was Lester Maddox, a florid, balding incarnation of Elmer Fudd. Maddox had made a name for himself in 1964 when he chased three black divinity students out of his chicken restaurant with an ax handle. Two years later he was governor of Georgia. "I never doubted I'd win," he liked to boast. "All I had to do was beat the state Democratic party, every major labor leader, the state Republican party, all one hundred fifty-nine courthouses, about four hundred city halls, all the politicians of rank—*every one* of 'em—every major newspaper, the television and radio stations, the railroads, all the major banks, all the major industries, the utility companies. So that's what I did. I beat *everybody.*" One of the people he beat was a little-known state senator and peanut farmer from Plains, who was in his first statewide race. Carter did not run well in that election, he was crushed, but he was a careful student of Maddox's use of symbols and his antiestablishment, outsider appeal.

Maddox was easily the most recognizable man in Georgia, and after George Wallace the most famous politician in the South. He was on the Dick Cavett show twice. His record album, *God, Family and Country*, sold five thousand copies in the first week. There was an off-Broadway musical review entitled *Red, White and Maddox*. The secret of his celebrity was his own utter inability to be embarrassed by who he was, combined with a general amazement that such a person could be elected to any office anywhere, even on a whim. And yet Maddox was a surprisingly good governor, honest, and successful in certain populist ways. He called himself a segregationist, but he appointed more blacks to state jobs than any previous governor. He was a patron saint to the state's huge prison population because of his penal reforms and large-scale reprieves. Under Georgia law Maddox could not succeed himself as governor, so he made a brief run for president (Georgia, the cradle of presidential candidates), then he prudently came home and got himself elected lieutenant governor. While he was in office he opened up a shop in Atlanta where he sold Lester Maddox memorabilia, such as autographed ax handles, Lester Maddox T-shirts, and the Lester Maddox Wake Up America alarm clock. For Christmas one year, my Georgia brother-in-law gave my parents a Lester Maddox toilet seat.

This was Jimmy Carter's political mentor, although the two men would become famous enemies. By whipping Carter, Maddox had taught him how to win in Georgia. The next time Carter stumped for governor he was a born-again Christian in a flannel shirt, running against the "liberal" Atlanta establishment and enjoying the support of most of the leading segregationists in the state, including Lester Maddox.

That was an education no national politician had ever received, because for the last century winning in Georgia had been an absolute bar to higher office. The South extracted compromises that no candidate could live with beyond its borders. The quandary of Jimmy Carter was that he wanted to go beyond. On the day of his inauguration as governor, he made a statement that would set him free of the South. "I say to you quite frankly that the time for racial

discrimination is over. Our people have already made this major
and difficult decision. . . . No poor, rural, weak, or black person
should ever have to bear the additional burden of being deprived
of the opportunity of an education, a job, or simple justice." That
speech got him on the cover of *Time* magazine. He was now a
national figure, of sorts, but he was curiously dead in Georgia.

I was covering the 1974 governor's race—the race to succeed
Carter—for *The Progressive*, a liberal northern monthly, which
viewed Georgia politics as a racial horror show. In the contest for
lieutenant governor, for instance, there was a Nazi who claimed
that "Hitler was too moderate" and a conservative black doctor
who went to jail in the middle of the campaign for contempt of
court (he neglected to pay his child support). However, I was just
learning that Georgia politics was far more subtle than it appeared
to the rest of the country, which would shortly be overwhelmed by
a man who learned his trade by courting votes among the small-
town bigots and the Lions Club bourgeoisie and the snake-handling
Christians of rural Georgia.

I caught up with Lester Maddox at a rally in Griffin. He marched
into the crowd in the middle of a team of majorettes, wearing a
Shriner's fez and throwing candy to the children. He made a quick
speech, pledging a war on crime, then he hopped on a bicycle and
peddled backward. It was his favorite campaign stunt, and thrilling
to witness. I was surprised to notice about a dozen black people in
the crowd, some of them wearing Maddox buttons and carrying
MADDOX WITHOUT A RUNOFF signs. Despite his assurance to voters
that he was "still a segregationist," Maddox was the only candidate
to advertise in black newspapers, and a Blacks for Maddox office
had just opened in Milledgeville.

He was in the contest with fifteen other men. One of them, a
former state employee in the Department of Corrections, said he
had been directed by God on two occasions, January 2 and 8, to
enter the race. Less-divine contenders included Bert Lance, the
North Georgia banker who was Carter's designated successor, and

George Busbee, the Georgia House majority leader. My favorite candidate was Ronnie "Machine Gun" Thompson, the mayor of Macon, who was entered in both the Republican and Democratic primaries. He was a political figure only Georgia could produce— that is, a white gospel singer who became mayor on a "shoot to kill" platform, and a segregationist who was a close friend of many black recording artists, including James Brown. Thompson got his nickname when he personally returned a sniper's fire with a spray from a police machine gun. His campaign song was "If You Don't Like Policemen, Call a Hippie."

Both Maddox and Thompson made the runoffs, Maddox as a Democrat and Thompson as a Republican. Maddox's opponent was the colorless moderate, George Busbee. Maddox opened the campaign by playing the racial gambit. He charged that Busbee was a tool of the black state representative, Julian Bond, who had become a national figure some years before when the Georgia House refused to seat him after his election. "The fellows I'll be in a runoff with are the two B's—Busbee and Bond," Maddox declared. "In South Georgia they are calling Busbee 'Julian Busbee.'" Bond did support Busbee, although not very significantly (like Carter, he was off running for president), but in Georgia it was a political sin for a white politician to appear to be courting the black vote. Once when a photograph of Lester Maddox and Julian Bond chatting in the capitol hallways was published in Georgia newspapers, Maddox had received a number of death threats, so the darker interpretation of the "Julian Busbee" ploy was that Maddox was trying to have his opponent murdered.

"I have made no special appeal to Julian Bond," Busbee declared. "If the lieutenant governor would bother to check the vote of the House, he would find that George Busbee voted against seating Julian Bond in the House because of the activities and the statements made by him on the draft cards and other matters concerning the war in Vietnam." That was Busbee's attempt to dodge the racial tag. In the meantime, Maddox had his own problems with a Ku Klux Klan endorsement, which is the donkey's tail for the pseudosegregationist. The candidate claimed that "Maddox-haters" had concocted the endorsement, and as a matter of fact Maddox "didn't even believe we have such an organization as the Ku Klux Klan in Georgia." That statement disgusted Grand Dragon James Lumpkin, who said that "every race Maddox has been in he's had the support of the Klan." Just when it began to look awkward for Maddox, the noisiest black activist in the state, the firebrand Hosea Williams, endorsed Busbee. Outraged, Busbee cried that he had never met or talked to Williams, and in fact he understood that Williams was secretly working for Maddox. Williams had to admit that he had twice referred to Maddox as "the best governor we've ever had" on Atlanta radio talk shows, but he claimed he was still endorsing Busbee, even if Busbee didn't want his support. "White folks have risen above that," Williams said when he was asked if this was a race-baiting tactic to bring down Busbee. "White folks ain't that stupid."

Busbee won the runoff and the general election, despite his unwanted black support. Maddox went on to join Bond and Carter in the presidential race, along with another Georgian, a black Republican who was running an antiprofanity campaign. It was still early in the presidential season, but already I had the feeling that Georgia politics had grown too sophisticated for the rest of the nation to withstand. Somebody from Georgia was bound to win.

Jimmy Carter was an enigma, and that is a frustrating quality in a politician. He was fortunate to be running for office at a time when people seemed to want qualities he seemed to have. He certainly didn't look like a president. "His countenance, unsmiling, resembles that of an intelligent gun dog," noticed the *Sunday Times* of London. His most attractive feature was his obscurity. Watergate had been such a tar baby that every politician in Washington was stuck to it, as was every lawyer. "I am not a professional politician," Carter would remind us. "I am not a lawyer." He did not live in Washington. He was not in any real sense a party man. In another year, what Carter was not would have been seen as liabilities, as they soon proved to be, but in 1976, our bicentennial year, we were longing for the lost innocence of our republic and looking for forgiveness. It was jokingly said that Jimmy Carter took his initials too seriously, but there was that religious air about him, and the unstated subtext of his campaign was that Carter was our political savior.

The first time I saw Jimmy Carter he was already a candidate for president. Roberta was an assistant book buyer at Rich's department store, and helped to arrange an autograph party for Carter's campaign book, *Why Not the Best?* Scarcely anyone came. Carter's four years as governor had been acrimonious. He had not been careful in the way a politician would be who intends to hold on to local power. He had been curt and inflexible. He had cultivated tastes that his constituents considered eccentric, such as the music of Bob Dylan and the philosophy of Reinhold Niebuhr. He had never been much of a hand-shaker or a baby kisser; he was not widely loved or even widely known. If Lester Maddox had held a book signing, the store would have been mobbed. Instead, there was Carter sitting alone on a small dais, grinning into space, cordoned off by gold ropes, and discreetly attended by Secret Service men. Given the department store setting, he reminded me of an unfrocked Santa waiting for kids to sit on his lap.

But there was also about him a peculiar radiance, which had partly to do with the lights shining on his orangish hair and partly to do with the glow of power and celebrity. Even a political dark horse like Carter acquires an aura when he announces for the presidency. One begins to read about the candidate in the papers, and soon grows acquainted with his family on television, and learns to recognize his voice and features—without really knowing him, one knows so much about him that it has a queer effect on nonpublic people like me. I wanted to go up to Carter, to talk to him and perhaps offer my support in his campaign, but his chances seemed so remote, and the radiance held me back.

The next time I saw Jimmy Carter was inauguration day. I was in Washington, perhaps the only journalist in town who was not writing about politics that week (I was working on water pollution). Sunday at noon on January 20, 1977, I was in Herman Talmadge's senatorial office with about a hundred other Georgians watching Carter take the oath of office on TV. He was only a block away in person, but the crowds were so great and the day so cold I had retreated indoors. As we watched the icy breath float from the mouth of the first southern president since the Civil War, a procession began to form in Talmadge's office; it was the Instamatic Line, an orderly queue of believers such as you might see at tent revivals and every Saturday night at "The Grand Ole Opry." They shuffled toward the senator's television set to kneel and flash a picture of Jimmy Carter on TV. It seemed to me a pledge of allegiance that the South had not been able to make to the rest of the nation since the reign of Andrew Jackson.

After the ceremony I walked outside into the brilliant, frigid day. The ground was covered with new snow, which squeaked when I stepped on it. I stood on Pennsylvania Avenue to watch the parade. At that point in my life I had seen only one American president, Dwight Eisenhower, who rode in a motorcade in the 1960 Boy Scout Jamboree. Eisenhower went by so quickly that I hardly got an impression of him, other than a smiling man standing in an open convertible, waving his arms over his head in that characteristic gesture of his as he raced past thousands of silent Boy Scouts. But the power of the presidency is such that I doubt there is a single one of those scouts who does not remember a quarter of a century later that he saw Eisenhower.

Now, however, the simple American action of watching a presidential parade drummed up old and complex fears in me, and an instinctive defensiveness. As we waited for Carter I prepared to make a quick mental snapshot of the passing limousine and to note the President's face. The marching bands came, and then the train of black Lincolns—and then a murmur in the crowd, a rustle of astonishment that caused me instinctively to cringe. But it was not a fearful sound; it was joyous. "He's walking!" people cried out. "He's walking!" Before we could disbelieve it, there he was, right in front of me, holding his wife's hand and walking down the center stripe of Pennsylvania Avenue. For many of us, it brought tears to our eyes. He was trusting us not to kill him.

* * *

The South was suddenly, briefly, chic. It had been discovered by the networks and the New York magazines. How wonderful, at last, to believe that I was in the center of life and not on its gray periphery. Everyone within the outer circle of the South was aware of it, this new sense of importance, and of acceptance, and of being in the spotlight.

The Deep South was emerging into the new world. You could see the skyscrapers sprouting in Charlotte and Atlanta, and the suburbs splashing across county lines. More than that, you could feel the juice surging through southern humanity, like an adrenal burst. To be in Georgia then was to be inside the inner circle. It reminded me of Texas a decade before, when Lyndon Johnson was president. Texas had become a real place then, an international dateline, and despite the moral complications of the assassination and the frequent embarrassment of watching Lyndon address his fell' Ummurrukuns, I had come to see myself as having an authentic heritage, however flawed and wrongheaded. I was a real person. Now that same feeling of coming to life was spreading across the South, and there was a sense of marveling at oneself and a humorous and forgiving feeling of being who one was after all.

We were living now in the New South, that is, the postracist South that had been promised since Georgia Senator Benjamin Hill coined the term during Reconstruction. It was essentially an advertising term, as in New, Improved South, which was designed to beckon industry and the balm of federal money. Investment in the South was booming, and a great image-reversal was taking place. School buses were being bombed in Denver and Detroit, while desegregation was succeeding in many southern schools. The entire country had lost a war now, not just the old Confederacy. The South now appeared prosperous, dynamic, and racially harmonious, while the North was languishing, losing its grip on industry, tumbling into racial despair.

Georgia was always the avant-garde of the civil rights movement, the homeplace of so many of its leaders; a battleground, certainly,

but the place where the ancient distress would finally resolve itself—through love. That was the electrifying message Carter delivered. No candidate or president I knew had ever said the word
aloud, but Carter said it boldly and all the time. Love as a political
doctrine was so raw it could only have sprung from the rural South,
a region where sophistication was not worshiped but Jehovah was;
where sudden death at the hands of passion was not an abstraction;
where people's daily lives were stultifying but whose spiritual lives
were filled with crude and spectacular intensity. There was this
particular irony that the rest of the country had not sorted out,
which was that while the rural South had resisted the politics of
the civil rights movement, it had been vulnerable to the spiritual
message, which was unconditional love. This was a revelation ec-
statically received in the churches of Calvary and Holiness and
Pentecost and Nazarene, and in the charismatic, deep-water Baptist church that Jimmy Carter attended. "Blacks have always
known that our best allies are those Southern whites," said Andrew
Young, "who have dared to live by their religious principles and
who have been through the fire of persecution because of it."

The epicenter of this great phenomenon, the reformation of the
South, was Plains. It was here that the Peanut Brigade formed up
and followed Carter through the primaries, paying their own expenses, knocking on doors of New Hampshire and Massachusetts
and walking the black wards of the big northern cities. They came
to spread the word about Carter and to disarm the old prejudices
about the South. It was a task Carter could not have accomplished
alone. Eventually, as Carter swept through the primaries behind
that famous grin of his, which was like the *Cutty Sark* under full
sail, reporters arrived to poke around Plains, to meet the other
Carters and to get a fix on this new political force. Very soon the
town of Plains, population 683, came to represent a vision of a lost
America, almost a preindustrial America of porch swings and soft-
ball games and Sunday school picnics. This was an America that
remained spiritually intact, unrushed, bound by profound family
ties and ruled by values deeply rooted in agrarian traditions that
seemed precious and, until now, nearly irretrievable. If the other

side of Plains—that is, the Klan and the White Citizens Council and the black tenant farmers on the Carter acreage—did occasionally lurch into view, it only added to the power of the metaphor Plains had become.

In its modest and frequently comical fashion, Jimmy Carter's hometown assumed a mythical, sitcom status in the national consciousness. Everyone knew the cast of characters, who were all Carters—Miz Lillian, the formidable mother; Ruth Carter Stapleton, the faith-healing evangelist; the redneck brother, Billy, who became a wisecracking, beer-guzzling antidote to the parson's manner of his elder brother—and so on, into the uncles and cousins twice removed, each of these characters being folksy and two-dimensional in exactly the ways that television characters would be, and each with his own constituency. I doubt, for instance, that Carter would have carried the Wallace voters without the image of the good ole boys sitting around Billy's filling station, or the women's vote without the forceful female figures of his mother and his wife. They reflected on Carter, as did his nanny and the black playmates of his youth. They were a part of him, and so we understood Carter's psyche as being partly redneck, partly female, and partly black.

Even before the election, Plains had become a roadside shrine, a stop on the way to Florida for many tourists who were drawn there by curiosity and nostalgia. It was a simple farm town, made possible by the conjunction of U.S. Highway 290 with two farm-to-market roads and the Seaboard Coast Line railroad. It was like a million such anonymous crossings in the web of America—like Seward, Kansas, my father's hometown, or Rutledge, Georgia, 120 miles north of Plains, my mother's birthplace—and because it was no more than it was, Plains seemed a part of me, a part of my ancestral, small-town past.

When a reporter asked Billy Carter on election night what he thought was going to happen to Plains now that his brother was standing on the steps of the railroad depot, tears streaming down his face, declaring victory, Billy predicted the town was "going to go to hell in a handbasket." That burst of candor was the only good laugh my father got in the entire election. We were watching the returns together in an Atlanta hotel room. He had voted for Ford, without much enthusiasm, and had watched Carter with increasing suspicion. "I will never lie to you," "Trust me," "If we could just have a government as good and as honest and as decent and as competent and as compassionate and as filled with love as are the American people—" my father heard these campaign statements from Carter with a cynicism I had not seen in him before. It was Nixon's legacy to him, this distrust.

For the first time since 1960, my mother voted for a Democrat— as how could she not, she still had the South in her mouth. When she heard Carter speaking, he was ratifying her origins as well as her accent. All of her life she had paid in incidental ways for being a Georgian; people had made unfair assumptions about her intelligence or sophistication; she had been judged as being racially biased because of her background. Now there was a man who forced everyone to understand the complexity and nobility and beauty of the Deep South experience.

I was a Carter man much as my father had been a Nixon man. Here was a candidate who talked about human rights, ecology, tax reform, arms control, mass transit, equal opportunity—issues that had animated me for most of my political life—as well as such nonliberal concerns as civil service reform, fiscal restraint, governmental reorganization, and deregulation, which had become more important to me as my faith in government began to wane. Carter described himself as being liberal on social issues, but also as a fiscal conservative, which suggested that he believed in social programs without wanting to pay for them. I had come to the same position myself.

For me, however, the real appeal of Jimmy Carter was spiritual. He promised to make America work again, which all candidates do, but he also promised to make it good again. Carter was fond of quoting Niebuhr's maxim that politics is the sad duty of establishing justice in a sinful world. In the anguish after Watergate, Carter's political theology promised to redeem a political system that had been corrupted by the small-minded, self-interested Washington insiders. He would sweep through the temple and chase away the money changers. He would bring to government the same redemptive love that had transformed the civil rights movement. He would restore our moral standing among nations.

To my father, who was as religious as Carter, and who did not believe America needed to justify itself to depraved old Europe, or the Communist world, or the corrupt and ruthless governments of the Third World, Carter's preachments were infuriating. But to me, who had come of age in a time of political murder and a bad war, and who had lost my own faith, Carter appeared to be the redeemer I sought. Perhaps the burden of my generation was to live in the reflected light of my father's time, when America had been, in our minds, purer and worthier, before pride led it astray. Jimmy Carter, in all humility, promised to make America holy again.

As president, Jimmy Carter will probably be seen as a transition between the end of Roosevelt liberalism and the beginning of Reagan conservatism, a small figure in the shadows of Johnson, Nixon, and Reagan, a pothole in the minds of students searching for the name of the thirty-ninth president. He cut the federal deficit in half (under Ford, the deficit was higher than it had ever been, $66 billion); he increased defense spending; he slowed the growth of welfare programs; he deregulated the airlines, the banks, the railroads, and the trucking and communication industries. In the process he alienated the Democratic liberals in Congress, and lost the support of his own party. His presidency was a precursor of the new world conservatism that would triumph four years later, bringing in Ronald Reagan and sweeping away the liberal war-horses of the Senate—Bayh, Church, McGovern—who were the center of resistance to Carter's legislative agenda.

Almost everyone agrees that Carter was a failure as President; he's been thrown onto the same heap with Nixon and Johnson; and yet for me Carter still represents unsolved problems concerning what I think about the presidency, and America's role in the world, and virtue as a goal of politics.

There was a conceit, when Carter came into office, that the presidency had grown too large, that it had thrown the powers of

government out of balance. Johnson and Nixon had waged undeclared wars; Nixon had attempted to impose a police state on the
country while corrupting the executive branch. And although both
men had been brought down by popular reaction, it did not seem
enough; the presidency itself must be bridled. There was significant
talk about turning to a parliamentary democracy, or, failing that,
adopting a single six-year term. The appurtenances of the presidency—the helicopter, the Marine Band, the Air Force jet, the
color blue—were more appropriate for a European monarch of
another era than a modern American head of state. The pomp of
the presidential arrival, not only in Paris or Bonn but also in
Cleveland or Fort Worth, was accompanied by an oxymoronic
sensation when *Air Force One* touched down, the carpet unfurled,
the band struck up "Hail to the Chief," and out stepped—well,
Lyndon Johnson or Richard Nixon or Gerald Ford. One felt fortunate that there was not a presidential costume, a robe and a crown.
Only Kennedy had the natural elegance to be an American king.

Jimmy Carter campaigned as a common citizen, carrying his
own luggage and sleeping in the homes of his supporters. Even his
faith in God was common, one could say primitive, despite his
interest in theology. He was "born again," something educated and
enlightened people didn't say. Toward God, and toward the American populace, he lowered his head. He was no more than one of
us, he said; he was no more decent and honest and sensible than
are the American people. His humility was appropriate for the
times. One believed that with Carter, at least, there would be no
war, no scandals; one asked very little more from him than that.
And indeed, he offered us little more than himself; his platform was
clean living and repentance.

When Gerald Ford stumbled, or fell on the ski slope, or got shot
at by women, he had seemed to diminish the presidency, because
we saw the occasionally clumsy human occupying the symbolic
office of America. Under Carter, the humanizing of the presidency
was a matter of policy. It seemed to be a part of his mandate to
make the presidency smaller, Carter-sized. One of his first actions
was to sell the presidential yacht, a symbolic action that had exactly

the opposite effect upon me than I might have supposed. He
lounged about in blue jeans, he gave a fireside chat wearing a
cardigan sweater. He liked to jog, and he entered a ten-kilometer
race that he failed to finish. His humanity was always on display,
disconcertingly so. He forced us to judge him as a person, not a
symbol. Some of his qualities were remarkable. For instance, I
never recall him saying "uh" in any of his numerous press conferences; he had such comprehensive, detailed responses to every
question that he reminded you of the best student you ever knew.
Like Kennedy, with whom he sought to be compared, he was a
voracious reader, swallowing huge briefs one after another—he
even found time to read the Bible in Spanish every night. But these
qualities were features of his insecurity; he was overcompensating;
he was mistaking omniscience for wisdom. During the first six
months of his presidency, according to his former speechwriter,
James Fallows, even such details as who would use the White
House tennis court each week were referred to Carter for his
approval. He wanted control, but he didn't really want power.

Congress quickly sensed this and learned to ignore him. The rest
of the world soon arrived at the same conclusion; attacks on America became hysterical at the very time when America was admitting
its faults. Even our allies treated us with contempt. All across the
globe antidemocratic forces discovered room to maneuver. No
doubt the trauma of Vietnam had left America in a state of semi-
paralysis, but by nature and religion Carter seemed disinclined to
respond forcibly to the humiliations America suffered during his
presidency.

At last, however, I believed that America was morally correct.
Carter proved himself a peacemaker by personally extracting a
Middle East settlement from Anwar Sadat and Menachem Begin
during an extraordinary thirteen-day arbitration at Camp David. It
was a triumph of Carter's best qualities: his persistence and his
unfailing belief in the fundamental goodness of all people. Even
though the agreement soon would cost Sadat his life, it was a great
achievement and one that meant much to me, with my fond
attachment to Egypt. Carter put a black civil rights preacher,

Andrew Young, in the United Nations, which had become a forum for anti-American complaints, and he made human rights the centerpiece of his foreign policy. His commitment to human rights was not really "absolute," as he had said in his inaugural address (the policy did not apply at all in the Philippines, for instance), but it was a criterion nonetheless: No longer would we prop up friendly dictators or military juntas that murdered their opponents in the name of anti-Communism. The point of the human rights policy was to look at the world as something other than a field of operations for American interests. Instead of saving the world for Coca-Cola, we would use our influence to aid the Soviet Jew or the Chilean dissident; in some respect every citizen in the world stood beneath the umbrella of Carter's new doctrine. We became the guarantors of freedom everywhere. Because it really was important to Carter, the policy had an effect. The number of Jews permitted to emigrate from Russia rose from 14,000 in 1976 to more than 50,000 in 1979 (then fell sharply after the Russian invasion of Afghanistan). Political prisoners began to surface in Argentina, Indonesia, even in Cuba. Despite the ridicule Carter received from the practitioners of Realpolitik, he was saving lives.

The unanticipated result of the human rights policy was that America became a court of appeal for every dissident group in the world. Already regarded as being close to omnipotence, we added to our powers the moral judgment of other governments—and at a time when our strongest instincts were to pull back from adventure and to settle into the family of nations like a rich uncle. This seemed to me a perfectly proper arrangement. After Vietnam, I had no desire to force my beliefs on other countries; I was not an isolationist, but I didn't believe we should be the world's policeman, either. I was uncomfortable with our running a world we knew so little about. Once we reached some decent understanding with the Soviets, we could withdraw from the inevitable conflicts of developing countries and the entangling alliances George Washington warned us against. We could let our will be known by rewarding our friends and criticizing our enemies. We would become like Europe—that is, less powerful, and less blameful.

Until the Soviet invasion of Afghanistan, Carter had similar views. "Our people have now learned the folly of our trying to inject our power into the internal affairs of other nations. It is time that our government learned that lesson too," he said during his first campaign. In one of his early presidential addresses, he said "We are free now of that inordinate fear of Communism which once led us to embrace any dictator in that fear." Then on Christmas Day in 1979, the Russians initiated a full-scale invasion of Afghanistan, and Jimmy Carter became a convert to the extreme anti-Soviet views of his national security adviser, Zbigniew Brzezinski. "My opinion of the Russians has changed more drastically in the last week than even the previous two and one half years before that," Carter said. We heard no more about human rights and the need to scale back our military expenditures. Instead, Carter asked Congress to reinstitute compulsory registration for the draft and began a military buildup that was without precedent in peacetime. He banned grain sales to the Soviet Union and ordered a boycott of the 1980 Olympic Games in Moscow. He also set about repairing relations with Pakistan's military dictator, Mohammad Zia ul-Haq, who had overthrown and then put to death the democratically elected prime minister of that country, Zulfikar Ali Bhutto. Carter had discovered, in the last year of his office, that morality as a foreign policy is limited by the assumption that the rest of the world will be bound by the same standards.

And anyway, despite our best efforts to do good, most of the world seemed to regard America as evil—indeed, as the source of evil itself. It was within our unlimited power, everyone supposed, to remove tyrants, eliminate poverty, and dispense justice—although we were also regarded as being responsible for those conditions in the first place. The attacks on America in the seventies were founded on this double premise: We had caused the problems, and we could cure them. How far from true this was may be seen in the example of Iran.

Iran was not an entirely real country to me. There was Iran, our devoted ally, the greedy OPEC partner, a newly industrialized country on Russia's southwestern border, and there was Persia, the

land of flying carpets and veiled women and Omar Khayyám singing in the wilderness. Over both of these entities ruled the shah,
Mohammed Reza Pahlevi, upon his Peacock Throne. I was opposed to the shah because I despised royalty on principle, even in
its vestigial forms, although Iran had been ruled by a monarchy for
2500 years, and the shah was a progressive leader. He had the
reputation of being a ruthless modernizer, who had given away the
royal lands to peasants, but who also bulldozed ancient villages to
make way for new agricultural collectives. He had advanced the
cause of women's rights and dispatched teams of teachers and
health workers to the countryside to improve the lives of the poor
farmers. He had even invited humanitarian groups, including Amnesty International and the Red Cross, to tour his prisons and
advise him on improving conditions there. Despite his liberal record, the shah was the world's most eager customer in the arms
market. During the Nixon administration, when he had carte
blanche to purchase even the most advanced weaponry, he spent
nearly $20 billion on American arms. Now, under Carter, who had
pledged to cut back on the weapons merchandising of the past, the
shah still accounted for one third of our foreign military sales.

On the day the shah arrived in Washington for a visit during
Carter's first year in office, four thousand anti-shah protesters
(mostly students), armed with clubs and staves, attacked the fifteen
hundred pro-shah supporters in Lafayette Park, opposite the White
House. More than a hundred people were injured. Washington
police dispersed the demonstrators with tear gas, which wafted
across the White House fence and onto the south lawn, where
President Carter was welcoming the shah and his wife. The newspapers the next day showed Carter wiping tears from his eyes as
he listened to the shah's remarks. To me that episode suggested
something about the amiable chaos of American democracy.
Carter seemed to feel the same way when he joked at the state
dinner that evening, "There is one thing I can say about the
shah—he knows how to draw a crowd." However, when reports of
the protests reached Tehran, opposition leaders interpreted them
as a sign from Carter that he had backed away from the shah, and

they immediately began to organize. They had been waiting for a signal to begin in earnest, and Carter's tears had provided it. This would be the great puzzle for Americans, that the Iranian revolution was directed not at the shah, who was already fatally wounded with cancer and who would spend his last year wandering the globe seeking sanctuary and medical treatment; it was instead a revolution directed at us and was waged to some extent for our benefit.

The students in Lafayette Park held us responsible for keeping the shah on his throne. They were followers of the exiled religious leader, the Ayatollah Ruhollah Khomeini, who called the United States "the great Satan," and who said Jimmy Carter was "the vilest man on Earth," because of his continuing support for the shah. For his part, the shah blamed Jimmy Carter for the demonstrations against his regime, in both America and Iran, which he thought were prompted by Carter's sermons on human rights. Later he suggested that his downfall was brought about by a conspiracy between American oil companies and the CIA in a scheme to raise oil prices. In the Iranian mind it was an article of faith that the CIA controlled everything. "Thus, long after Khomeini returned to Iran and U.S.-Iranian relations lay in ruins," wrote Gary Sick, who was on Carter's National Security Council, "it was common to meet sophisticated, well-educated Iranians whose inevitable question would be, 'Why did the United States want to bring Khomeini to power?' "

There were certain parallels between Carter and Khomeini, which suggested that similar currents were moving in both countries. The Iranian revolution, led by holy men, was entirely novel and bizarre to us, and yet more than any president in our history, Carter was a religious leader. He had not lived in exile, as Khomeini had, but he had been so far on the fringe of national power that his election was at least the representation of an overthrow of the existing order. Both men came to power because of popular distress with the direction in which their countries were moving, and both represented a spiritual appeal to an earlier time, when values were firmer and easier to grasp.

To most Americans the rage directed at their country by the

Iranians was simply wild, a form of religious hallucination. We were not a colonial power in Iran, but Khomeini spoke of us as an "oppressor," a "plunderer," the source of all Iranian problems. "This is not a struggle between the U.S. and Iran," Khomeini contended. "It is a struggle between Islam and blasphemy."

On November 4, 1979, a mob of as many as three thousand students scaled the walls of the American embassy in Tehran and held captive the seventy-six American employees trapped inside. It was at first merely a symbolic action, spurred by the anti-American speeches of the Ayatollah. The students who led the takeover of the embassy did it in the spirit of theater, not expecting that Khomeini would endorse their action or that for the next fourteen months the American hostages would become the central issue of the Iranian revolution.

I recall a scene on television of a young Iranian woman wearing a dark blue head scarf (some of the other female militants wore a full chador) piecing together the mutilated documents that the embassy staff had shredded during the siege. We would learn later that all the most sensitive documents had been captured intact, so that this painstaking assembly of the destroyed files was mostly a show of fanaticism. I had two quite vivid thoughts. One was that the students certainly had the goods on America now. I was predisposed to believe in America's guilt; I expected a deluge of embarrassing revelations. The other thought was, what kind of revolution is this, that revolves backward in time, back into the age of religious oppression and veiled women? Iran was turning back into Persia.

Night after night we saw screaming mobs of Iranians pouring out their hatred for America, using our flag to carry out the trash, hanging Carter's effigy, and occasionally producing some helpless blindfolded hostage. In part it was all a performance, done for the benefit of the television camera, which would turn a docile crowd into maniacs as soon as the lens was trained upon them. But there was also about these crowds an eager curiosity; despite their rage, they would often look into the camera as they might peer into a one-way mirror, looking for the Americans in their fabled living rooms on the other side.

After two weeks Khomeini released the black and female hostages who were not suspected of being spies. He assumed that American blacks would respond sympathetically. Indeed, the most profound misconception of the Iranian revolutionaries was that the American people would rally to their cause once their case against the U.S. government had been fully explained. "If the facts penetrate the Zionist-imperialist propaganda screen, if we succeed in explaining the truth to the American citizenry through the mass media, then the Americans will most probably have a change of heart about us," Khomeini said in his *Time* magazine Man of the Year interview. Many of the students in the embassy and some top officials in the revolutionary government had attended American universities during the sixties and early seventies, when protests against the Vietnam War and the U.S. government were at a peak, and they had returned to Iran believing that, like them, Americans were just waiting for a signal to overthrow their own government.

In fact, their anti-American revolution had exactly the opposite effect, even on me, who was still willing to believe the worst about my country. The taking of American hostages was an international crime, widely condemned, but when Carter asked our allies to apply sanctions to Iran, they quietly refused. One came to feel, as an American, intensely alone. The Iranians seemed to be saying something about us that the rest of the world tacitly believed, which was that we controlled their lives, we were evil, whatever went wrong in the world was our fault.

America was, of course, modern, and the Iranian revolution loathed the modern world. Perhaps it is because Americans have so little past of our own that we rush toward the future, but in a country like Iran, with a past that reaches back to the birth of civilization, the homogenizing American future must look like cultural extinction.

America equals change. One can understand the resentment in a country where every new fashion, every new industry, every new idea, makes a person incrementally more American than he was before. To avoid becoming American, one must avoid newness; innovation must be despised. This is absurd, of course, it will not work; to live against modernity is to become a cult, not a culture. But this was the impossible posture Iran had chosen, to retreat two hundred years into itself, into a pre-American world. This was the sympathetic chord that kept our allies from punishing Iran; yes, they had economic reasons as well, but they too were nostalgic for a life that was once more French, more German, more Japanese, less American.

What makes America such a powerful agent for change is that, being a nation of immigrants, it is more international than any other country; it has roots in all nations. As a result, it has divided all other countries into two countries. There is, for instance, Italy, and there is the Italy that is inside America, in Brooklyn and Providence; there is Poland and there is the Poland of Chicago and Milwaukee; and so on. Iran exists similarly divided. Between these two countries, Iran and Iran-America, there is the natural antagonism of siblings. One does well at the other's expense. This must be one cause of anti-Americanism everywhere, the resentment a person feels for his successful relative.

America not only divides countries, it divides personalities. One thinks of the 60,000 Iranian students in the United States, some of whom stayed here and continued to demonstrate for Khomeini, risking the fury of offended citizens. I noticed several of the militants in the embassy wearing American army field jackets, just as I had when I was a student. I identified with them that way, and I understood that they identified with me. Part of them was American. The revolution was going on inside them, between their American selves and their Iranian selves, and it made unconscious sense that this battle would be fought on the only patch of American soil in Iran.

I identified, as I say, with the American selves of these Iranian revolutionaries, but I also responded to that other resentful, anti-American side of them. What I understood about their Iranian selves was their sense of insignificance, the feeling of being less than a complete human being because one is not at the center of life. It was a similar resentment I felt growing up in Texas, believing that my life was unimportant because it was being lived offstage, and not in Paris, London, someplace central and vital. I now imagined what it must be like to live in a world in which there is America, and not to be an American.

I was still waiting for the revelations from the documents. Every night we attended lectures on television by the Iranian president, Abolhassan Bani-Sadr, or the foreign minister, Sadegh Ghotbzadeh, a highly self-assured man who had once flunked out of Georgetown University. They spoke to us about the crimes of America. In 1953 the CIA had staged a coup to keep the shah in power, and the Iranians had never forgiven us. It was a crime, no doubt, perhaps not so great a crime as the British invasion of Iran during the previous decade, or the Russian occupation, but it ended any claims of American innocence. According to Bani-Sadr, the American embassy was "the real center of power in Iran"; the shah was only an American puppet. But when the documents were finally published, eventually totaling forty volumes, there was scarcely any evidence that the United States had controlled or even strongly influenced Iranian affairs for the thirty-eight years the shah was on the throne. "The students who captured the embassy were convinced that the United States had secretly managed political events in Iran for years, that it had directed the shah's campaign against the revolution, and that it was engaged in efforts to destabilize Iran and undermine Khomeini's regime through nefarious contacts with dissident tribes and disaffected political elements," wrote Sick. "In fact, the most striking feature about the many volumes of material published . . . was the absence of anything sensational."

This was curious. Like a juror, I sensed a verdict arising from my soul, and it astonished me. America was not innocent, but it was also not guilty. It was not good but it was also not evil.

For me, the important result of the Iranian revolution was that it brought down Jimmy Carter. The morning after the 1980 presidential election a friend called and said, "There's not a liberal left in town." The country had renounced Carter because he appeared to be weak and because it could not bear the mortification it had endured in Iran. Carter had handled the crisis with patience and nobility; it was a true spiritual trial, and in some respects his finest achievement, but people had stopped believing in him. His rescue attempt came to an embarrassing, fatal end in the Iranian desert, when a helicopter crashed into one of the transport planes carrying American soldiers; and it was there, in a superheated fireball in a remote, Iranian desert, that Carter's presidency was consumed.

He had been the one president I called mine. America had turned against him, and I felt that it had also turned against me. But I also felt a sense of relief, which I did not want to admit. One wants to believe in a president's karma, and Carter, as his party chairman sadly observed, had used up all his luck getting elected. I knew that the experiment with morality was over. Even Carter, at the end, had learned about the compromises nations must make just to exist in the world, and the conflicting ideas different peoples have about how and why they want to live their lives. The world would be harder to fit into now. We had been led into Vietnam by pride, and perhaps into Iran by humility. Where could we turn next? We were confounded. And yet on the day the hostages finally came home, 444 days after their capture and moments after Ronald Reagan's inauguration, it seemed to me that America had broken loose from a guilty image of itself and had once again, in the miraculous American fashion, made itself new.

16 / RETURNINGS

In 1979 I passed through Texas on assignment for *Look* magazine to write about the twelve men who had walked on the moon. One of the twelve, Charlie Duke, was walking now on New Braunfels, a German settlement south of Austin, where he was intending to build shopping centers. Duke is an ingenuous man with wide brown eyes and a face you probably wouldn't recognize. Recently, he said, he had been touched by God, not on the moon, as one of the other astronauts claimed, but on State Highway 46. I rode with him and his wife, Dottie, to an Episcopal church in Austin where Charlie was giving a talk about his religious experience and his voyage on Apollo 16.

It had been ten years since the first man, an American, set foot on the moon, a Cold War adventure that John Kennedy had proposed in my childhood. I was in the eighth grade when Yuri Gagarin became the first man in space and sent Americans into an identity crisis that could be resolved only by planting the Stars and Stripes in the lunar soil. The moon program cost $25 billion and had left me feeling alienated from one of history's great achievements. Astronauts were heroes when Kennedy was alive, but they had come to be, in my mind, naive and faceless projections of the Chamber of Commerce and the military-industrial complex. On Christmas Eve, 1968, I had sat with my parents in Dallas watching Frank Borman read from Genesis as Apollo 8 circled the moon, and although I was moved by the words and awed by the setting, it had seemed bizarrely out of touch with the America of the sixties, the murdered leaders, the burning ghettos, the burgeoning war.

But now that the sixties were in the grave of memory and the seventies were passing away, it was easier to see the space program as a part of a separate history, that of the universal urge to explore and push on, which has always been the sport of great nations. In another life, if one wanted to surrender to such thoughts, Charlie Duke might have been a crewman on the ships of Magellan or Captain Cook.

"I'm gonna prob'ly cry tonight, okay?" he warned me.

He was asking me not to condemn him. It is the journalist's power to make others appear large or small, intelligent or fatuous, worthy or contemptible. Also, as a class, reporters are famous agnostics and not likely to respond to religious displays. For years I had been repelled by the treacly sentiments of Christianity, which in my experience had an opposite face of intolerance and greed. I could choose to apply these sentiments to Charlie Duke, as I rode along taking notes in the backseat of his Mercedes-Benz, or else, what is more natural to journalism, I could forgive his religiousness and draw him up a bit larger than he really was.

I was speculating on the vagaries of the American quest for celebrity, which had made the name of Neil Armstrong immortal, while leaving Charlie Duke among the footnotes. The very idea of celebrity, that we would raise one above the others, especially one above equals, stood against what was really important about the American experiment, which was the wonderful accomplishments of ordinary men and women. Of the two, I might have preferred Duke to have been the person history remembered as the first man to stand on the moon, rather than Armstrong, but Charlie seemed happy to be free of this burden and allowed to live unnoticed. He had come close enough to immortality when he set out to establish the lunar high-jump record. "I squatted down and leaped," he told the teenaged audience in the church that afternoon, "and I got about five feet up in the air, and my backpack began pulling me over." His feet had risen up in an awful slow-motion roll, and he found himself falling backward, away from the earth. "I landed flat on my back, just like a turtle. If my suit had split open I would have been dead just like that. But you had confidence in your material—even though everything was made by the lowest bidder."

As we drove into Austin I was looking at the license plates of the traffic passing by, which said Texas, Texas, Texas. When I was a child and traveled with my family we often played the license-plate game, and all my life I have noticed where cars are from. By now I had bolted on to my own cars the plates of five different states, and each time it involved a modification of identity, which went with the new driver's license, the new telephone number, the new checking account, the new friends. In the fourteen years since I had graduated from college, I had changed addresses twelve times. I imagined my entry in a friend's address book, scratched out again and again, Myrtle Street, Marian Street, Forrest Road, the apartment numbers I couldn't remember now, the phone numbers I might not recognize. In none of these places did I feel at home. I was always passing through, on my way—where?

My uncle had died that year, and he was buried in Atlanta with my mother's relatives. After the ceremony she and I walked among the tombstones of her mother and father, her aunts and uncles, and people she had known. One of the graves belonged to my sister Marilyn, who had died before I was born. I did not feel at home here, but Mother did, and some of her grief at that moment was the knowledge that she would not in the end lie down with her ancestors, nor would she have her children around her. She would be buried in Dallas, where none of her kinfolk lived. And she felt estranged.

It was not really a "modern" condition. Our forebears had been immigrants and pioneers; they had broken with their native countries; their children had left the farms and entered the cities; their children's children had moved to the new world; their great-grandchildren were alive and adrift. We had become a rootless tribe; one would have to go back to Wales and Scotland and England and France to find the generations stacked up in the churchyards. By now it would seem that even the instinct for ancestral ties would have been bred out of me, but it was not.

For years I had been living in cities that I didn't wish to be caught dead in. "What does it matter where you're buried?" asked Roberta, who is unsentimental about death, and the answer was of course it didn't matter where you died, it mattered where you lived. But it seemed to me that if you were living in a place where you didn't want to be buried, you were not really at home. I didn't want to feel like Charlie Duke on the moon, facing death and realizing that home is far, far away.

Texas, Texas, Texas. I knew its history, its traditions, its nasal accents, its drab landscape. I knew it well enough to hate it more than any place in the world. What a mean and provincial land, how stupidly rich, how desperately insecure, how endless and physically unrewarding! And yet, as we came into Austin, I felt more at home than I had in years.

Charlie gave his speech, and cried when he talked about God, and afterward he put on a white robe and gave the Eucharist to those who wished to receive it. I didn't know what this ceremony meant to me any longer, but I went forward and accepted the wafer and the wine. I was grateful, even if it meant nothing at all.

A month later, in one of those coincidences that govern life, the editor of *Texas Monthly* magazine called and offered me a job in Austin. "Come home," he said. It was a summons I couldn't resist.

I was crossing the Congress Avenue bridge in Austin on March 30, 1981, when I learned that President Reagan had been shot. By the time I crossed the river I was sobbing and pounding the steering wheel. Seventeen and a half years ago I heard a similar bulletin in Dallas and thought my prayers were answered, something had happened at last. But I had had enough of tragedy now. I could not bear another martyr.

Then details emerged about the assassin's Dallas background. With every assassination I had waited for exactly this news. That is the mark of the native son; I had come to expect the worst; I believed that somehow the finger would point at me.

The Hinckleys, like my own family, had come to the new world from a small town—Ardmore, Oklahoma—and like us they had been blessed by the boom. Jack Hinckley, the father, was an oilman, an entrepreneur, exactly the kind of man Dallas celebrates and rewards with its admiration. He personified the city's spirit—stern, religious, politically conservative—and he made money without apology. He worked hard, perhaps too hard, but if that was a sin, what hustling man in Dallas could blame him? He provided his family with comfort, opportunity, and eventually real wealth.

The Hinckleys may have been more successful than most families in Dallas, but their values—their religious materialism, for lack of a better term—were characteristic of the city. They moved to Highland Park, the most exclusive close-in suburb in the city. They bought a yellow-brick house on Beverly Drive, which sported the first private pool ever built in Highland Park and a fully equipped commercial soda fountain. They played golf at the Dallas Country Club and socialized with the city's elite. On Sundays they went to the Episcopal church. "The Hinckleys fit into the pattern of the parish—redneck Republican, ultraconservative, as I am," recalled their pastor, Charles V. Westapher. "A solid family, I can see them in my mind's eye, standing there with their children around them. There was nothing outstanding about John Junior. He wasn't an achiever. He wasn't in trouble. He just fades into the mists of time."

John Hinckley, Jr., was eight years old when Kennedy was killed. He ran home from school to tell his mother the news and was disappointed when she already knew. Then he asked her what the word "assassin" meant.

After Hinckley graduated from Highland Park High School, his parents moved to Colorado and he went to Texas Tech. He was assigned a black roommate. "My naive, race-mixed ideology was forever lad [sic] to rest," Hinckley wrote about himself. "By the summer of 1978, at the age of 23, I was an all-out anti-Semite and white racialist." He read *Mein Kampf*, and then, like Oswald, he formed his own political group that no one else cared to join. Hinckley advertised in gun magazines and urged prospective members to move to Dallas, where he kept his national headquarters. "There will be plenty of friendly help available to those of you who are unfamiliar with the city," he wrote. "We are even considering opening up a barracks." He was deluded, of course. However, Hinckley's politics were not an aberration in Dallas. Politically, he was little different from General Walker.

Hinckley compiled a small library on assassination. In a college paper he wrote a report on Jim Bishop's book, *The Day Kennedy Was Shot,* recalling the "oceans of ink and mountains of newsprint" that had been devoted to the president's murder. It had been the most impressive event in Hinckley's life. Perhaps his identification with the assassination was increased by the fact that his birthday was the same as Kennedy's. Later, he purchased the same kind of rifle that Oswald had used.

In 1980 Hinckley dropped out of school and told his family that he was working on the copy desk of the *Dallas Morning News.* Instead, he soon left town and began stalking President Carter, deciding on two occasions not to kill him, despite opportunities. In Nashville he was arrested when he tried to slip through airport security with a suitcase full of guns. He paid a sixty-two-dollar fine and flew back to Dallas—"back," one of his psychiatrists testified, "to replenish the arsenal." He went to Rocky's Pawn Shop on Elm, the same street that runs past the Texas School Book Depository, and bought two .22-caliber revolvers for forty-seven dollars each. He used one of them to shoot Ronald Reagan and three other men on a rainy sidewalk outside the Washington Hilton.

Who was John Hinckley, Jr.? In the minds of many of us who were in Dallas on November 22, 1963, there was something dreadfully familiar about him. He was the assassin we had imagined for ourselves, the right-wing Dallas killer we had thought was in the School Book Depository. He was the killer who would have given justice to the accusation that Dallas killed Kennedy. He was the monster of our guilty dreams. And isn't that the nature of tragedy, that all our dreams come true?

Five days before he was shot, Ronald Reagan attended a "command performance" at Ford's Theater in Washington. It was a strange episode: an American president, himself an actor, applauding and being applauded by other actors, in a place where actors will always be disgraced. He seemed to be taunting fate. Already he was being stalked by Hinckley, who had made his own pilgrimage to Ford's Theater a few months before.

As a child I watched Reagan on television every week, hosting "General Electric Theater" or "Death Valley Days." When my father was president of the Ponca City, Oklahoma, Chamber of Commerce, he invited Reagan to speak, and afterward Mother came home with a signed program, utterly starstruck. I was ten years old and had never seen my parents so dazzled. "He's so *commanding*" was the phrase my mother used. My father had sat next to him on the dais, and was strongly impressed and charmed.

But it was Kennedy, not Reagan, who became my hero, more in death than in life. Since then I had yearned for a great man to come forward; instead, Johnson, Nixon, Ford, Carter—all failed in diverse and tragic ways, and I stopped waiting for heroes. Their failure was a part of the struggle of the new world to take control from the old Establishment—Kennedy's Establishment. With Reagan's election the transfer of power was finally accomplished.

There was, as one looked at them now, not that much difference between the politics of Kennedy and those of Reagan. Whatever his intent, Kennedy's primary goals in office had been to build up the national defenses, stand up to the Soviets, cut taxes, and cure the deficits through growth. Twenty years before, Kennedy's politics sounded like liberalism, but after two decades of liberal presidents, the same agenda in Reagan's hands was seen as reactionary conservatism. One felt the extreme gravity of the center.

Coming into office each man brought with him large preconceptions about what kind of country we were, expectations about what kind of future we might have. Reagan himself often looked back to Kennedy, and the Kennedy moment, as a prelude to his own presidency. During his reelection campaign, Reagan spoke in Waterbury, Connecticut, and recalled Kennedy's own speech in that town twenty-four years before. "It was three o'clock in the morning, his campaign was near ending, and he was exhausted," Reagan said. "But the night was bright with lights and they lit the faces of tens of thousands of people below.

"And even though it was the fall, it seemed like springtime, those days. I see our country today, and I think it is springtime for America once again."

Yes, there was hope again, and one did remember those exciting days when America seemed about to bloom—until Kennedy went to Dallas to meet death and the hopes he had excited rained upon us like the fallout from a nuclear blast. Since then I had been afraid to give myself to a political leader, because it was love of that sort, love of a great symbol, that awakened the assassins. Then Reagan came, a man I had looked upon for much of my life as a nemesis. Perhaps because he wasn't my president at all, in the way Carter had been—I released some reservation inside me that I had been holding back for so long. Like Kennedy, Reagan's personality—his strength and wit and charm—overwhelmed his politics. Like Kennedy, he was more illusion than reality, more myth than man, but after the many mortal failures who occupied the space between the two men, I was ready for someone to survive that dreadful office.

And now, like Kennedy, he was shot by a Dallasite, and once again I was washed over with humiliation. No one could say Dallas hated Reagan; he had carried the city by a landslide in 1980, and Highland Park gave him the largest majority of any section of town. Before he fired, Hinckley called out "President Reagan! President Reagan!" It was a respectful cry. Then he knelt in a shooting posture and the shots—such small noises—popped and popped and men fell. The scene recalled the basement of the Dallas city hall, when Ruby murdered Oswald on TV. It was all happening again. And what would follow? Confusion, despair, guilt, and once again, the dolorous funeral, the gathering of princes, the enduring sense of vacancy, the rain of exploded promises.

But this time the President lived. He had enough of the Hollywood hero left in him to write his own ending to the nightmare. It seemed to me that an evil spell had been broken.

Because Reagan survived, Dallas was spared in the press. The Republican party even decided to hold its 1984 convention there.

In Dallas, the convention was seen as a chance for redemption, an opportunity to show the world that Dallas was forgiven at last.

I approached Dallas cautiously. Although I had come home to the new world, I had not yet made peace with my hometown. I had noted on my occasional visits that the city was growing up, diversifying, becoming in various ways more like the rest of the nation. It was a city now of fine restaurants and galleries, international flights, compelling architecture—that was a destiny it was bound to have. But it was also a city of funky nightclubs, arty movies, experimental theater—a place with texture at last. Although it was still overseen by a white male mayor, at a time when cities all over the country were changing the guard, one could not say it was just a white man's town. It had been changed, like all cities, by the flood of immigrants, who brought their own customs and their own restaurants and grocery stores, and their energy and expectations. The monopoly of opinion and belief had been broken. The newspapers were the best in the state. Dissent spoke in a louder voice now.

I was surprised to find my own father the object of community protests. When we first moved to Dallas, my father was dismayed, as everyone is, by its lack of natural beauty; physically, the city is like a mail-order bride. East Dallas, which stretches between Lakewood and downtown, had some of the most charming homes in the city, but they were decayed and chopped into tenements. My father decided to risk loan money in the area, which had been redlined by every financial institution in town. His bank made loans to young couples with no more equity than their willingness to rehabilitate those old houses. At the same time, the Lakewood shopping center, which encompassed my father's bank, was run-down and neglected, and he went to every shopkeeper and asked him personally to spruce up his store, to remove the piles of trash in back, to consider planting trees and taking down obtrusive signs. *Life* magazine publicized his clean-up campaign with a photograph of my father holding a broom: "The garbage king of Dallas," he was called. He had an effect. He persuaded the city to landscape the traffic islands. His lending program became a model for the nation. After a while Lakewood got to be a more attractive place to live, not lovely but respectable, with a small-town charm that is unique in the city. To a considerable degree this was the result of my father's efforts. So when he proposed to tear down a portion of the shopping center to build a tower for his bank, he was astounded by the outcry he heard in the community. I listened to my father's side of the story with mixed feelings. I knew how much he had poured himself into the neighborhood, but I was also sympathetic with his opponents. They have a vision that is different from his. The new world they desire is not one of shiny office towers but old stucco hardware stores. It was a sign, I thought, of a better city that such arguments were taking place.

On the other hand—of course the office tower would be built. Dallas is an urge toward the future. There is a price to pay for living in a city that is continually being born, and it can be measured in the lost feeling of rootedness that old hardware stores provide. To love Dallas is to be able to live without the consolations of the past. To love Dallas is to celebrate the thrill of the new, to smile at the building cranes on the horizon and the bulldozers clearing the pasture beyond the latest development. It takes courage to live in a city that never pauses. It's a kind of courage I don't think I have.

In the days before the convention people were talking nervously about the city's image. The Dallas police announced that they would not give jaywalking tickets to out-of-towners. The mayor lectured cabdrivers about hospitality. Dallas still hated disorder, which national conventions naturally attract. Its approach was to make friendly overtures to the protest leaders and then corral them in a makeshift campground on the Trinity River levee, directly behind the jail. A "protest square" was set aside for the Gay-Lesbian Alliance, the Iranian students, the International Women for Justice, the Gray Panthers, et cetera—it was Dallas's way of imposing order on chaos. Despite these efforts one could sense the anxiety in the city as the delegates swarmed into town. The city police borrowed reserve officers from the suburbs. The jail was cleared to make room for mass arrests. Even the local punk rockers were concerned about the city's image and put out the word to visiting punkers to "cool it" during the convention. Once again the eyes of the world were turning to Dallas, and there was an unstated feeling that disaster awaited, that the city was jinxed.

Dallas built its capacious new convention center on a rise above the old municipal cemetery, which was now patrolled by mounted policemen. Their horses nibbled the grass around the graves of dead Confederates. Behind the new center is the old Memorial Auditorium, where Adlai Stevenson was assaulted. A block away stands the Kennedy memorial. There were ghosts all around.

This was a convention with nothing to decide. Ronald Reagan would be renominated; George Bush would be his running mate— a California-Texas, new world ticket that was certain to win. The reporters were bored. I spent most of my time on the periphery, going to meetings in hotels, talking to protesters in the tent city; I even went to a fashion show for Republican wives.

In one of the hotels, to my amazement and delight, I met the man who got my first presidential vote, Eldridge Cleaver. I had followed his career since then with occasional interest; I heard he was back from his exile in Algeria, that he had experienced a religious conversion, and that he was in Republican politics in California. He was graying now, and he wore a pin-striped suit with a red club tie. I was reminded of his brief excursion as a fashion designer, which was notable mainly because of his use of codpieces in men's pants. These days he designed clothing only as a hobby, Cleaver told me. "I should have met some Republicans before I went into business," he said with a quick, self-deprecating grin. To make a living now he fabricates flowerpots in his backyard. He was here to speak for the Populist Conservative Tax Coalition, a group of far-right Republicans who oppose, among other things, welfare, income tax, and what Cleaver, the former Marxist, described as the Communist effort to destabilize our government.

Outside, in the protest square, I went to hear a punk band called the Dead Kennedys. "We'd like to do a song for you called 'Religious Vomit,' " one of them said. The young people around me reminded me of myself not so long ago. They were celebrating absurdity. I stood there, not understanding their music but really savoring the perversity of the moment, which could not have meant so much outside of Dallas. One of the Dead Kennedys looked out at the skyscrapers, which stood like gleaming monoliths of mirrored glass. "Cop glass," he called it, and it did look like the reflective sunglasses favored by the policemen who surrounded the square and watched from rooftops and sat on the tombstones on the hillside. Like them, the buildings were cool and official, impenetrable; there was about them the same protective need for order, a loathing for weirdness, a smug sense of power and of the capacity for retribution, which is all in the face of the new world.

In the crowd, punks with pink hair and pierced noses wandered among the Concerned Christians for Reagan and the Young Americans for Freedom and various delegates who had slipped out of the convention to hear the music. I met Richard Jacobs, who was standing aside and shaking his head—not at the punks, he said, but at himself. "I was a hippie in California. I lived in a commune and had a beard down to here. The person I am today I probably wouldn't have talked to twelve years ago." He was now a gas distributor and a Republican delegate from Jackson, Tennessee. Then we began to chat with Mark Von Zenicht, who wore a spiked Mohawk seven inches high, chains, handcuffs, a safety pin in his ear, and a black cross on his forehead. Mark owns an apartment building in Oak Cliff, Oswald's old neighborhood. In a moment he and Richard were complaining together about government regulation. I thought again about what a strange country I was living in, how we all change, how surprised we seem to be about who we are. In the background the Dead Kennedys were singing "Everybody knows this country's gonna blow, and it's gonna blow—sky high!" It was a refrain I had sung myself in another form, in another time, when I was romantic, existential, violent, when I craved disorder and change, but as I listened to Richard and Mark talk about property rights, the revolution seemed like an old dead dream no one really wanted.

* * *

I stood in the press gallery in the convention hall and stared out at the mass of Republican faces, noticing the tiny glints of diamonds among them. They were the same people I had grown up with in Dallas; they were proud, decent, religious, provincial, but now they were in power. It had taken them a quarter of a century, but here they were, victorious already and certain of victory again, and speaking of their own revolution, the Reagan revolution.

The power of America had shifted to the new world. The 1980 census found a majority of Americans living in the South and West. The same electoral base Nixon lost with in 1960 would have brought him victory now. Within a few years a quarter of the population would be living in Florida and Texas and California alone. What would the new world do with this power? It was still raw and brooding, more comfortable being on the resentful margins of power than in the complex center. The qualities that brought the new world to power were those of the grasping outsider. What it had offered to the country until now was cheap land and cheap labor. It had grown wealthy not through the establishment of great industries but by selling off its oil and gas and timber. It had little of the institutional or cultural maturity of the Northeast and few political leaders whose scope of vision extended beyond their own precincts. And yet the future of the country—and to a large extent, I fear, the future of the world—depended on the capacity of the new world to lead America. I had only to look inside myself to sense the uncertainty of that challenge.

Before Reagan came to the podium to accept the Republican nomination, there was a film about his rise to power, from Illinois to Hollywood to the California governor's mansion, and after three tries, to the White House. One image caught my eye: it was Reagan on his ranch in Santa Barbara, riding a white horse. I remembered that old call for a "man on horseback" to lead the nation; that was what Ted Dealey, the publisher of the *Dallas Morning News*, had said to Kennedy. It was a curious, recurring image in new world politics, and now I saw it as a prophecy.

Buried in the image itself is a Hollywood-manufactured ideal of innocent America, a nostalgia for fallen values of the frontier, and a call for a man from the West. Reagan was the man the new world had wanted all along. And suddenly there he was above me, smiling, giving his modest nod as the cheers poured down upon him. It was a long circle from 1960 to now, when the new world I had discovered growing inside America had come at last to its full stride.

Reagan was the latest and, I suddenly thought, probably the last expression of the World War II generation, which had found its first champion in Kennedy. Even as I looked at Reagan glorying in his moment, I sensed an end in sight—the end of my parents' time, and the coming of my own.

During the convention I went on a bus with some of the delegates to tour the assassination sites. We traced the route of Kennedy's motorcade from Love Field, where he landed, to Parkland Hospital, where he was declared dead. We drove down Mockingbird Lane past the Coca-Cola bottling plant and turned onto Lemmon Avenue. In 1963 this was where the crowds had begun to swell, and several times along here Kennedy stopped to shake hands. "They were mostly schoolchildren and housewives," our guide told us. We went down Turtle Creek Boulevard, the loveliest street in Dallas, where General Walker lived before he sold his house to the Hare Krishnas. We cruised past immense construction pits on Cedar Springs Road, then we turned onto Harwood Street and entered downtown, which loomed above us like a geologic fault. I could imagine what the Secret Service men were thinking as they stared up at the million windows. We rode past the old Municipal Building, where Ruby shot Oswald. Ruby's nightclub used to be nearby, the guide was saying, but it since has been torn down. It was odd for me to see my hometown this way, as a tourist, and to realize that the assassination had given Dallas something it had always lacked, and always needed: a history.

We stopped at the Texas School Book Depository, which the

guide described as a "Greek and Roman commercial building." One wouldn't have looked at it twice if Oswald hadn't been here. There is that word "hallowed," which only means sacred or holy but which has always had the connotation of being haunted. Battlefields are hallowed. Ford's Theater is hallowed. Death imposes itself on the imagination; even the scene of a traffic accident or a gangland slaying has this feeling of being in sharper focus. I remember riding on the old two-lane highways of the rural South when I was a child and seeing the white wooden crosses to mark the places where life has made a sudden exit. It is an instinctive mark one wants to leave for others to notice: someone died here, this place is hallowed.

There have been many attempts to have the building torn down, but it has been preserved, in the Dallas fashion, because it is hallowed, and because it is a tourist attraction. It is being used now for county offices. The delegates stood outside and stared at the window from which Oswald fired. "I was in law school at the time," remembered Buzz Elkins, a state senator from Tennessee. "I walked into the E&E Drug Store across the street from the University of Tennessee, and everybody was crying. It was like somebody hit the whole city with a hammer." Dolores Brooks, a delegate from Ohio, said she was watching a soap opera while her daughter slept, "and suddenly Cronkite broke in." I had become a subsidiary guide, pointing out the Grassy Knoll, the spot where Zapruder stood, the Triple Underpass. It's a function nearly every Dallasite has served. People come from out of town, they stand in Dealey Plaza, and they tell you where they were when it happened. It's a memory they offer up involuntarily. And you listen, and receive it, because that's your special privilege as a Dallasite, to be the bearer of their stories.

After the tour was over, I went back to the depository. "It's just as it was," said the historian who accompanied me to the sixth floor. "The plywood floor you see partly finished was being laid down on the day of the assassination." Some cardboard boxes were shoved to one side.

There was a green window with a blue ledge. Bits of the brick around the window had been chipped away by souvenir hunters. There were water stains on the floor. "People remark on how small it is, how close the environment is," said the historian. I looked out the window from Oswald's perspective. A hot breeze stirred. Above the Triple Underpass a train was crossing. In the street below tourists were gesturing, and some of them brought flowers. There was a bare spot on the grass where people stood to have their pictures taken.

Before me was Dallas. It was not at all the city it had been when I came here, so long ago now. Kennedy had spoken in the 1960 campaign of "a new world to be won—a world of peace and good will, a world of hope and abundance." In the melodrama we had made of Kennedy's death it seemed that the promise of America had been extinguished in Dallas. But as I saw the city now, bursting with "vigor," as Kennedy would have said, I saw the new world he promised fulfilled in the place of his death. It was not the world he would have made. It was ambitious but flawed, no longer innocent. I mourned Kennedy once again. And yet I would not call him back. I could not see into that other world, the America that might have been, the me I might have been.

I suddenly saw the ghosts rise up and depart.

ACKNOWLEDGMENTS AND
NOTES ON SOURCES

As the reader knows by now, this book is neither a formal history nor a straightforward memoir, but a half-breed offspring of both genres. It began as an essay for *Texas Monthly* about growing up in Dallas in the years preceding the assassination of President Kennedy. I found myself writing in a vein that was both personal and historical. I did not intend to make myself a character so much as a guiding sensibility to the thoughts and passions of the moment.

When I was asked by the editor of this book, Ann Close, to continue this narrative into recent history, I suddenly began to grope for precedents. I have always enjoyed the art of autobiography, from *The Diary of Samuel Pepys* to *North Toward Home*, but there was no more unlikely autobiographer than myself. In my reading experience, people who write about themselves are either famous for other reasons, or they have undergone some profound experience that needs to be shared, or else they have an inward vision that often precludes them from writing about anything else. I did not see my life as being interesting, even to me; it was, at best, representative of my time and my generation. That is the book I have attempted to write, the story of an extraordinary generation as witnessed by one rather ordinary member of it.

If it were more of a history, it would arrive footnoted and indexed; if it were more of a memoir, it would not require an essay such as this. However, since it is neither one nor the other, I believe I owe the reader some explanation of my sources of information and inspiration.

I am grateful to my friends and colleagues who contributed their time and insight. In particular I should like to thank Stephen Harrigan, my friend and reliable sounding board; Gregory Curtis, who commissioned the article that later gave shape to the book; Jan McInroy, who examined the manuscript with her careful eye and provided so many insightful suggestions; Dan Okrent, Jon Larsen, and Jim Fallows, who gave me friendly but unsparing editorial advice; my sisters, Rosalind Wright and Kathleen Minnix, who reminded me of so many forgotten incidents; my parents, Don and Dorothy Wright, who patiently and honestly

recalled for me many of the episodes recorded here; and finally my life's companion, Roberta, who went back to work to make this book possible and whose love
and support have given my life, so far, a happy ending.

1 / A NEW AMERICA

In the rather small department of literature about Dallas, Texas, I place at the
top of the list *Dallas, Public and Private* by Warren Leslie (Grossman, 1964), a
book that was written after the assassination to explain Dallas to itself and to the
nation. Also invaluable to me were Stanley Marcus's memoir, *Minding the Store*
(Little, Brown, 1974), and A. C. Greene's *Dallas USA* (Texas Monthly Press,
1984). There is, in addition, a fine history of the city as told through its buildings
and builders, in *Dallas Architecture,* by David Dillon, with photographs by Doug
Tomlinson (Texas Monthly Press, 1985). An angry treatise on Dallas race relations
may be found in *The Accommodation* by Jim Schutze (Citadel Press, 1986). *The
Super-Americans,* by John Bainbridge (Holt, Rinehart and Winston, 1961), offers
an amusing and informative look at Texas before the assassination. On the political importance of the new world, see Kirkpatrick Sale in *Power Shift: The Rise
of the Southern Rim and Its Challenge to the Eastern Establishment* (Random
House, 1975). The anti-Communist hysteria of the fifties in Texas, particularly
in Houston, is nicely described in *Red Scare!* by Don Carleton (Texas Monthly
Press, 1985). The best book on preassassination Texas politics is George Norris
Green's *The Establishment in Texas Politics* (Greenwood Press, 1979). The
emigration figures showing the rise of Sunbelt cities and the corresponding decline
of the urban Northeast came from Kevin Phillips's *The Emerging Republican
Majority* (Arlington House, 1969), which is by now a well-established classic of
political science. Anyone interested in the bizarre life of H. L. Hunt will enjoy
Texas Rich (W. W. Norton, 1981) by Harry Hurt III, the standard biography
of this anarchistic personality. There is also an insightful glance at Hunt in Robert
Sherrill's *The Accidental President* (Grossman, 1967). The true dimensions of
Hunt's mansion, as well as his relationship to Lily Pons, are mentioned in *Dallas
USA*. Some information about Dan Smoot may be found in Arnold Forster and
Benjamin R. Epstein's *Danger on the Right* (Random House, 1964). The Life
Line editorial about firearms is in Sherrill. A hard look at Dr. Criswell is Dick J.
Reavis's article, "The Politics of Armageddon," in the October 1984 issue of
Texas Monthly. The quote about Kennedy's election being "the end of religious
freedom" is in Hurt. More on Criswell and the religious scene may be found in
Joe Edward Barnhart's *The Southern Baptist Holy War* (Texas Monthly Press,
1986). The anecdote about Arthur Ashe and the building of the public tennis
courts in Dallas was reported years ago on the KERA-TV "Newsroom" show, and
was reconfirmed for me by a longtime member of the Dallas Country Club. The
account of the desegregation of the Zodiac Room, as well as the information about
the banning of art and literature in Dallas, came from Leslie. The Edna Ferber

incident is recounted by A. C. Greene. Earle Cabell's relationship to the John
Birch Society is mentioned in William Manchester's *Death of a President* (Harper
& Row, 1967), which is a reliable source for much of the worst that can be said
about the city.

2 / 1 9 6 0

Much of my information about Bruce Alger came from interviews with two of
Dallas's most notable journalists, A. C. Greene and Hugh Aynesworth. There is
additional information to be found in John R. Knaggs's *Two-Party Texas* (Eakin
Press, 1986), and in George Norris Green. The files of the *Texas Observer* were
also helpful (the February 7, 1964, issue in particular). Of course, the enduring
account of the 1960 campaign is Theodore H. White's *The Making of the
President 1960.* Among the contemporary books that look back at that campaign,
I was influenced by Allen J. Matusow in *The Unraveling of America* (Harper &
Row, 1984); Charles R. Morris in *A Time of Passion* (Harper & Row, 1984); and
Godfrey Hodgson in *America in Our Time* (Doubleday, 1976). Since each of these
books covers a span of time also accounted for in this book, I can only say that
I am grateful that the authors wrote their books before I wrote mine. Their
influence may be felt throughout this work. In reference to the voluminous
literature concerning both Kennedy and Nixon, I have benefited from a multitude
of authors. There are too many "standard" works to name here, and to do so would
obscure the writers who most affected me. On the subject of Kennedy, I would
point to two extraordinary books, *The Kennedy Promise,* by Henry Fairlie (Doubleday, 1972), and *The Kennedy Imprisonment,* by Garry Wills (Little, Brown,
1982). Nixon had the benefit of surviving to write his own memoirs, *Six Crises*
(Doubleday, 1962), and *RN* (Grosset & Dunlap, 1978). To my mind, the single
most incisive book about Nixon is also by Garry Wills, *Nixon Agonistes* (Houghton Mifflin, 1970). Dr. Criswell's "Ha-ha" is quoted in the September 14, 1960,
Dallas Morning News. For the liberal eastern attitude toward Lyndon Johnson,
see Eric F. Goldman's *The Tragedy of Lyndon Johnson* (Knopf, 1968). The
Adolphus incident is recounted in newspapers of the time, as well as in Leslie,
and in Merle Miller's oral biography, *Lyndon* (G. P. Putnam's Sons, 1980). Judge
Irving Goldberg of Dallas, who was at the Adolphus with Johnson, shared his
memory of the occasion with me. There are also invaluable records and photographs in the collection of the Lyndon B. Johnson Library. Incidentally, Nixon
never lost the feeling that Johnson had set up the entire episode. According to
William Safire in *Before the Fall* (Doubleday, 1975), the lesson Nixon drew from
the incident, which he passed along to Vice President Agnew, was "If anybody
pushes your wife, tell her to fall down." John Tower's presence at the affair, long
a rumor in Dallas, was confirmed to me through his press secretary.

3 / A MAN ON HORSEBACK

A good look at the *Dallas Morning News* and its history is Peter Elkind's article "The Legacy of Citizen Robert" in the July 1985 *Texas Monthly*. On the subject of celebrity, I refer the reader in particular to Daniel J. Boorstin's *The Image* (Atheneum, 1962), which appeared at the height of the Kennedy phenomenon. A good account of the Ole Miss riots and General Walker's involvement is in Arthur M. Schlesinger's *A Thousand Days* (Houghton Mifflin, The Riverside Press, 1965). Also see *Life* magazine, October 12, 1962. Walker was charged with public lewdness in two Dallas parks, on June 23, 1976, and March 15, 1977. In the first instance, he pleaded no contest and received a suspended sentence and paid a thousand-dollar fine. There was no conviction following the second arrest. The best source about Oswald's attempt on General Walker's life is in *Marina and Lee*, by Priscilla Johnson McMillan (Harper & Row, 1977), which is also the source for many of the details I have included about Oswald's life. It is, I believe, the most insightful book available on the subject of Oswald's character. *Lee: A Portrait of Lee Harvey Oswald*, by his brother Robert Oswald, with Myrick and Barbara Land (Coward-McCann, 1967) is helpful, as is, of course, the *Report of the Warren Commission on the Assassination of President Kennedy* (McGraw-Hill, 1964). On the National Indignation Convention and the right-wing scene in general, see *Newsweek*, December 4, 1961 ("Thunder on the Right"), and *Life*, February 9, 1962 ("Who's Who in the Tumult of the Far Right"). There is a fine eyewitness report on the assault on Adlai Stevenson in the *Texas Observer* ("An Early Hallowe'en in Big D,"), November 1, 1963. I have benefited from personal accounts by friends who were at the Memorial Auditorium that night. Stanley Marcus also recalls the episode in his memoirs. The assertion that Oswald was present at the Stevenson incident comes from the December 13, 1963, *Texas Observer* ("Who Was Lee Harvey Oswald?") and the December 27, 1963, *Texas Observer* ("Oswald and Others: Persisting Suspicions"), in which Ronnie Dugger reports that "two Dallas women say they saw [Oswald] leading a group of five or six or so pickets before the Stevenson meeting opened." The "Who Was Lee Harvey Oswald?" article also refers to Oswald's speech to the ACLU. A psychological "quasi symposium" on the subject of Oswald may be found in the *Journal of Individual Psychology*, vol. 23, May 1967. See also David Abrahamsen, "A Study of Lee Harvey Oswald: Psychological Capability of Murder" in the October 1967 *Bulletin of the New York Academy of Medicine*. The "pseudocommunity" is described in a paper published in *Psychiatry*, vol. 32, no. 1, February 1969 ("Symbolic Aspects of Presidential Assassination"), by Edwin A. Weinstein and Olga G. Lyerly. For Oswald in Russia, I consulted McMillan, and also *Legend: The Secret World of Lee Harvey Oswald*, by Edward Jay Epstein (Reader's Digest Press, McGraw-Hill, 1978). For Goldwater, I relied on Richard Rovere, *The Goldwater Caper* (Harcourt-Brace & World, 1963). On the subject of Texas politics in 1963, I have been greatly assisted by the patient recollections of former senator Ralph Yarborough. See also Knaggs, Schlesinger, Manchester, Miller, and Charles Ashman, *Connally: The Adventures of Big Bad John* (William Morrow, 1974). Yarborough, incidentally, has always disputed the report that Kennedy came to Texas to resolve the quarrel between him and Connally; indeed, this is one subject where Yarborough and Connally find agreement. On the paralysis of the Kennedy administration, I referred to Hodgson, I. F. Stone's *In a Time of Torment* (Random House, 1967), Morris, Fairlie, and Charles Murray's *Losing Ground: American Social Policy, 1950–1980* (Basic Books, 1984).

4 / GOD AND THE BOMB

Thomas Hine makes an interesting point in his book *Populuxe* (Knopf, 1986) about the shift in emphasis from air-raid shelters to suburban fallout shelters, which made the family the unit of survival, not the community. Six months after he began the campaign for home shelters, Kennedy tried to call off the program. "Let us concentrate on keeping enemy bombers and missiles away from our shores and less on keeping neighbors away from our shelters," he said, but by then, as Hine points out, the idea of nuclear holocaust had been redefined as "a radical form of suburbanization by other means." On Kennedy's war record, I consulted Wills (1982); Joan and L. Clay Blair, Jr.'s, *The Search for JFK* (Berkley, 1976); and Victor Lasky, *J.F.K.: The Man and the Myth* (Dell paperback, 1977). The assertions about the authorship of *Profiles in Courage* come from Wills. For the game-show and payola scandals, I referred to *The Glory and the Dream*, by William Manchester (Little, Brown, 1973).

The subject of fraud in the 1960 campaign has been a source of frustration for many reporters (including myself), who would like to establish the truth, finally, about who really won that election. For contemporary accounts of the fraud, see December 1 and 11, 1960, *Chicago Tribune;* December 4, 5, and 6, 1960, *New York Herald Tribune;* December 15, 1960, *The New York Times;* November 22, 26, 28, 29, and December 1 and 10, 1960, *Houston Chronicle;* November 20, 22, and 26, and December 1, 6, 7, 8, 9, 10, 13, and 18, 1960, *Houston Post;* December 10 and 11, 1960, *Austin Statesman;* November 20, 26, and December 8, 1960, *Dallas Morning News;* November 30, and December 1, 1960, *Lufkin News;* and the December 2, 1960, *Christian Science Monitor.* See also Richard Wilson in *Look* magazine for February 14, 1961 ("How to Steal an Election"). White (1961) discusses the subject of fraud, and again in *Breach of Faith* (Atheneum, Reader's Digest, 1975). Lasky mentions it in *It Didn't Start with Watergate* (Dial Press, 1977). See also John H. Davis's *The Kennedys: Dynasty and Disaster* (McGraw-Hill paperback, 1985). For an analysis of the manipulation of the "river ward" votes in Chicago, see William Brashler's *The Don: The Life and Death of Sam Giancana* (Harper & Row, 1977). I have also benefited from several interviews with Austin attorney Hardy Hollers, who handled the court case on behalf of the Republican party, which sought a recount of the Texas vote. The petition was refused. "We knew what happened," says Hollers, "but we couldn't prove it. We couldn't prove it because we couldn't get into the ballots."

On Governor Shivers's advice to Nixon, see Sam Kinch and Stuart Long, *Allan Shivers: The Pied Piper of Texas Politics* (Shoal Creek, 1973).

Richard Nixon himself never lost the feeling that he was cheated of victory in the 1960 election. He made sure that it would never happen again. Curt Gentry, J. Edgar Hoover's biographer, interviewed former FBI agent Louis Nichols (since deceased), who was hired by Nixon to prevent the 1968 election from being stolen as well. According to Gentry: "Nixon appointed Nichols to his six-man advisory board, placing him in charge of ballot security. Nichols in turn (with Hoover's secret cooperation) recruited a task force of former FBI agents to monitor key precincts. Again according to Nichols . . . although Texas was stolen, his program 'saved Illinois, New Jersey and several other states.' " Following the election, "the president-elect summoned Nichols to his suite in the Hotel Pierre, where he told him: 'Lou, you saved the election for us . . .' " (Letter to the author from Gentry.) About the 1960 election, Nixon himself has noted, in a letter forwarded to me, that "Eisenhower strongly urged that the election be contested and offered to raise the money needed for recounts in Illinois and Texas." Nixon goes on to say: "I think there is a good chance that we could have won in the courts, but in the process the damage to the country would have been enormous. When a House or Senate seat is involved, which party wins that seat has only marginal effect. Where the Presidency is concerned a void, particularly in foreign policy, for even a few weeks, let alone a year or so, is simply unacceptable." In response to my query about the 1960 vote fraud possibly contributing to the paranoia that led to the Watergate scandals, Nixon responds: "Certainly, my close political associates were all determined that we make sure that we not be counted out again. But those precautions were necessary in 1968, which we knew was going to be a close election, rather than in 1972, when a landslide was assured from the time that we knew McGovern had the Democratic nomination locked up. I suppose it could be argued that because we knew from experience that Larry O'Brien and his associates played rough, we had to develop the capability to meet them on their own ground. But I believe that [the author] would be reaching to develop the thesis that the 1960 vote frauds directly led to Watergate."

5 / S O M E T H I N G   H A P P E N S

I am aware that the Warren Commission states that the "wanted poster" handbill appeared on the streets of Dallas on the day before the assassination, but my own memory is that I found it on our doorstep on November 22. Nellie Connally has told her story to the Warren Commission, and to Michael Drury in the August 1964 *McCall's* magazine ("Since That Day in Dallas"). My memory of the church service on November 24 was refreshed by conversations with my former pastor, Bishop Robert Goodrich, who died several months after my interview with him. He recalled that many preachers in town had received anonymous phone calls that Sunday, warning them "not to say anything to damage the image of Dallas." For the "dearth of dreams" following the assassination, see Joseph Katz in *Journal of Individual Psychology*, May 1967, vol. 23 ("President Kennedy's Assassination: Freudian Comments"). For a larger picture of political assassination in various contexts, I referred to *Society and the Assassin*, by Bernhardt J. Hurwood (Parent's Magazine Press, 1970), and particularly *American Assassins*, by James W. Clarke (Princeton University Press, 1982). Cardinal Spellman is quoted in Gerald W. Johnson's *America Watching* (Stemmer House, 1976). Oswald's glance at Jack Ruby was noticed by Ronnie Dugger in the December 27, 1963, *Texas Observer* ("Oswald and Others . . ."). About Jack Ruby, I consulted the Warren Commission reports, Melvin Belli's book, and *Jack Ruby* by Garry Wills and Ovid Demaris (New American Library, 1968). On assassination literature in general, I have been most strongly influenced by the work of Edward Jay Epstein, in *Inquest* (Viking, 1966), *Counterplot: The Garrison Case* (Viking, 1969), and particularly the aforementioned *Legend*, an engrossing study of Oswald and his relationships with the intelligence agencies of both the United States and Russia. Epstein satisfies, for me, the physical questions concerning the path of the bullets, and the elapsed time of the assassination, which he shows was not 5.6 seconds, as postulated by the Warren Commission, but 7 seconds. He is also persuasive in overruling the "single bullet" theory, showing that Kennedy and Connally were hit by two separate bullets, and that a third bullet then struck Kennedy—all of them fired from Oswald's rifle (see Epstein's Appendix A). A sympathetic and knowing overview of assassination theories in general can be found in the November 1983 *Texas Monthly*, by Ron Rosenbaum ("Still on the Case").

6 / ESCAPE

According to Mary Ferrell, an assassination researcher and archivist, Delilah (Marilyn Magyar Miranda Moone Walle) married Leonard Walle of New Orleans, who shot her eight times on August 31, 1966, on their honeymoon in Omaha, Nebraska. Ferrell says that Ruby's sister, Eva Grant, reported that Ruby was upset about Delilah's testimony before the Warren Commission, but Ferrell has been unable to find any such testimony. Omaha police records show that Leonard Walle was arrested September 1, 1966, and charged with second-degree murder. He received a life sentence. On the Garrison investigation, I referred to his own account, *Heritage of Stone* (Berkley, 1970); Epstein (1969); Robert Sam Anson in *"They've Killed the President!"* (Bantam paperback, 1975); and James Kirkwood's *American Grotesque* (Simon and Schuster, 1970). A sardonic look at the Garrison case from an investigator who worked for him is by Tom Bethell in the March 1975 *Washington Monthly* ("Was Sirhan Sirhan on the Grassy

Knoll?"). About Carlos Marcello and Bobby Kennedy, see Rosenbaum's article, and *The Kennedys: An American Drama,* by Peter Collier and David Horowitz (Summit, 1984). Warren Rogers in the August 26, 1969, *Look* ("The Persecution of Clay Shaw") notes that Garrison had been discharged from the army in 1952, suffering from chronic, moderate anxiety reaction, characterized by hypochondria, exhaustion syndrome, gastrointestinal discomfort, and an allergy to lint. "He was also found to have a mother dependency," writes Rogers. "He was diagnosed as totally incapacitated for military service and moderately impaired for civilian life. Long-term psychotherapy was recommended." Later, after Clay Shaw's acquittal, Garrison himself was accused of sexually molesting a boy in a New Orleans athletic club, according to Jack Anderson's column of February 23, 1970. Anson notes that Garrison was acquitted of that charge, as he was of subsequent federal charges of income-tax evasion and conspiring to protect pinball operators. Charles Whitman, "nation's youngest Eagle Scout," as noted in his police file, quoted in the July 6, 1986, *Austin American-Statesman* ("Secret File Describes UT Sniper").

7 / FATHER AND SON

The Eisenhower quote is in William B. Ewald's *Eisenhower the President* (Prentice-Hall, 1981). I was drawn to this book by a citation in Tom Wicker's insightful article in the December 1983 *Esquire,* which glances back at the presidential decisions that led America into Vietnam ("Hey, Hey, LBJ . . ."). See Wicker also on Kennedy's decision to go into Vietnam in *JFK and LBJ* (William Morrow, 1968); Manchester (1974); "John F. Kennedy" in the CBS News Collector's Series (1981); George McT. Kahin's *Intervention* (Knopf, 1986); and David Halberstam's *The Best and the Brightest* (Random House, 1972). Halberstam and Wicker (1968) differ on the number of U.S. advisers in Vietnam at the time of Kennedy's death: Wicker says "about 25,000"; Halberstam says 16,900. Kahin says "over sixteen thousand." I rely on Halberstam, which remains in my opinion the most compelling account of America's entry into Vietnam. Hodgson is especially good on the cost of the war. About the pessimism of youth, see Barbara Cummiskey in the May 25, 1962, *Life* ("The Voice of the Nego"). The "nego," besides being a phrase that never caught on, was defined as "a young man who cannot find any basis for the standards of morality most adults take for granted: faith in life, religion, ethics, judgments of right and wrong."

8 / EXISTENTIAL POLITICS

On Johnson and the Kennedy circle, I consulted Lawrence O'Brien's *No Final Victories* (Doubleday, 1974); Hodgson; Doris Kearns's biography, *Lyndon Johnson and the American Dream* (Harper & Row, 1976); Wicker (1968); Halberstam;

and Kahin. I have also enjoyed frequent conversations with Michael Gillette, Chief of Oral History and Acquisitions at the Lyndon B. Johnson Library, and benefited from the generous access to their files. Liz Carpenter's quote is in Miller. She has also shared her memories personally with me on several occasions. Johnson's quote about Bobby Kennedy's calculating how to prevent him from assuming the presidency is in the oral history files of the Lyndon B. Johnson Library (August 12, 1969, conversation with William J. Jorden). The invention of the Camelot myth is revealed in Theodore H. White's autobiography, *In Search of History* (Harper & Row, 1978). About Bobby Kennedy and the 1968 election, I relied on *An American Melodrama* by Lewis Chester, Godfrey Hodgson, and Bruce Page (Viking, 1969); also Matusow; Jack Newfield in *Robert Kennedy: A Memoir* (Dutton, 1969); Hodgson (1978); Jean Stein and George Plimpton, editors, in *American Journey: The Life and Times of Robert Kennedy* (Harcourt Brace Jovanovich, 1970); Victor Lasky in *Robert F. Kennedy: The Myth and the Man* (Pocket Books paperback, 1971); Arthur M. Schlesinger, Jr., in *Robert Kennedy and His Times* (Houghton Mifflin, 1978); David Halberstam in *The Unfinished Odyssey of Robert Kennedy* (Random House, 1968); William L. O'Neill in *Coming Apart* (Quadrangle, 1971); and Theodore H. White, *The Making of the President 1968* (Atheneum, 1969). On McCarthy and Humphrey, besides many of the same sources cited above, I used *Miami and the Siege of Chicago,* by Norman Mailer (New American Library, 1968); Phillips; Morris; and Curt Smith in *Long Time Gone: The Years of Turmoil Remembered* (Icarus Press, 1982). On Bobby Kennedy and Marilyn Monroe, I referred to the BBC documentary "Marilyn: Say Goodbye to the President," which details Marilyn's relations with the Kennedy brothers, and Jimmy Hoffa's knowledge of the affairs. Stokeley Carmichael's quote comes from Carmichael and Charles V. Hamilton in *Black Power* (Vintage paperback, 1967). The figures detailing the violence that followed Martin Luther King's death are from Schlesinger (1978) and Gerald W. Johnson. I have learned much about the history of the civil rights movement from the passionate recountings of Pat Watters in *The South and the Nation* (Pantheon, 1969), *Down to Now* (Pantheon, 1971), and, with Reese Cleghorn, in *Climbing Jacob's Ladder* (Harcourt, Brace & World, 1967). Another valued work is the oral history *My Soul Is Rested,* by Howell Raines (Putnam, 1977), which was especially helpful on Martin Luther King. I also used David Levering Lewis's biography, *King* (University of Illinois, 1970). Lincoln's dream is in *Life of Abraham Lincoln,* by Ward Hill Lamon (Osgood & Co., 1872). For diverging contemporary interpretations of it, see *Patricide in the House Divided,* by George B. Forgie (Norton, 1979), and Dwight G. Anderson's *Abraham Lincoln: The Quest for Immortality* (Knopf, 1982). The assertion that Lincoln's hat was twice shot off is in John Cottrell's *Anatomy of an Assassination* (Funk and Wagnalls, 1966). Kennedy's premonition is in Manchester (1967). Theodore C. Sorenson, incidentally, goes out of his way in the epilogue to *Kennedy* (Harper & Row, 1965) to refute the notion that Kennedy foresaw his death, or that he had a morbid fascination with it, as so many historians believe. For King's last day, see Ralph

David Abernathy's moving account in Raines (1977). The quotes from Reagan and Nixon about Bobby Kennedy are in Lasky (1971). About Sirhan I consulted Clarke, Godfrey Jansen in *Why Robert Kennedy Was Killed* (The Third Press, 1970), and Robert Blair Kaiser in *"R.F.K. Must Die!"* (Dutton, 1970). The quotes from Quinn and McCarthy come from Stein and Plimpton.

9 / UN-AMERICA

On the subject of Johnson's secret summit, I was assisted by conversations with Michael Gillette at the Johnson Library, and with former White House press secretary George Christian.

10 / CHOOSING

One of my friends who avoided the draft wrote a brave and penetrating essay on his experience, and the social distortions caused by the draft: see James Fallows in the October 1975 *Washington Monthly* ("What Did You Do in the Class War, Daddy?"). About the draft in general, the most useful source for me was Lawrence Baskir and William A. Strauss's *Chance and Circumstance: The Draft, the War, and the Vietnam Generation* (Knopf, 1978). I also relied on Myra MacPherson in *Long Time Passing: Vietnam and the Haunted Generation* (Doubleday, 1984) and John Wheeler in *Touched with Fire: The Future of the Vietnam Generation* (Franklin Watts, 1984). Muhammad Ali's draft experience is recounted in his autobiography, *The Greatest* (with Richard Durham; Random House, 1975); also by Irwin Shaw in the June 1983 *Esquire* ("The Conscience of a Heavyweight").

11 / EGYPT LAND

About Nasser, I used Anthony Nutting's biography, *Nasser* (Dutton, 1972) and *Egypt: Military Society,* by Anouar Abdel-Malek (Random House, 1968).

12 / WHITE MAN

On the Baby Boom, I referred to Landon Y. Jones, *Great Expectations: America and the Baby Boom Generation* (Coward, McCann & Geoghegan, 1980). The views on Georgia's farm economy reflect interviews with former Georgia agriculture commissioner Tommy Irvin, and the legendary secretary of state, Ben Fortsen (since deceased). For more on Will Campbell, see Thomas L. Connelly's biography, *Will Campbell and the Soul of the South* (Continuum, 1982); Frye

Gaillard in *Race, Rock & Religion* (East Woods Press, 1982); Marshall Frady in *Southerners* (New American Library, 1980); and Campbell's own memoir, *Brother to a Dragonfly* (Seabury Press, 1977).

<h2>1 3 / T H E   N I X O N   A G E</h2>

Leo Rangell's quote comes from his book, *The Mind of Watergate* (Norton, 1980). Kennedy's "no class" quote is from the 1960 campaign and is mentioned in White (1975). On Nixon's constituency, see Fawn M. Brodie in *Richard Nixon: The Shaping of His Character* (Norton, 1981); and especially Safire, who is also insightful on Nixon versus the Eastern Establishment, as is Henry Kissinger in *White House Years* (Little, Brown, 1979); and Leonard and Mark Silk in *The American Establishment* (Basic Books, 1980). About Hiss I consulted Brodie; Wills (1971); Earl Mazo in *Richard Nixon: A Political and Personal Portrait* (Harper & Brothers, 1959); as well as Nixon (1962 and 1978). For the Checkers speech I used the same sources, as well as Henry D. Spalding in *The Nixon Nobody Knows* (Jonathan David, 1972). I also referred to Herbert G. Klein, *Making It Perfectly Clear* (Doubleday, 1980), on Old Nixon versus New. Candidate Nixon patting his breast pocket was observed by Halberstam. Nixon's liberalism is detailed in Murray; Curt Smith; White (1975); Morris; Gary Allen in *Richard Nixon: The Man Behind the Mask* (Western Islands paperback, 1971); and in *The Great Nixon Turnaround*, Lloyd C. Gardner, editor (New Viewpoints paperback, 1973). See also Representative Richard Cheney's comments in Jack W. Germond and Jules Witcover's *Wake Us When It's Over* (Macmillan, 1985). Nixon's secret plan is in H. R. Haldeman's *The Ends of Power* (New York Times Books, 1978). The chronology of the Watergate developments is found in Rangell; also in *The Breaking of a President: The Nixon Connection*, Marvin Miller, compiler (Classic Publications, 1975). About McGovern, I referred to Theodore H. White, *The Making of the President 1972* (Atheneum, 1973) and Norman Mailer in *St. George and the Godfather* (New American Library paperback, 1972). I was also assisted in conversation with former McGovern aide Allan Stone. Safire is especially insightful on the 1972 election. Dean's story is told in *Blind Ambition* by John W. Dean III (Simon and Schuster, 1976). The bug under the bed at Camp David is revealed in the May 19, 1986, *Newsweek* ("The Road Back"). I referred to the Watergate transcripts compiled by the *Washington Post* in *The Presidential Transcripts* (Dell paperback, 1974). The Kleindienst episode is detailed in Marvin Miller. On Agnew, see his account in *Go Quietly . . . or Else* (Morrow, 1980); also Richard M. Cohen, Jack W. Germond, and Jules Witcover in *A Heartbeat Away* (Viking, 1974). Andrew Johnson's impeachment is an ancient prejudice of mine, and if one wishes to pursue the scheming of Edwin Stanton, that mysterious and morbid personality, consult *Stanton: The Life and Times of Lincoln's Secretary of War*, by Benjamin P. Thomas and Harold M. Hyman (Knopf, 1962). The impeachment proceedings are reproduced in *The*

Impeachment and Trial of Andrew Johnson, President of the United States (Dover paperback, 1974, a reproduction of the 1868 version published by T. B. Peterson & Brothers).

1 4 / T U R N I N G S

On Manson I referred to *Helter Skelter,* by Vincent Bugliosi, with Curt Gentry (Norton, 1974); and David Felton and David Dalton in the June 25, 1970, *Rolling Stone* ("Charles Manson: The Incredible Story of the Most Dangerous Man Alive"). Jerry Rubin's account is in *We Are Everywhere* (Harper & Row, 1971). The transcendental meditationist episode is in *Somoza,* by Bernard Diederich (Dutton, 1981). Figures on the Great Society came from a forum on the subject at the Johnson Library in 1985; also from Murray and Matusow. On the New York City blackout, see Charles E. Silberman, *Criminal Violence, Criminal Justice* (Random House, 1978). My first account of the Lazy B 3 ("Trials of Justice") was in the August 4, 1972, *American Report,* a publication of the Clergy and Laymen Concerned. The second account is in the June 27, 1975, *New Times* ("The Lazy B 3 in Black and White"). The detail about the money being burned on the roof of the American embassy during the fall of Saigon came from an interview with an intelligence officer who was in the embassy compound. See also Stanley Karnow's authoritative *Vietnam* (Century, 1983) and Richard Nixon's *No More Vietnams* (Arbor House, 1985)—a book one should not read with much trust. I also consulted *The New York Times* during that period. On the boat people, I referred to *Newsweek* on April 17, 1978 ("The Debris of Our War"), June 25, 1979 ("Boat People Backlash"), July 2, 1979 ("Agony of the Boat People" and "Home of the Brave"); and to *Time* on July 2, 1979 ("Facing a 'Liquid Auschwitz' "). UN Ambassador Vernon Walters places the number of boat people at two million in the May 31, 1985, *New York Times.* Morris is insightful on the consequences of the Communist takeover, as is Kissinger. The Vietnamese birth rates are quoted in Norman Podhoretz, *Why We Were in Vietnam* (Simon and Schuster, 1983).

1 5 / M Y P R E S I D E N T

On Lester Maddox, see Marshall Frady in *Southerners,* and Bruce Galphin in *The Riddle of Lester Maddox* (Camelot, 1968). My brief account of that gubernatorial election is in the August 1974 *Progressive* ("Lester's Loose Again"). The best reference for the New South during this period is *The Americanization of Dixie,* by John Egerton (Harper's Magazine Press, 1974). On Carter, I relied on his own memoirs, *Why Not the Best?* (Broadman, 1975) and *Keeping Faith* (Bantam, 1982); also James Wooton in *Dasher: The Roots and Rising of Jimmy Carter* (Summit Books, 1978); Leslie Wheeler in *Jimmy Who?* (Barron's paperback, 1976); Victor Lasky in *Jimmy Carter: The Man and the Myth* (Richard Marek, 1979); and Garry Wills in the June 1976 *Atlantic Monthly* ("The Plains Truth"). About the spiritual appeal of Carter, see the curious *Jimmy Carter and American Fantasy,* edited by Lloyd deMause and Henry Ebel (Two Continents/Psychohistory Press, 1977). Lewis Lapham, in *Fortune's Child* (Doubleday, 1980), is interesting on the subject of Carter as a focus for popular discontent with the Eastern Establishment. The most influential article, for me, during the Carter campaign was Hunter Thompson's account of Carter's Law Day speech, which is in the June 3, 1976, *Rolling Stone* ("Fear and Loathing on the Campaign Trail, Third-Rate Romance, Low-Rent Rendezvous"). On the failure of the Carter administration, see James Fallows in the May and June, 1979, *Atlantic Monthly* ("The Passionless Presidency"). A good account of Carter's presidency is Frye Gaillard's series in the July 7–11, 1985, *Charlotte Observer.* On human rights and Carter's foreign policy, I used Gaddis Smith's sympathetic and perceptive account in *Morality, Reason, and Power: American Diplomacy in the Carter Years* (Hill and Wang, 1986). The best source on America's role in the Iranian revolution is Gary Sick's *All Fall Down* (Random House, 1985); also useful is Barry Rubin's *Paved with Good Intentions: The American Experience in Iran* (Oxford, 1980). Khomeini's Man of the Year interview is in *Time,* January 7, 1980 ("The Mystic Who Lit the Fires of Hatred"). A good perspective on Iran before and after the shah is in Paul Johnson's monumental history, *Modern Times* (Harper & Row, 1983). On the effect of Iran on Carter's reelection bid, see John F. Stack, *Watershed: The Campaign for the Presidency, 1980* (Times Books, 1981).

1 6 / R E T U R N I N G S

My account of the Apollo astronauts is in the July 1979 *Look* ("Ten Years Later . . . The Moonwalkers"). On John Hinckley and his family, I consulted court records; I interviewed his father, Jack Hinckley, and the family pastor, Charles V. Westapher; I interviewed psychiatrists who analyzed Hinckley, including Dr. David Michael Bear, Dr. Tom Goldman, Dr. Jonas Rappaport, and Dr. Park Dietz; I also consulted Jack and JoAnn Hinckley's memoir, *Breaking Points* (with Elizabeth Sherrill, Chosen Books, 1985). Aaron Latham's profile of Hinckley in the August 5, 1982, *Rolling Stone* ("The Dark Side of the American Dream") is helpful. The detail about Hinckley purchasing the same kind of gun Oswald used is from the testimony of his personal psychiatrist, William T. Carpenter, Jr., as is the "replenish the arsenal" quote. Reagan's presence at Ford's Theater was footnoted in an editorial by Lewis Lapham in the June 1981 *Harper's* ("Shooting Stars"). On the similarity of Reagan and Kennedy, I referred to Lou Cannon in *Reagan* (Putnam, 1982) and Morris. Reagan's Waterbury speech is quoted in the September 20, 1984, *Austin American-Statesman* ("President Remembers JFK in Connecticut"). V. S. Naipaul has an interesting account of the GOP Convention in the October 25, 1984, *New York Review of Books* ("Among the Republicans"). Apparently Naipaul was listening to my interview with Cleaver when he reports that "the very simplicity of [Cleaver] . . . made the journalists ask only the obvious questions." I am grateful to historian Conover Hunt for her guided tour of the Texas School Book Depository.

A NOTE ON THE TYPE

The text of this book was set in a digitized version of Electra, a typeface designed by W(illiam) A(ddison) Dwiggins for the Mergenthaler Linotype company and first made available in 1935. Electra cannot be classified as either "modern" or "old-style." It is not based on any historical model, and hence does not echo any particular period or style of type design. It avoids the extreme contrast between thick and thin elements that marks most modern faces, and is without eccentricities that interfere with reading. In general, Electra is a simple, readable typeface that attempts to give a feeling of fluidity, power, and speed.

Composed by The Haddon Craftsmen,
Scranton, Pennsylvania

Printed and bound by
Fairfield Graphics, Fairfield, Pennsylvania

Typography and binding design by
Dorothy Schmiderer